I0820644

Praise for *The Ayatollah Begs to Differ*

"Perhaps the best book yet written on the contradictions of contemporary Iran. . . . It captures like no book in recent memory the ethos of the country, in elegant and precise prose."
—Reza Aslan, *Los Angeles Times*

"Illuminating. . . . Captivating. . . . A discerning guide to a complex country."
—Joseph Richard Preville, *The Christian Science Monitor*

"Essential reading for anyone wanting to understand the paradox that is Iran (as well as America) in the post-Bush world."
—*GQ*

"In this delightful book, Hooman Majd, a gifted storyteller, takes us on a tour of his own private Persia, which is also the Iran of Mahmoud Ahmadinejad. The results are illuminating, humorous, sobering, and ultimately reassuring."
—Jon Lee Anderson

"Great books can be bridges too, and a prime proof of this is Iranian author Hooman Majd's wonderfully informed and enlightening new book, *The Ayatollah Begs to Differ: The Paradox of Modern Iran*. . . . He writes elegantly about the art of ta'arouf, the polite dance of self-deprecation—a kind of one-downmanship—that dominates social interactions. He expertly dissects Iran's superiority/inferiority complex, born of centuries of manipulation by the West and a stunted nationalism. . . . A refreshing and mind-opening book, a nuanced and informed portrait of one of our most misunderstood global neighbors."
—Don George, *National Geographic Traveler, Book of the Month*

"Profound in insight . . . Hooman Majd's delightfully unclassifiable book, *The Ayatollah Begs to Differ* [is] part travelogue, part reminiscence, and shifting between bemusement, grudging respect, and despair. . . . While blithely exposing hypocrisies and paradoxes, Majd does not spare the Islamic Republic's critics, either."
—Max Rodenbeck, *The New York Review of Books*

"The book is particularly strong on class and social identity in the maturing Iranian revolution. . . . He is also very strong on the relationships among Shiite theology, history, and contemporary Iranian culture, both secular and religious. What makes the book urgent now, however, is its peculiar angle of vision. . . . His carefully observed case against the assumptions of the regime-change crowd in the West is a very important contribution; one hopes that American policymakers will take the time to absorb this book."
—Steve Coll, *The New Yorker*

Praise for *The Ayatollahs' Democracy*

"Majd offers a nimble take on Iran's fraught political landscape. . . . Majd, an Iranian diplomat's son who was largely educated in America, has impeccable connections and is able to infiltrate the official and nonofficial camps fluidly."
—*Kirkus Reviews*

"Intriguing. . . . His books are worth reading because they offer acute, almost 'insider' analyses of Iranian policies and intra-regime rivalries."
—Roland Elliott Brown, *The Guardian*

Praise for *The Ministry of Guidance Invites You to Not Stay*

"Few people are better positioned to offer insight into U.S.-Iranian relations than Iranian-American journalist Hooman Majd. . . . *The Ministry of Guidance Invites You to Not Stay* offers a street-level view of life, culture, politics and political repression in Iran today."
—Terry Gross, NPR

"Not just a book about Iran—it's a personal story that will speak to any readers who have ever been disassociated from home . . . struggled to navigate a new culture . . . or attempted to come to terms with their own foreignness. . . . Reveals an Iran far more nuanced, sophisticated and affluent than most Western readers might imagine. . . . *The Ministry of Guidance Invites You to Not Stay* completes a trilogy that illuminates the politics, society, and culture of modern Iran through the eyes of the decidedly hip, well-connected Majd."
—Jon Letman, *The Christian Science Monitor*

"No one takes you inside Iran like Hooman Majd, whose keen observations and rich writing tell the story of an illuminating, delightful, and at times, horrifying journey."
—Ann Curry

"A dark story, rivetingly told. . . . As a gifted writer and the grandson of an ayatollah, Majd is well-placed to probe the role of cultural pride in Iranian diplomacy and the Shia exceptionalism that makes Iran both a fundamentalist state and a less tedious place to be during Ramadan than Dubai."
—Azadeh Moaveni, *Financial Times*

"A breezy, down-to-earth account of everyday domestic life in the polluted, congested, tense and utterly fascinating megapolis that is modern Tehran. . . . Majd goes on to build a sympathetic and nuanced picture of a complex society too often misinterpreted by the outside world. . . . An insightful study of how politics and religion intersect with daily life in the Middle East's oldest and most culturally rich state."
—Ed O Loughlin, *The Telegraph*

"Written in Majd's wry, laconic style, in which gentle comical lampooning combines with the relaying of facts. . . . The political insights are fascinating. . . . An insightful, appealing read."
—Leyla Sanai, *The Independent*

"Bold and discerning. . . . Hooman Majd's new book on Iran, *The Ministry of Guidance Invites You to Not Stay*, is his best yet."
—Roland Elliott Brown, *The Spectator*

"Majd's account is useful and elucidating. . . . [He offers] insightful glimpses of the complex Iranian character."
—*Publishers Weekly*

"A vibrant, witty account."
—Kate Tuttle, *The Boston Globe*

Also by Hooman Majd

The Ayatollah Begs to Differ
The Ayatollahs' Democracy
The Ministry of Guidance Invites You to Not Stay

MINISTER *without* PORTFOLIO

MEMOIR OF A RELUCTANT EXILE

PUBLISHED BY
Ze Books of Houston, TX
(in partnership with Unnamed Press of Los Angeles, CA)
3262 Westheimer Road, #467 Houston, TX 77098
www.zebooks.com

BOOK SERIES DESIGN
With Projects, Inc.

ISBN
979-8-9886700-6-3

Library of Congress control number available upon request.
Manufactured in China

FIRST ZE BOOKS PRINTING
September 2025
2 4 6 8 9 7 5 3 1
First Edition

Contents

MINISTER *without* PORTFOLIO

MEMOIR OF A RELUCTANT EXILE

HOOMAN MAJD

Author's Note

I was born fortunate: to two parents, both educated, both with careers. My mother, unusual for her time and place, was a university graduate and an English high school teacher, and by the time I entered this world my father was a career foreign-service officer, a trilingual diplomat with a bright future in Imperial Iran. This was in Tehran, at a time when the Shah of Iran, Mohammad Reza Pahlavi—having been recently restored to power largely courtesy of the CIA and MI6—was about to embark on his modernization drive, although I was never in a position to witness it. Living my life abroad, away from Iran and without any "home," left me with a confused identity. But as I grew up, I learned to live by my wits, whether at boarding school or when the Islamic revolution changed my life forever, and I suppose that is why I've had such highs and lows in my life since—the highs being, yes, spectacular, and the lows usually short-lived. Most are in this book.

As an Iranian, I have no illusions that my lows

were anywhere near as traumatic as those so many of my compatriots experienced and, in many cases, still experience today. Such as the hundreds of thousands who perished in the eight-year Iran-Iraq War amid trench warfare redolent of World War I and from chemical weapons used by Saddam Hussein. His invasion of Iran would not have been undertaken had he not, *because* of the revolution, perceived the vulnerability of the Iranian army. Thousands of Iranians have also died as a direct result of Ayatollah Khomeini's revolution, and many die today due to sanctions blocking access to medicines and proper health care. They and their families suffer much more than I ever have.

But I've had many experiences—as an Iranian, as a hyphenated American, and as *just* an American—that I consider worth sharing here: from my peripatetic childhood as the Shah's diplomat's son, to English boarding school, to losing my country and homeland, to my status as an illegal alien in the United States; to odd jobs, Beverly Hills real estate, and then to political asylum; to the music business, to film production, to journalism and writing books and opinion pieces on Iran, to the Iran politics I've witnessed up close, and to the U.S. nuclear negotiations with that country.

I have kept some names out of this memoir to protect their privacy, but not because I didn't consider them important, or important in my life. Everything I write, though, is, to paraphrase Walter Cronkite, *the way it was*.

MINISTER *without* PORTFOLIO

MEMOIR OF A RELUCTANT EXILE

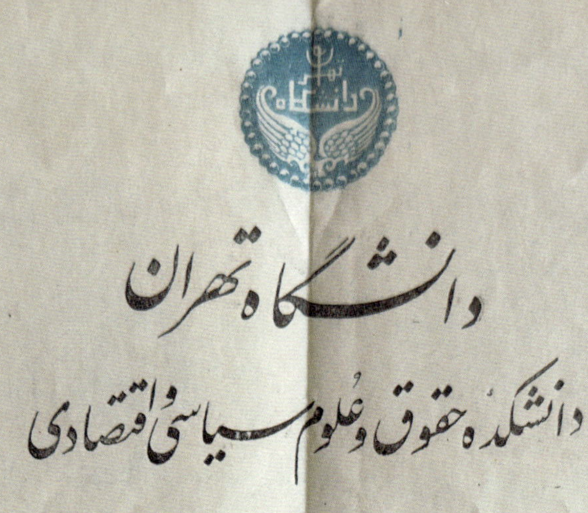

دانشگاه تهران

دانشکده حقوق و علوم سیاسی و اقتصادی

…وّب هشتم خرداد هزار و سیصد و سیزده

دانشکده حقوق و علوم سیاسی و اقتصادی مصوّب شورای دانشگاه

…لد ۱۳۰۷ در یزد دارنده شناسنامه شماره ۹۵۶ صادر از حوزه ۴ یزد در تاریخ شهریور ماه ۲۸

…ر تاریخ ۱۳۲۸/۹/۱۲ با درجه بسیار خوب گذرانیده و از تاریخ ۱۳۲۸/۹/۱۲

…ن دانشنامه با درجه لیسانس در رشته قضائی داده میشود که از مزایای قانونی آن بهره م…

تهران - بتاریخ

رئیس دانشگاه تهران

دانشگاه تهران

Chapter 1

Flight

My first memory (at least one that I've always been able to recall) is getting off an airplane, heavy in my mother's arms. I was told when I was much older that it was in Ankara, Turkey, a stop on either the Pan Am Clipper or BOAC route that went from Tehran to London via several cities in the Middle East and Europe. I don't think my parents ever remembered which airline—it would have been not just *my* first time on an airplane, but my mother's, too. It was the spring of 1958 and my mother, Mansoureh Assar (from childhood called "Badri"), my older brother, Saman, and I were heading to London to join my father on his first posting abroad as a diplomat in the Shah's foreign ministry; his own flight had also been *his* first time on an airplane. Oddly I have no memories of arriving in London, being greeted by my father, or indeed any memories of our three-year stay in England except for even vaguer, fuzzier ones of a babysitter, birthday parties, and riding a tricycle in the courtyard of our rented flat in Barons Court.

I didn't know it at the time, of course, but the airplane was to figure significantly in my life; a peripatetic one as the son of a diplomat whose foreign ministry was, in the aftermath of the 1953 U.S.- and U.K.-sponsored coup that brought the Shah of Iran back from exile and to absolute power, a fraction the size it is today. I also couldn't know then, in London, that the concept of home would be alien to me for most of my life, and that in my adult years I would have contradictory and often confusing notions of what or where my home was or lay.

My father, Nasser, who had a law degree from the University of Tehran and who joined the foreign ministry only after it instituted what was its inaugural entrance exam—previously, it had been the preserve of the aristocracy—spoke French and had a decent command of English, which meant that with a small cadre of diplomats, the ministry would keep him in Anglophone or Francophone countries for as long as it could afford to. London, therefore, was a natural fit for a young man at the start of his career, and, coming from a small desert town, Ardakan, that he considered backward and had fled as soon as he could, he took to the Western lifestyle like the proverbial duck to water. His blue eyes, fair skin, and light hair, inherited from his mother, and his elegant style made him appear—and forgive the overused phrase—straight out of central casting, for not just a Middle Eastern diplomat, but perhaps a European one, too. I know he enjoyed being mistaken for a Westerner not only because it amused him, but also as it only took him even further from the dusty village of his childhood.

As a student in Tehran in the 1940s, my father had become, like many of his peers (including his future wife, my mother), a leftist with sympathies for the Tudeh Party—Communists opposed to the monarchy—and later for Jebhe-ye-Melli, or National Front, the party founded by the future prime minister Mohammad Mosaddeq. After college, while performing his national service in the Imperial Cavalry and based in Bojnourd, a small village near Mashhad in the northeast, he became close friends with an army doctor there, Esmail Bazargan, who was a staunch Communist, as

وزارت فرهنگ

دانشگاه تهران

دانشکده حقوق و علوم سیاسی و اقتصادی

نظر بقانون تاسیس دانشگاه مصوب هشتم خرداد هزار و سیصد و سیزده

نظر باساسنامه و آیین نامه دانشکده حقوق و علوم سیاسی و اقتصادی مصوب شورای دانشگاه

چون آقای ناصر مجد اردکانی متولد ۱۳۰۷ در یزد دارنده شناسنامه شماره ۹۰۶ صادره از حوزه یزد در تاریخ شهریور ماه ۱۳۲۸ از عهده امتحانات رشته قضائی

برآمده و پایان نامه تحصیلی خود را در تاریخ ۱۳۲۸/۹/۱۲ با درجه بسیار خوب گذرانیده و از تاریخ ۱۳۲۸/۹/۱۲ شایستگی دریافت درجه لیسانس را

احراز کرده است بموجب این دانشنامه با درجه لیسانس در رشته قضائی داده میشود که از مزایای قانونی آن بهره مند گردد

شماره ۷۳۲۶

رئیس دانشکده حقوق و علوم سیاسی و اقتصادی

رئیس دانشگاه تهران

وزیر فرهنگ

01.

02.

01.
The author's father's diploma from the College of Law, University of Tehran

02.
Dr. Bazargan, army doctor, with unidentified man and the author's father, cavalry officer on the right, Bojnourd, early 1950s

many career officers were at the time. Iranian Communists generally supported Mosaddeq over the Shah in their conflict, which wasn't—at least for Mosaddeq, who came from an aristocratic family himself—about overthrowing the monarchy and creating a republic. Rather, it was about adherence to the constitution, which, like those of some European countries, rested political power in an elected government and not the monarch.

After the 1953 coup that returned the Shah to Tehran from Rome, where he had fled into what he had thought would be permanent exile, members of the Tudeh Party and many National Front members were thrown in jail, including Dr. Bazargan. My father, who had joined neither party, decided that, as the saying goes, if he couldn't beat them, he'd join them: he competed in the inaugural exam for entrance to the foreign ministry—the most prestigious ministry, previously reserved for the aristocracy. Yet his affection and loyalty toward his friend meant that every Friday on visiting day, he would head to the prison and see Bazargan. In the visitors' book, he would sign his name and his place of employment: Ministry of Foreign Affairs. That might have easily resulted in his firing from the ministry, for no government employee ordinarily dared to associate with political prisoners in the aftermath of the coup, but fortuitously he suffered no consequence. Unlike, say, his expulsion from Iran's most prestigious boarding school—Alborz, known by some as the Persian Eton—the consequence of having punched the headmaster in the face after the headmaster slapped his older brother's ears for some minor infraction.

Years later, on our second tour of duty at the embassy in London, Dr. Bazargan and his family also moved there, and my brother and I became close friends with his sons. After the Islamic revolution of 1979, Peyman Bazargan, the younger son, having lived most of his life in the U.K., nevertheless joined the Mujahedin-e-Khalq—better known in the West as the MEK—onetime Islamic Marxists opposed to the Shah and now also opposed to Khomeini. The MEK conducted terror attacks against the regime and fled to Iraq when its bid for power failed. Peyman was sent to Iraq by the organization to be its English-language press officer when it was preparing a military attack across the border with arms supplied by Saddam Hussein, who was himself engaged in war with Iran. But along with every other able-bodied man and woman, Peyman was ordered into battle, and he died in a furious clash with Iranian troops that resulted in the decimation of the MEK fighting force. His body was never recovered. His death came as a shock to me—the first childhood friend I'd lose—and to my father, who was visiting me in California at the time. I had never seen him cry until then.

Chapter 2

Coming to America

From London, we went in 1960 to San Francisco, where Iran's west-coast consulate was located and where my father had little of a political or even consular nature to do: it was a time when few Iranians emigrated to the United States, let alone required consular services in California. At the time, San Francisco was the commercial and financial hub of the state, while Los Angeles was the entertainment center; Iran, like many other less wealthy countries, decided that if it could afford to maintain only one consulate, San Francisco was better, as it was closer to Sacramento, the state capital. There were, of course, nowhere near the number of Iranians in Los Angeles then as there are now.

My brother and I took to San Francisco, and I have a handful of vivid memories of our time there. I went to kindergarten and first grade in the public school system, and I remember the layout of our apartment, on a steep hill (naturally), quite well. I also remember our neighbor Ann Parenti,

01.

SAN FRANCISCO UNIFIED SCHOOL DISTRICT
PROGRESS REPORT
for
GRADES ONE AND TWO

Pupil Hooman Majd
Teacher Vera L. Humphreys
School MADISON SCHOOL
Principal DOROTHY ROBERTSON
Grade L1 Term Ending Feb. 1, 1962

ASSIGNMENT FOR NEXT TERM

Hooman is assigned to the H1 Grade for the Spring Term, 1962

NOTE TO PARENT OR GUARDIAN

San Francisco is proud of her public schools as shown by the active public interest and support. The high standards reflect close home-school relationships and co-operation. Parents are welcome in the schools at all times; and in the case of conferences with teachers, time is saved by making such arrangements with the principal.

In the sound and sympathetic preparation of your child for the future, there is no substitute for your close interest and participation in the work of the school.

Harold Spears
Superintendent of Schools

02.

01.
San Francisco school photo,
the author at top far right

02.
School report card

a senior Italian American with no children of her own, who treated us kids as if we were her grandchildren. My mother seemed to love her, which made us grow so fond of her that for years after we left the city, my mother, brother, and I all corresponded with her. I had hoped to see her again, even promised her, but of course sadly never did. That was how it always was: I suppose I never wanted to acknowledge that I was leaving friends behind for good when we left a place and a country, even as I must've known that it would be the case. From California we went to Tehran, for my father had to do a short stint at the ministry before being sent out into the world again. But now America was a part of me. San Francisco had greatly affected me, from our weekend drives out of the city to have brunch at a diner—pancakes with maple syrup!—to our time with Ann Parenti; even down to the beat cop whose name I can't recall but whose image is implanted in my brain, who walked our street and would cheerfully say hello to us boys every day. And New York, where we stayed on our way back to Iran, fascinated me, especially when we walked up the steps inside the Statue of Liberty, and saw the city from the top of the Empire State Building; my strongest memories of my first time in the place I now call home.

Chapter 3

Home, Part One

Of our brief time—less than a year—that we spent in Tehran, I have only the vaguest of memories. Hard to imagine now, but this was a time when Iran was the closest of allies of the United States, and not just because the CIA had installed the Shah firmly back on the Peacock Throne. The Shah was West-oriented; he had been educated in Switzerland, enjoyed champagne, fast cars, and beautiful women—two of which were prohibited to him as a married man by his Shia Muslim faith—and was, like his father before him, determined to drag Iran out of her Middle Ages and into the twentieth century.

America was a natural partner, and while the Shah was less enamored of President John F. Kennedy, who pressed him to extend his modernity to human rights, relations were such that my brother and I could attend the American School in Tehran—home to American "diplobrats" and the children of military and, presumably, CIA station officers. I remember the building well and the drive there in my father's Renault Dauphine—the compact French car he could afford on a junior diplomat's salary at the time. On weekends (Fridays, according to the Muslim week) we visited my maternal grandfather's house. We lived in a rented apartment (of which I have no recollection), while my grandfather, grandmother, and grandmother's widowed sister all lived in a house on Iran Street that to me seemed like a huge mansion, with a large walled garden in the back, which my grandfather had bought before my mother was born. My grandfather was an *allameh*—meaning "learned" in Arabic—an Islamic title for a scholar or lettered person—and was recognized by many in the clergy as an ayatollah, albeit one without a seminary in either Qom or Mashhad, Iran's centers of Islamic learning. Instead, he devoted his life to teaching philosophy and Islamic jurisprudence at Tehran University in his clerical garb. When in the 1930s the Shah declared turban-wearing in public illegal, rather than obey, my grandfather stayed home and taught his students in his book-lined library on a mezzanine of the house, a room I would visit to see him when I was a child.

My brother and I loved visiting his house. We could play in the backyard, dip our feet in the small, blue-tiled pond, and generally run about as we pleased with no one to tell us what to do. The food that my mother's aunt cooked was delicious and plentiful—rice with stews such as *ghormeh sabzi* or the pomegranate-and-walnut *fesenjoon*, or my favorite rice-and-lima-beans dish, *baghali polo*—and more often than not other family members showed up at lunch or dinnertime. The house played an important role again in 1967, when we were stationed back in Tehran for a year. This time, my father decided that we would not go back to the American School; rather, we would enroll in a new English-language school called Iranzamin that was popular among diplomats and other upper-class Iranians keen on their children receiving an American education. That academic year, again living in a rented flat, we would spend many a weekend at our grandparents', and my grandmother would often take my brother and me on a walk to a patisserie and treat us to whatever we wanted while my mother spent time with her father and her aunt in the house that truly was her home. We'd also stay in the house on our summer vacations, as my parents never owned property in the city. In the hot, dry Tehran summers, my brother and I slept at night on beds covered with mosquito nets, in the backyard along with the entire family and whomever else might be visiting.

Among the four siblings who inherited the house in 1979 soon after the Islamic revolution when my grandmother and her sister died, it was decided that my mother, Badri, should travel to Iran to dispose of the property. Her eldest brother, Nassir Assar, a former ambassador and deputy prime minister who escaped the country dressed as a woman in a chador, was wanted by the new regime, and her sister, Shusha Guppy, was a singer and writer in London who didn't dare show her face at Mehrabad International Airport. Her younger brother, Nasser, was a painter living in Paris who had been a favorite of the Shah's wife, the Shahbanou, and who was regularly invited by the empress to participate in the Shiraz Festival, an arts festival she founded. While my mother was married to an ambassador of the ancien régime who was in exile in London, she argued that, as a wife with no particular political affiliation for more than twenty-five years and a former public high school teacher, she wouldn't be in any serious danger, and she traveled to Tehran a few months after the revolution, ignoring my father's misgivings and quiet disapproval. Strong-willed and fiercely protective of her family, my mother wouldn't have dreamed of not fulfilling this last obligation, no matter the potential danger. She quickly sold the family house that she had loved her whole life, knowing the country was no longer hers, either. My mother soon enough returned safely to London, but until the time she died in 2022, she never again returned to the house on Iran Street, nor set foot in her homeland again.

In 2005, during my first visit to Tehran after a thirty-plus-year absence, I tried to find my grandparents' street, though I knew that the house itself—like many others dating to the early twentieth century—had been torn down soon after my mother had arranged for its sale decades earlier. Although I've had family in Iran continuously since the revolution, who remembered the house and the neighborhood in now unfashionable downtown Tehran, Abbasabad-e Eine-doleh, none of them could tell me where to find the street, long renamed for a "martyr" in the Iran-Iraq War of the 1980s. I walked around the neighborhood anyway, hoping an alley, a street, or a still-standing house would awaken a memory. It seemed familiar, but apartment blocks now stood where once there were walled gardens. I inquired at several convenience stores—a feature of downtown Tehran neighborhoods that has survived modernization—and in a small auto repair shop I was mistaken by an old man for my fugitive uncle when I asked him if he knew where the Assar house was. But no one, not even an old man who had lived and worked there for decades, could tell me how to get to the street once named after the country itself, Iran, where my mother was born.

01.

01.
Their maternal grandfather, Mohammad Kazem Assar, with the author and his brother, Saman (left), in the walled garden of their mother's childhood home in Tehran

Chapter 4

Eastward and Westward

It was from my grandparents' house on Iran Street in 1963, having given up our rental apartment, that we left for New Delhi and a new posting for my father. And again, off we went, me and my brother, to the American school, populated as usual by U.S. embassy staffers' children plus a handful of offspring of close allies. Having lived in apartments for as long as I could remember, in India we suddenly had a house in the Diplomatic Enclave, including a backyard and green square around which houses had been built. We also had a staff, which even my junior diplomat father could afford in the India of the early sixties.

My father, the ex-cavalryman, also told my brother and me that we were now old enough to learn how to ride, and he arranged private lessons for us. But this being India, we didn't need to go to a stable; a groom would bring horses to the park and my father would instruct us in the basics: essentially, how to mount a horse, walk it, trot, and get off without falling.

"*Saaf besheen*," he would say to me (sit up straight), or tell me I needed to give the horse a little kick to get it to trot. I remember one particular hot, sunny Sunday morning, having my father's full attention on me while I sat in a saddle on a horse that was probably more the size of pony, but to me seemed impossibly tall.

I would walk to school with a servant who would put her hands over our eyes if there was a sight she didn't want us to witness, such as dead animals or beggars missing limbs or even dying in the street; once I saw a half-naked man lying immobile before she managed to cover my eyes. I recall Sikhs taking off their turbans and immersing their long hair in a bucket, filled, my mother later claimed, with coconut oil. But one of the strongest memories is of the day (or at least the day in India's time zone) that we heard President Kennedy had been assassinated. We were let off from school, and I vividly remember walking with a couple of American friends, arms over each other's shoulders, in silence and sadness. And I remember my mother's sad eyes and teary face, the first time I had seen her cry—for even proud Iranians grieved his death.

Our sojourn in India was cut short by a new assignment for my father: Morocco, where the ambassador had requested him. But before we left, Prime Minister Jawaharlal Nehru died, and my father attended his funeral pyre on a bank of the Yamuna River. For a man raised in Islam but irreligious, cremation was a revelation. He later told me that contrary to Muslim practice, he wanted to be cremated when he died, and his ashes discarded in any way we, his survivors, pleased. In his old age he feared visiting family and friends in Iran in case he passed away there, for he would by law be buried in the Muslim tradition, wrapped in cloth but with no casket, anathema to him. He especially forbade any ceremony or memorial, other than our presence at his cremation itself. We did our best when he died, holding a small gathering after the cremation for our own benefit, but in Tehran there was a memorial for him at a mosque that I was unable to prevent.

In Morocco, we'd be stationed in a Francophone country where his French, better than his English, would be employed at the embassy in Rabat. We dutifully made our way from Delhi to Tehran, staying at my grandparents' house while our furniture and household goods were shipped off to Morocco. But before we could embark on the journey west, my father's assignment changed: Tunisia. The ambassador there, Agha-ye Rashidi as we came to know him, had requested my father as his deputy. Agha-ye Rashidi was a divorcé with an adult daughter who visited only occasionally, and I later came to believe his choice of my father, a family man, was partly to bring a female hostess into the embassy's social events, a role my mother could play exceptionally well. And for a man who had no children of his own—in Iran then it was still culturally significant and a source of pride for a man to have sons—the opportunity to act as a father-figure. And so our container of household goods, already halfway to Rabat, was diverted to Tunis, and we settled in a whitewashed rental villa in Carthage. Another house with backyard, this time with a fence that separated the villa from the actual ruins of Carthage, and one that I eventually realized I could crawl under and roam about the ruins, all the way to the sea, without going through the main gate and paying a fee to enter. Fascinated mostly by broken mosaics (I even once found a large piece in our yard), I imagined a time when Roman soldiers marched on the very same ground I scampered over.

Tunis was a blissful moment we never wanted to end. From a work perspective my father had little pressure; we lived in a big house by the sea, had a maid-housekeeper-sitter, Aisha, whom we adored, and had friends at the American school we attended on the main highway between Tunis and La Marsa. The school buildings included a villa and a barn next to two orchards, and unusually for our family, we remained in contact with those we left behind decades later, my brother traveling back to Tunis from London to visit his best friend, Rhys Payne. My parents, while they were alive, stayed in touch with an American diplomat, Zach Geneas, and his wife, Vivian, all their lives, and Vivian visited my parents in Tehran in 1972 from her husband's later posting in Athens. (My parents also became close to a British diplomat and his wife, the Mallets, and they stayed in touch for the rest of my parents' lives.) We had a car pool going to the school, and I don't know how we managed to fit four growing kids in our VW Beetle. The other families had American station wagons, and in a larger car, my brother and Rhys Payne could more readily torture Fay Lynne Geneas, the only girl in the group.

I'm sure that for my father the Tunisian idyll was made all the more idyllic by his annual September assignment to the ministry's delegation to the United Nations General Assembly (UNGA) in New York, a month of

01.

02.

01.
Ambassador Rashidi, the author and his brother (left), and an unidentified woman, Tunisia beach, 1960s

02.
The author (right foreground) at the American School in Tunis

03.
The Summit Hotel in New York in the 1960s, my father's home away from home

03.

respite from Tunis and the family. I'm confident he enjoyed himself in the big city, staying at the Summit Hotel on Lexington Avenue, a stunning Morris Lapidus structure that I knew only because of the postcards he would send or bring back with him, along with jeans, shirts, and tees that he'd buy for us at Sears, Roebuck. After spending months in what was then the small capital of a country that had gained independence (from France) only eight years before we arrived, going to New York must have been exciting for a young diplomat.

Our idyll was momentarily shattered at the onset of the Six-Day War in June 1967 between Israel and the Arab states of Egypt, Jordan, and Syria. While Tunisia under its first president, Habib Bourghiba, whose palace grounds were across the street from our villa, was an Arab, Muslim state, it had a large Jewish population too, and had never been openly antagonistic toward the state of Israel. And yet both the U.S. Embassy and the American School, as well as many Jewish-owned targets, came under unexpected attack by mobs of Tunisians, and my father rushed to the school in his VW Beetle to take us and our friends to our homes (I would fit sideways in the "trunk" behind the back seats). Much later in life, when I applied for political asylum in the United States and had to present evidence that I would be in danger were I to return to Iran, I asked Zach Geneas, longtime foreign service officer and World War II veteran, if he would write a letter of recommendation for me. I found out only then that he, stuck at the U.S. Embassy in lockdown at the time of the attack, had called my father to see if he could go to the school and get the car pool children away to safety. Zach considered this a sign of my family being a friend of America, and he wrote that he believed this would put me in danger in Iran. When I told my father of the letter's contents, he warned me to never let it get in the hands of the Islamic Republic authorities, and in fact when I applied for an Iranian passport some two decades later, when there was an opening of sorts for Iranian exiles, I simply neglected to sign a document that would give the Iranian Interests Section in Washington, housed at the Pakistani Embassy, authority to access my asylum file at the U.S. Immigration and Naturalization Service (superseded by USCIS that very same year). Zach's letter, along with others extolling my father's virtue and by extension mine, remain buried somewhere at USCIS, or has been lost forever. I regret not making copies.

During the Six-Day War our school remained closed for a few days, but the war was soon forgotten by us kids if not by our parents or by the Tunisian Jews who had lived in North Africa for centuries, but who were now less certain of their safety as a minority in an Arab land at war with the Jewish state. (While Tunisia never joined the war, I do recall a parade of soldiers marching past the presidential palace and in front of our villa, far too late to make it to the front, after Bourguiba had made a speech promising solidarity with his Arab brethren.) After the war, many of Tunisia's Jews left for Israel or France, and today the country's Jewish population is a tiny fraction of what it was, much like other Arab countries where Jews were expelled, encouraged or forced to leave, ever since the creation of the state of Israel and its subsequent wars with Arab nations.

Almost every summer we lived in Tunis, my uncle Nasser Assar, the painter, would visit us from Paris, where he'd lived since the late 1940s. He spoke English with us boys, even though our own French had become semi-fluent. All the Tunisians we met spoke French, and at the American School it was taught in all grades. My brother and I looked forward to his visits; he was a fun-loving, carefree bachelor then, and sometimes he would show up with a friend for a few weeks of vacation. He taught us chess and would take us swimming in the Mediterranean every day. On foot we'd go to the beach, where a buoy bobbed in the sea, presumably to warn boats of shallow water. My uncle would challenge us to swim out to it and back to shore, and this remains the strongest memory of our daily excursions to what was mostly a deserted beach during the week.

When we left Tunis for good, on our way to Tehran we took the ferry to Palermo and then went on to Paris, where we saw our uncle in his tiny flat, surrounded by his paints and canvases of modern art, mostly abstract landscapes. I remember being surprised at the way he lived, having always imagined that he had a grander life as a French painter. I was especially sad that we had left Aisha behind in Tunis. I had grown extremely fond of her, and the whole family shed tears at the dock. I promised her I'd come back to visit her, but of course this remains a ten-year-old's unkept promise.

We were at the dock about to board the ferry with my father's brand-new Mercedes. He always bought a fancy new car at the end of each tour of duty—usually a Mercedes-Benz at the low end of the range and way

01.

01.
The author in his
dad's Mercedes

beyond his means—but not because he was a spendthrift or car fanatic; rather, it was to sell on return to Iran. Custom duties on foreign cars and household goods, such as furniture and kitchen equipment, stood at 100 percent at the time, and diplomats, whose pay would shrink drastically when back in the home office, had a onetime exemption on paying duties on any goods, including automobiles, imported upon the completion of a foreign tour. Foreign cars were sought-after commodities in Tehran among the wealthy and the elite, and a diplomat would profit enough from a sale to enable him and his family to live as they were accustomed to, including sending children to private schools. I remember sitting in the car on the drive to Paris, which impressed me after the VW Bug, before my father would undertake to drive it all the way to Tehran and deliver it to its proud new owner. Later in life I wondered how my father, having only temporary ownership of cars he so admired, could so readily accept that he would never own one himself, for his salary couldn't accommodate a Mercedes in a family with boys in private schools.

After an academic year in Tehran at Iranzamin, the new Tehran International School—a year that witnessed the Shah's coronation, which we watched on our small black-and-white television, for school was out that day—our next home was to be London again, ten years after my father's first posting there. We said our goodbyes to family again at the house on Iran Street, our temporary home before we left for England. I couldn't have imagined it at the time, but I would see that house, my grandparents, and my mother's family only once more, during Christmas holidays four years later.

Chapter 5

London, Redux

London already felt like a second or third home to us. While in Tunisia (which itself felt like a vacation), during some summer holidays we would spend two weeks or so in London to shop for new clothes and for my parents to see friends and get a taste of western culture. We would stay at a bed-and-breakfast on my father's modest salary, in a house in Vicarage Gate—walking distance to Kensington Gardens, Hyde Park, and of course the shops and restaurants in Kensington. Having been deprived of fast food for the time we had just spent in Tunis—Tunisia was not yet a market for the American burger or fried-chicken chains—we boys would look forward to eating at the Wimpy hamburger outlet on Kensington Church Street where, in the days before McDonald's conquered Europe, we could scarf down burgers, milkshakes, and fries in that simulacrum of an American fast-food joint in swinging London.

Britain in 1968 was little changed, but I would soon experience the shock of going to an English school rather than an American one. And while my father had every intention to send me and my brother to a proper private school—or *public* school as they're inconveniently known in Britain—he discovered that we had arrived in London too late to be admitted to the day schools—St. Paul's or Westminster—that he had researched and wanted us to attend. After asking around at the embassy and among friends as to which state school was best, he found himself persuading the headmaster of St. Marylebone Grammar School to take two Iranian boys, educated at American schools, into his academy despite our residence in Bayswater, where the state-run Holland Park Comprehensive would have been the more logical, and easier, choice. (Neither school exists today.)

The shock of wearing a uniform that included a blazer and necktie, going to school in a building that looked like something out of *Oliver Twist*, and now having Latin—taught by the headmaster, no less—included in my syllabus was trivial compared to the jolt I received on the ancient courtyard, where the schoolboys' aggression bore no resemblance to the far more genteel behavior of American diplomats' young offspring. On my first day, two boys came up to me and asked which football club I supported. Responding with an American accent that I didn't support any club, as I knew nothing about football (or soccer, as I thought of it) or the English league, apparently wasn't satisfactory, for one of the boys landed a hard punch to my stomach and said, "If anyone ever asks you, Yank, you say *Arsenal*!" After catching my breath, I was terrified that other boys my age and older would do the same thing, perhaps even worse, if I said Arsenal and they hated the team, so for the rest of the academic year I skulked in the corner of the yard hoping to avoid any football fans—probably the entire student body. There was more general bullying, alternately being called a Yank and a wog (derogatory for Middle Easterner or Arab), a few scuffles here and there leading to tears, and my mother angrily demanding that the headmaster, Harry Llewellyn-Smith, a kindly, older man who also taught history, do something about the bullies. He asked me who they were, and I told him basically everyone in my class, and while he did indeed put a stop to the bullying, it had the unfortunate side effect of leaving me with no friends at all for the year I spent in Marylebone.

One of the more refreshing discoveries for me as I entered fourth form, the first grade (equivalent to eighth grade in America) at St. Paul's School, where my father had again persuaded the High Master (what the principal was called there) to admit his two sons in 1969, was that the school didn't play football. The chief sport there was rugby, slightly alarming to a sheltered Iranian boy educated in the American system, yes, but at least I wouldn't be tormented by soccer-mad boys or subjected to their arguments about whose team was better than whose. There were more boys at St. Paul's from different backgrounds and countries, which despite the strict social and academic atmosphere made it feel more welcoming to me than St. Marylebone, where it seemed all the boys came from the same working- and middle-class London backgrounds. I don't know how my father persuaded the school's High Master to accept us without us taking the entrance exam, but there we landed at a time when Iran was respected—and I suppose having diplomats' sons who might one day be ambassadors or ministers was good for the empire. There were Americans at St. Paul's, too, and my brother became fast friends with Richard Kent and David Smith. David even traveled with us to Iran for Christmas holidays in 1972, though I suspect his memory of that trip today is restricted to the horrible bout of diarrhea he had after a group meal that, of course, affected none of us Persians. To be fair, he probably also remembers the T.B.T. bus trip we took together (sans parents) to Isfahan and to Shiraz and Persepolis, staying in hotels by ourselves and seeing the UNESCO World Heritage sites; a first for all three of us teens. (Curiously, my father never recommended we stop at Yazd—the big city to small-town Ardakan and where he finished school—which conveniently is on the way. I finally saw it in 2005.)

I made friends quickly with foreign students such as Raja Jarrah, the Palestinian son of a Kuwaiti ambassador, and Britain-born students visibly of foreign extraction such as Kwok Li, whose parents spoke no English and were from Hong Kong SAR, China, and Anjan Gupta, whose Indian heritage was evident from his name and complexion. I had fewer relationships with the English boys, who already had long-term attachments to one another. A good English—*very* English—friend was Fred Grundy, who I later discovered was the son of Air Marshal Sir Edouard Grundy, who preceded

01.

02.

01.
T.B.T. bus matches, 1960s

02.
St. Paul's School Rowing Colts (junior varsity eight), 1972, with the author, standing on left, and his brother, seated second from left

his son at St. Paul's and whose house I was in, attending a party in 1973, when the police evacuated us due to an IRA bomb threat. Fred always knew he would follow in his father's footsteps, and although we soon lost contact, I later learned that he became a well-known RAF pilot himself. David Winner was another acquaintance I lost contact with, who I later enjoyed reading when he became a journalist and author. Lord Anthony Rufus-Isaacs was the first peer I'd met in my short life. He later became an attorney in Beverly Hills, of all places, and he seemingly no longer uses the title. (Knowing the English public-school attitudes of the time, I'm confident that St. Paul's wouldn't have let him *not* use his title.) Daniel Pinter, son of the playwright Harold, was a contemporary I did not become close with; he seemed to be a sad boy, foretelling his later life, estranged from his father and a recluse.

A relatively cosseted twelve-year-old, I soon became familiar with a less-welcome fact of life at St. Paul's: sexual advances and even abuse by masters (as teachers were called) toward young boys. The first time was at the start of term in fourth-form mathematics class, when the teacher, an older man whose name now escapes me, would ask the boys to come to his desk while he graded our tests. While doing so with one hand holding a pencil, he would rub the inside of the boy's thigh with the other, although careful, at least with me, not to venture too close to the genitals. The same teacher coached junior rugby; he would line us up and one by one pull open our shorts to, in his words, "see if you have your jockstraps on." Since I couldn't imagine *not* wearing a mildly protective undergarment while playing a decidedly violent sport, I wasn't particularly concerned with his peering down my pants, and in fact I remember laughing about it with fellow students. I remember one day a boy referring to him as an "old queer," and my sudden recognition of what that meant.

Later another teacher, Paul Rogers, who taught English literature at "O level"—what one part of GCSE exams were called then—and was also the fencing and swimming coach, who was known among the boys to be homosexual, would offer me a choice of punishment when I did something to annoy him in class: after-school detention, or a private caning at the swimming pool. I chose detention. Caning was still practiced at St. Paul's, and I ended up on the receiving end of the stick twice. One time was during physics class, taught by David "Paddy" Porteus (who was also a rowing coach), who yelled "MAJD!" when I muttered "Jesus Christ" under my breath after he had announced a lengthy assignment. "*Fetch the cane!*" I looked at him quizzically. "*Blaspheming!*" he shouted, as I walked out the classroom and down the stairs to the porter's room where the "cane" was kept. (One had to ask for the cane, and the porter would inevitably smirk as he handed it to you, furthering the humiliation.) Had I known at the time that my father had punched his school's headmaster, I might have been tempted to throw a punch at Porteus, post-caning, although it could have gotten me expelled, as it did my father.

During my later years at school I came to know the philosophy and divinity master, the Reverend Dr. Edward Ryan, who, unlike other masters, treated the boys as adults and was highly popular for that reason. I enjoyed the philosophy classes I took, but it wasn't long before the boys realized that Ryan's unconventional attitude hid something quite different: a desire for sexual relations with students. He lived in a flat near the school, and often invited the older boys to his home for a chat. He had a permissive attitude toward underage drinking, and boys who went to his home were offered sherry. He never propositioned me, though decades later he was accused of coerced sexual relations by boys who attended St. Paul's in the years I did. (I was contacted by Scotland Yard when the St. Paul's abuse revelations became a scandal in Britain, in the mid-2010s, but since I had not been abused by any of the masters myself, I had little to offer the authorities other than what they already knew, in some cases in more detail than I did.)

When we first moved to London we were living in a rented flat in Bayswater—a large one with formal living and dining rooms—at the corner of Queensway that also had an ice-skating rink in the basement, where we learned to skate. I shared a room with my brother, and it was convenient both for the park, Kensington Gardens, across the street, and the two underground stations mere feet from the entrance. But we were forced to leave after two years when the landlord decided to sell the building as individual apartments—condominiums—and my father was offered an insider's discount of 10 percent, bringing the reduced price to £18,000. I remember my mother trying to persuade him to buy the apartment, perhaps in the hope that we'd have a home we could call our own *somewhere*, but he, despite his fondness for living in the West, insisted that he didn't have the money, and besides, we'd be leaving London in a couple of years. So we moved to Upper Richmond Road, almost a suburb then, and lived in a town house where for the first time in my life I had my own bedroom. It was an easier commute to school in Barnes, too; a walk across a park and then a simple bus ride away.

Chapter 6

Anglo-American Iranian

Perhaps the most rewarding thing about attending St. Paul's was that in the sixth form, in 1971–72, I met an American from New York who would become my lifelong friend. (St. Paul's, like some other English public schools, had its own unique system of naming grades, and sixth was the form in which one took O levels. "A levels" were taken in the middle eighth form. For some inexplicable but wholly English reason, there was no seventh form at St. Paul's; rather, from sixth you went to lower eighth.) Davitt Sigerson arrived at school in 1971, his parents escapees from the United States of Richard Nixon. We became friends, for we had much in common in our love for R&B and for parties, and very little enthusiasm for the sports culture so predominant at English public schools. We both detested rugby and especially cross-country running, which in my case was mostly cross-country *walking*, often in the freezing rain. Later I did enjoy rowing, which seemed to me a much more civilized form of exertion among the choices offered, although I quit that sport when the coach of what we might call the varsity "A" crew in America, and what was called the 1st VIII at St. Paul's, didn't put me in his boat, and I decided if I couldn't be in the best boat, I wouldn't row at all. Although sports were no longer mandatory in my grade, I did play basketball, which was unusual in British schools at that time (and the masters all wrote it "Basket-Ball") but reminded me of the States and my American schooling. As bad a player as I was—and I was awful by American school standards—I was better than the British boys who joined in.

At some point Davitt discovered the St. Paul's Anglo-American Society, founded by John Weitz, the American menswear designer and an Old Pauline who attended the school in the thirties, whose purpose was to provide a refuge of sorts for American students in a dedicated room where they could feel the sort of privilege and elitism that many of the British students already enjoyed. Davitt became the "president" of the society and appointed me "vice president," a title that I don't believe existed. We would spend lunch breaks in the room—Davitt would simply not eat the glop that was served in the cafeteria, and his mother, Yola, made packed lunches for him every day—and when I became a boarder in 1972, she would pack extra food so that I wouldn't be obliged to eat all my meals at the dreaded cafeteria.

Another factor that brought us close was our being non-Christians (or non-Anglicans, more precisely), Davitt a Jew and me a Muslim, though neither of us was religious. We would spend some twenty or thirty minutes in a common room with the other Jewish Paulines (my brother and I were among perhaps three or four other Muslims then, and there may have been a Hindu or two as well), while our fellow Christian students had to attend morning chapel. We were supposed to spend the time in contemplation, but of course we did nothing of the sort. One day when Davitt and I were being boisterous schoolboys and Davitt was singing "Ball of Confusion" by the Temptations extremely loudly, a master, Dave Pirkis, strode into the room and asked who was singing. When Davitt confessed, Pirkis punched him in the face and stormed out of the room. We were both in shock. I believe that was the first and last time Davitt has ever been punched. But the shock led to laughter, for the utter preposterousness of it all. We have both told our children about the episode, who were highly amused.

In 1971 my brother decided he was old enough to get a summer job, and he applied to be a salesman at the Scotch House in Knightsbridge, a purveyor of woolens, cashmere, and tartans mostly purchased by tourists who also shopped at the great department store Harrods, just down the street. (The Scotch House, at some point owned by Burberry's, later became its flagship store in London, and still stands there.) I wanted in on the game and so he recommended me, his fourteen-year-old brother, to the manager and I was quickly hired too. The managers knew we were at St. Paul's, and it seems that was qualification enough for a snobbish store in the West End. A friend of ours in Saman's year, Steve Springer, one of only two Black students at the school, asked us if we'd recommend him, too, which of course Saman did. His manager told him that of course another Pauline would be welcome to work at the Scotch House, and that he should stop by to get sorted out for his summer employment. When Steve showed up, however, impeccably dressed as he always was (one of the few boys we knew who would wear custom gray trousers and a tailored black blazer with the school badge sewn on in lieu of the school-supplied sack of a uniform), he was told by his interviewer that, sadly, there was no position available at the store.

I knew all about racism, having been called a wog many times, and Steve had told me that the reason he had to keep his hair cropped close to his scalp was that his father, an Oxford don, insisted that the only way his son would be taken seriously in British society was not to wear a popular afro style, or be dressed in any way other than that of an English gentleman. My own father was distressed that we had taken jobs as *salesmen*, peddling sweaters and scarves to tourists—well below our station, he thought. The evenings we were all at home, he would ask us nothing about the store, but would show his disapproval by simply saying, "*Ja-ye shoma neest*"—it's not your place. Before the summer was up, he put an end to our employment, insisting we quit. If it was money we wanted, he would provide. *What if an Iranian comes into the store and sees a Majd son as a salesman?* For us, more exciting than the money had been feeling like grown-ups and heading to work every day, spending the luncheon vouchers we were given for sandwiches and Cokes at the nearby cafés.

In 1971, for the first time in my father's career he had completed the standard four-year tour abroad and was returning to Tehran with my mother and our baby sister, Marjan, born in London the previous year. He arranged for Saman and me to board at St. Paul's, which had two boardinghouses, for both weekday and full-time boarders. (Most boys went home on weekends, and those two days were especially lonely until we were a little older and could escape into town.) My brother and I ended up at School House (the other house was named "High," though not due to a greater consumption of cannabis by its residents), and our housemaster was the very kind Philip McGuinness, who lived with his family in a ground-floor flat in the building. Anthony Retallack was the housemaster at High House, which also housed Undermaster Keith Perry, the extremely popular history teacher who decades later was convicted and given a suspended sentence over his vast collection of child pornography, discovered, apparently, by students in his rooms.

In a way, boarding school was liberating, with my parents thousands of miles away. I can recall Housemaster McGuinness calling them only once, when I asked for the seemingly preposterous sum of two pounds for a haircut at Vidal Sassoon in the West End. (We could draw cash from the funds our parents deposited with the house but had to justify our expenses.) My parents insisted that we call them, collect, once a week, from the house phone—I'm sure McGuinness thought that expense rather extravagant, too—and during one phone call I asked my father to please explain to the master that my haircuts were, in fact, an expense he approved of.

Being older than many boys who started boarding as soon as they entered school, I knew I had a relatively easy time ahead of me, and other than the first term in a six-bed dormitory, I had a private bedroom and was even made house prefect in my last year and could boss younger boys around, which I did only occasionally if they were being especially annoying. My friend Raja Jarrah had a stash of vodka nestled above the ceiling tiles (undoubtedly asbestos-laden), and having a room on the ground floor also meant an easy escape through the window after lights-out and an excursion into town or to a party on the weekend. We never got caught. In my later years the greatest parties were always at Davitt's apartment in Chelsea, where he had the best record collection, the nicest duplex flat, top-shelf liquor, the cutest girls, and the most permissive parents, who would stay in their bedroom upstairs until the early hours of the morning when his mother would descend the stairs and offer to make any stragglers a hot breakfast. I was inevitably a straggler.

Unlike most students at St. Paul's, I had no intention of sitting for the Oxbridge exam (for entrance to Oxford or Cambridge Universities) after finishing my A levels. St. Paul's had a form, *upper* eighth, after finishing one's A levels, dedicated to preparing boys for the exam to ensure that its stellar record for Oxbridge places would not falter. As such and unlike most other universities in the world, admitted students didn't enter Oxford or Cambridge until the year after graduating, and had an enforced "gap year." I wanted nothing to do with the system and started applying to U.S. universities, although both my brother and Davitt sat for the exam and both attended Oxford.

In 1973, my last year at school, my father was requested as DCM (deputy chief of mission) at Iran's embassy in Washington, which made going to an American college even more attractive. Ardeshir Zahedi, the Iranian ambassador, offered my father unprecedented privileges for a number two in the foreign ministry hierarchy—a house, a car and chauffeur, and an expense account with practically no limit—to entice him to the job. And for Christmas break in 1973 my brother and I flew to D.C. and stayed at the Wellington with my parents and sister in what was a furnished, serviced apartment a few blocks from the embassy on Massachusetts Avenue while my parents went about looking for a house to buy for the DCM post, which had hitherto not included a residence.

Chapter 7

Back to America

Ardeshir Zahedi, a former foreign minister and the Shah's ex-son-in-law, who had served as ambassador in both Washington and London, himself had privileges no other ambassador of the Shah did at the time. He insisted that my father buy—with the embassy's money, of course—a Mercedes or other luxury car, and buy an elegant house for Iran's DCM somewhere in Northwest Washington, perhaps even on Embassy Row. My father bought a Cadillac DeVille sedan—not the top model—and a house in Bethesda, which he thought more appropriate to a deputy and less flashy, though it was a disappointment to Zahedi, who wanted the embassy and the diplomats' appearances to befit the empire they represented. Bethesda was more to my father's liking, for American suburbia to him was the pinnacle of relaxed, comfortable, clean, and efficient living—the antithesis of the village of his birth. We also got a chauffeur and a maid, and, sensing an agreeable future living arrangement, I decided to live at home again.

IRAN—Imperial Embassy of Iran

Chancery: 3005 Massachusetts Ave. NW., 20008 (483-5500 and 483-3070).
National Holiday: Birthday of the Shahanshah Aryamehr, October 26.

His Excellency Ardeshir ZAHEDI, Ambassador E. and P., 3003 Massachusetts Ave. NW. 20008 (AD 4-3003).

Mr. Nasser MAJD, Minister Counselor, 3005 Massachusetts Ave. NW. 20008 (483-5500); Mrs. Majd.

Major General Mokhateb RAFII, Counselor (Head of Secretariat), 1510 Baylor Ave., Rockville, Md. 20850 (424-2391); Mrs. Rafii.

Mr. Nasser SHIRAZI, Counselor (Political), 4201 Cathedral Ave. NW. 20016 (363-1639).

Dr. Assad HOMAYOUN, Counselor (Political), 4201 Cathedral Ave. NW. 20016 (966-7133); Mrs. Homayoun.

Mr. Ahmad MOSHAVEGH-ZADE, Counselor (Political), 5599 Seminary Rd., Falls Church, Va. 22040 (578-4065); Mrs. Moshavegh-zade.

Mr. Youssef AKBAR, Counselor (Political), 4501 Cathedral Ave. NW. 20016 (EM 3-0173); Mrs. Akbar.

Mr. Manoutchehr ARDALAN, Counselor (Political), 10201 Grosvenor Pl., Rockville, Md. 20852 (493-5543); Mrs. Ardalan.

Mr. Bahram PANAHI, First Secretary (Political Affairs), 6007

01.

01.
Partial page from 1974 Diplomatic List published by the State Department

I applied to George Washington University, less highly ranked than Georgetown, for its engineering school. I had neither love nor special aptitude for science or engineering, but during school in England, where one had to choose the sciences or the liberal arts at the age of fifteen or sixteen, my father had strongly recommended that my brother and I pursue science—both because it was considered prestigious among Iranians and because, my father insisted, with a science degree we'd have guaranteed employment anywhere in the world. While my brother had a flair for the sciences, for my part I simply didn't want to disappoint my father. I preferred English courses at school (and scored better grades in them), and enjoyed writing essays, but I didn't challenge my father, as I had no idea how one made a career out of writing and accepted that he must know best.

In the summer of 1974, after receiving poor grades in my science A levels, I left St. Paul's for good and met Saman—who had spent his gap year in Tours, France—in Le Havre to board the SS *France* for New York. We had student tickets and shared a tiny cabin, but I was thrilled to be leaving a continent on which I had never felt fully at home, a place where I knew I would always be a foreigner and never a local. It was my second time sailing across the Atlantic to America, though I had no memory of the first—on the *Queen Mary* in 1961 on our way to San Francisco, when my mother spent the entire journey seasick in bed.

My brother and I had U.S. A-1 diplomatic visas stamped in our Iranian passports, which the Iranian embassy in London had arranged at my father's request, and customs at the docks in New York waved us through to a waiting Lincoln Town Car to take us to the train station for the trip to Washington, courtesy of the Iranian consulate and my father's close friend Mr. Goodarzi, the consul general in New York. (I had once spent a night at the consul's official residence at 34 East 69th Street on my way back to London after Christmas holidays, as the Goodarzis were among my parents' best friends. That town house was seized by the U.S. government when diplomatic relations with Iran were severed in 1980 following the hostage crisis of 1979, and was, I discovered years later, rented by the State Department to none other than Jeffrey Epstein.) In Washington, we were picked up at Union Station by our chauffeur in the navy-blue embassy

Cadillac and whisked off to Bethesda and what was to be my new home, at least for as long as my father remained in D.C. Zahedi himself was absent from Washington for long stretches, spending time with the Shah in Iran or on his ski trips, or in Switzerland at his estate in Montreux. This left my father as the chargé d'affaires of the Imperial Embassy of Iran, as powerful a position as almost any in the foreign ministry of the Shah, who viewed his relationship with the USA as Iran's paramount one.

When Zahedi *was* at his office, he was easily the most popular ambassador in Washington. His parties were legendary, the invitations highly sought after. From politicians to Hollywood types, there was a party of some sort—a small gathering or a fete celebrating one thing or another—almost every week. Caviar—the Iranian Imperial Beluga reserved for the Shah's court—was served by the kilo, there were Dom Perignon bottles and magnums in endless supply, and Chivas Regal Royal Salute was the whisky of choice. Zahedi had a secret budget for dispensing favors—a budget no other ambassador had and which, I'm confident, was limitless. He had a Rolls-Royce Silver Shadow sedan as the official embassy vehicle at a time when Rolls-Royce cars were not allowed to be registered in Iran *at all*, being reserved for the Royal Court. Zahedi and his father, Fazlollah, were instrumental in the 1953 coup that brought the Shah back to power, after which Fazlollah became prime minister. Ardeshir married the Shah's daughter Shahnaz (from his wife, Princess Fawzia of Egypt) in 1957 and gave the Shah his first grandchild. He divorced her in 1964, but it didn't affect his relationship with the Shah in the least: Zahedi was untouchable.

Within weeks of arriving in Washington I was introduced to Zahedi, and when he came over for Sunday brunch and a swim, I was duly impressed when he took a call from the Shah at our house. He was known to not be on speaking terms with either the foreign minister at the time, Abbas Ali Khalatbari, a friend of my father's, or Prime Minister Amir Abbas Hoveyda, preferring to go straight to the top. Prime minister was not a position he aspired to, knowing full well it held little actual power. (Khalatbari was replaced as foreign minister in 1978, months before the revolution, and he was executed by the new regime in April 1979, to the great distress of my father and many other career diplomats. He was no von Ribbentrop, yet hard-liners in the new regime viewed him and Hoveyda so.)

I was taken with Zahedi, who I thought was doing Iran proud, giving it name recognition and a sophisticated reputation, while I, growing up, had never really sensed its importance on the world stage. But this was the capital of the United States, and everyone knew who the Iranian ambassador was—and *everyone* wanted to go to his dinners and cocktail parties. My father, however, while he liked Zahedi personally and considered him a friend, found it increasingly difficult to work with a personality such as his. The stress of trying to manage the embassy, the political and diplomatic work that needed to get done, and the whims of an ambassador who led a chaotic life soon overtook him. He began taking Valium to sleep at night and his health was deteriorating. Only two years into his term, he asked to retire, which he was entitled to do after two decades of service. Zahedi was disappointed but didn't stand in his way, and my family left for England to await official retirement before deciding on where to settle. I was disappointed, too, having hoped that my father would rise further in the foreign service. I did not yet understand Persian culture well enough to know that he had wanted to be *refused* retirement and be begged to continue as, naturally, a vitally important diplomat.

In the meantime, I had become friends with the embassy secretaries, young Iranian women who would invite me to their parties, which were eye-opening to a seventeen-year-old who had only ever experienced my father's diplomatic receptions or high school parties where drunkenness and awkward sexual embraces (but rarely sexual *healings*) took place. I found the women beautiful and sexy, and their parties great fun except for their insistence that I get up and dance with them—Persian style to Persian music—and I would beg off a little too insistently. Persian *ta'arouf*—politesse or etiquette—demands that one refuse an entreaty but eventually succumb, which I couldn't do with Persian dancing, not even after many drinks, and the women soon understood that as someone who hadn't grown up in Iran and whose Farsi still left much to be desired, I should be excused. My sense of a national identity—Persianness—was growing with these friends, but was not yet fully formed. When my family was preparing to leave for England, I had to find an apartment, as after boarding school I had no intention of living in a dorm in my sophomore year at college. I settled on a studio—what they called an "efficiency" in Washington—in

01.

01.
Iranian Embassy entrance at 3005 Massachusetts Avenue, N.W., in Washington, D.C.

Arlington, across the bridge from Washington and a ten-minute drive to school. It meant that I needed to have a car, so my father bought me a Toyota Corolla, at the time one of the least-expensive cars in America. The embassy had it registered for me with diplomatic plates, and when I picked it up, I was happily surprised to see that the license number was DPL 3005, coincidentally the address of the embassy chancery on Massachusetts Avenue. I was sad to give it up, along with my diplomatic visa and D.C. diplomatic driver's license, after my father departed his post.

Even after my father departed as DCM, replaced by his friend Jamshid Tavallali, Ardeshir Zahedi invited me to parties every now and then, and I always wondered at the long line of cars on Massachusetts Avenue, snaking toward the embassy to discharge the invitees. I would never stay very long, sensing that the scene wasn't exactly a teenager's. The people there mostly ignored me, and I was too shy to start a conversation with a congressman or senator or even a socialite, but I did enjoy the food and appreciated that Zahedi thought to include me. He also jumped into action in the runup to the Islamic revolution when I, despite having some friends who were either Communists or opposed to the Shah, began receiving anonymous phone calls, and got the FBI involved. The death threats were, the FBI tried to reassure me, likely just meant to intimidate the son of a diplomat. The agent who spoke to me did suggest, however, that I look under my car before getting into it in the mornings. "You know, just in case."

Years later, Zahedi sent me very nice letters from his home in Montreux when he happened to come across one of my books, magazine articles, or op-ed in *The New York Times*. He also sent me a gracious, kind condolence letter when my father died in 2012.

Zahedi was, as ever, gracious to the end, passing away in 2021. I know he enjoyed his lunches with my father at Villa Les Roses, which he'd host whenever my father would visit his longtime friend and former ambassador to the U.N. in Geneva, Manouchehr Fartash, who had stayed in the city after the Islamic revolution. Zahedi's defense of Iran—even under a regime that despised him—caused many die-hard monarchists to criticize him in his later years, but he was unfazed and remained a patriot to the core. He once told me on the phone when I was covering the Iran nuclear talks for NBC News in Geneva in 2013, when President Obama had authorized

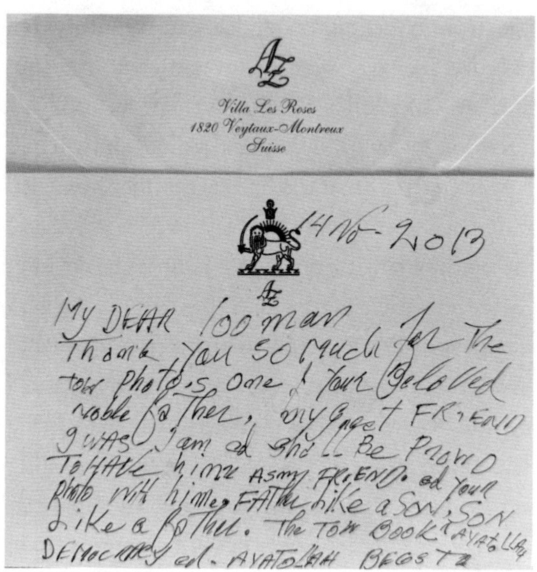
Villa Les Roses
1820 Veytaux-Montreux
Suisse

14 Nov-2013

My DEAR 100man
Thank you so much for the
two photos, one of your beloved
noble father, my great FRIEND
I WAS, I am and shall be PROUD
TO HAVE him AS my FRIEND and your
photo with him. FATHER like a SON, SON
like a father. The two BOOK "AYATOLLAH
DEMOCRACY and AYATOLLAH BEGS TO

01.

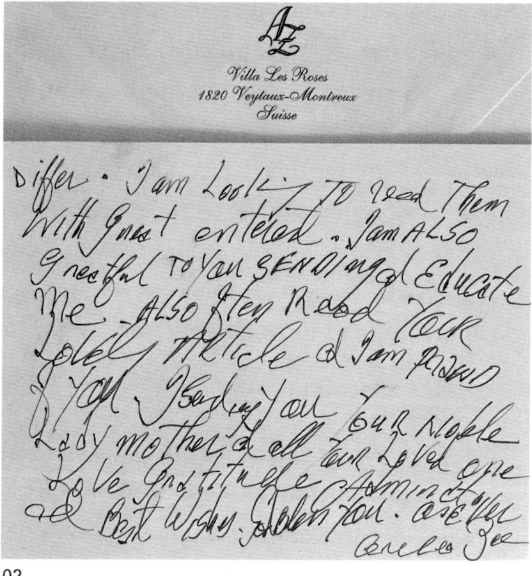
Villa Les Roses
1820 Veytaux-Montreux
Suisse

differ. I am looking to read them
with great interest. I am ALSO
grateful to you sending and educate
me. ALSO I have read your
lovely article and I am PROUD
of you. I sending you, your noble
lady mother and all your loved one
Love, Gratitude, Admiration
and Best Wishes. God bless you. As ever
Ardeshir Zahedi

02.

01. & 02.
Ardeshir Zahedi
correspondence

03.
Ardeshir Zahedi email

» My dear beloved Hooman,

Truly: Like father, Like son!

My cousin Tino very kindly has sent me your article in Washington Post.

I would very much like to call you and talk to you, but I happen to be in hospital currently, like a prisoner - with covid19. Suffering from terrible pain, caused by a festering pneumonia, as I am told.

So I thought, through my cousin, to send you my admiration, my love, my respect and wish you joy, happyness and continuous success, for you and your beloved family. I look forward to overcome my affliction and be released from hospital soon, to be able to personally hug you.

In a way, despite the trouble this horrible desease gives me, I am not unhappy to have contracted it, since it reminds me vividly of the pain and anguish our beloved compatriots are going through. I therefore consider it as a blessing, for me to be able to feel with them.

I do hope, in the present political situation, as you said yourself, we shall be able to solve the problems of our country nobely, with justice and honesty.

I hug you and send you my very best wishes.

You are like a son to me,

Ardeshir «

03.

direct contact with Iran to resolve the crisis that he thought Mohammad Javad Zarif, tasked with the negotiations, the finest and most capable Iranian foreign minister in memory. Considering that he himself had been foreign minister under the Shah, it was quite a statement. A true gentleman, Zahedi never publicly criticized Empress Farah, the Shah's wife, for keeping her distance from him after Pahlavi's death, despite having introduced her to the Shah in the first place. And he never, of course, criticized the Shah directly, even after Pahlavi's harsh words about Zahedi in his memoir published after the revolution. Neither the Shah nor his wife and children deserved Zahedi's unwavering loyalty and love.

Nostalgia still lingers for the time of Pahlavi's reign among many Iranians in the face of today's Islamic Republic. Yet when the Shah blamed Zahedi for the lack of U.S. support during the revolution, it was indicative of Pahlavi's tragic misreading of the sentiments of the Iranian people.

Chapter 8

Tehran on the Potomac

As I settled into life alone, staying friends with the embassy secretaries and some of the younger diplomats, I also connected with Iranian students at George Washington. It was revelatory to me: here I was, someone who had spent his entire life among foreigners, someone without a fully formed sense of national identity, who was now suddenly accepted among a group of perhaps the most cliquish people on the planet. The Iranian students at university—and their numbers increased exponentially as the Shah's government expanded scholarships and as the middle class grew in step with the oil-bonanza economy—didn't generally make friends with non-Iranians, didn't tend to date Americans, and stayed a tight-knit community of kids biding their time in the United States before they would return to Iran. At one point the Iranian government offered every Iranian student in the States $200 a month for expenses, as long as they signed a document promising to work for the government for as many years as they received the stipend. The embassy encouraged me to sign up for the handout and I did, receiving my first check for $600, three months' payment, shortly thereafter (rent for my studio apartment in Arlington at the time was $230 a month).

I became very close with a handful of Iranians with whom I shared interests, but also with Communists, Islamist students, and of course students whose fathers, like mine, worked for the Shah. Hossein Valian and I, for example, became close; his father, Abdolazim Valian, was a former minister and then the governor of Khorasan Province in the northeast, which encompassed Mashhad, Iran's second-biggest city and home to the Imam Reza shrine, an important Shia pilgrimage site. While immersed in an Iranian community for the first time in my life, some other acquaintances whispered to me that Valian's father was known to be deeply corrupt as well as someone with close ties to SAVAK, the Shah's secret police, but I didn't let it interfere with my friendship with his son, whose father's sins I didn't think should be visited upon him. I became fast friends with the Jalali brothers—Bahman and Behzad—and through them with Khosro Etemadi, who lived in California and with whom I reconnected in Tehran when I visited for the first time in more than thirty years. I've stayed at his house on Safi Alishah Street in downtown Tehran, and we remain in close contact today.

As a young adult, I was finally finding an identity, one that would give me a home, too. I exclusively dated Iranian women, whom I found exotic—they almost all wore full makeup to class and dressed sexily, even when in jeans and T-shirts. One girlfriend, Mandana Motlagh—my first serious relationship—I met at a party, and she influenced my desire to become fully Iranian, as it were, and less of a fish out of water among my people. I began to believe that my future lay with Iran, and not America.

My spoken Persian, or Farsi as it's known in Iran, improved dramatically, as I used it every day and not just occasionally with my parents. I was fascinated with a language that was much more complex than I knew. With girls, I learned that the words for "I love you" could be the same as "I like you," which made no sense unless you also knew that there was a word for love, *eshgh*, that could be used to describe *passionate* love. The secretaries at the embassy always disapproved of my choices in women, arguing that I should be exclusively dating members of the upper, and not the middle (or lower) class. Mandana was firmly middle-class—her father was an engineer with the National Iranian Oil Company—but her family were Baha'i, and as such, like Jews, Christians, and Zoroastrians, they could be free, successful, and wealthy but not aristocrats in Shia Iran, not even under the Shah. Iran was, and still is, a very hierarchical society, especially among the aristocracy and upper class (who were mostly interchangeable then). My father also disapproved of my romantic choices. He wouldn't say it at the time, but my mother later told me that he had been concerned in 1975 that Mandana would pressure me into marriage. It was hard for either of my parents (or indeed most of their generation) to imagine that any "good" Persian woman would have sex of *any* kind before marriage, and they witnessed her entering my bedroom and closing the door enough times to confirm the disreputable nature of the relationship.

So, that summer, my father bought me an airline ticket to Europe and gave me $500 cash—a substantial sum back then—to sow some wild oats and get Iranian women out of my mind. I think my parents were hoping to arrange for the "right" Persian girls (daughters of friends) to be introduced to their sons or, failing that, if we were to marry strangers, that they be aristocratic Europeans or at least from a distinguished American family. (In his worry about my girlfriend, my father wasn't entirely wrong. After the revolution and a long absence, Mandana returned to Washington and told me that I would have to marry her if I wanted to resume seeing her. After I declined and we parted as friends, I received an invitation to her wedding to another man, about a month later.)

Thinking my father especially generous, I went to London first. I stayed at the flat of a close friend of my parents, Shamsi Assef, whom my siblings and I thought of as an aunt, and still do. She was in Iran for the summer, and so I arranged a party in the flat and invited Davitt and some other comrades from my days at St. Paul's. Davitt was at the end of his gap year and about to go to Oxford in the fall; a girl we both had had crushes on (and whom he later dated), Maria Schleger, came to the party and we flirted. I was ready to break with Persian girls, I told her, if she would be my girlfriend, but she had no interest in seeing someone who lived in America. Many years later I reconnected and had tea with her in London after she had become a deaconess, *Reverend* Maria Schleger, in the Church of England.

I went on to Paris after a day or two, not sure what exactly I was going to do, and met up with my uncle Nasser. I decided then that I would go to the Riviera and spend time on a Mediterranean beach, which I thought would be reminiscent of the Tunisian beaches I had loved as a child. Nasser approved of my plan and drove me to the entrance of the A6 Autoroute not too far from his flat at 65 rue la Fontaine, where I could hitchhike to points south. My father, who I called collect from a post office, told me that I should call one of his good friends, Mostafa Farzaneh (known in France as Maxime Feri Farzaneh), a writer and filmmaker who lived in Paris, and who also ran the French branch of the Iranian Bank Saderat and spent his summers in Cannes. I made my way to Cannes comfortably with only three or four stops and spent the first night in a cheap hotel in town, away from the beach, with a shared bathroom down the hall.

I decided I would rather sleep on the beach, having seen the backpackers from America, Australia, and various European countries seemingly happy to do so. The beach at Cannes had one small "public" section (that even had a shower) next to the private sections run by the luxury hotels such as the Carlton or Majestic, with cafés on the sand. It meant one could swim in the same waters as the wealthy and superwealthy (who in fact rarely swam). Surrounded by fellow backpackers forming a kind of community of freethinking and adventurous youths every night, I slept comfortably under the stars—something I had not done since childhood in my grandparents' garden. Sleeping on the beach was illegal, though, and the police would show up every now and then, usually after midnight, to round up backpackers and transport them to the train station. They seemed to take the greatest pleasure in forcing Americans to stand up and gather their belongings. When it came to my turn, though, my Iranian passport would elicit a surprise "*Vous êtes Iranien?!*" whereupon they'd hand it back and leave me alone. On those nights, I would be the only person on the beach until the others staggered back in groups from the station. It was, I thought, a mark of the prestige France afforded Imperial Iran, and the shock of the French police, in seeing an *Iranian* doing what hippie *Americans* or *Australians* did, made me momentarily proud to be a citizen, even though it wasn't my home.

I did call Mr. Farzaneh on the next-to-last day of my stay on the Riviera, where I rented cheap mopeds and explored the different towns, or stayed in one place and swam in the sea while trying to figure out what to eat to get me through the day—mostly baguettes with cheese or a *pan bagnat* sandwich. He asked me to lunch at one of the beach cafés that I had considered beyond my budget. I had met him before, and he was charming, telling me to order whatever I wanted and asking about my plans. When I told him I was going to hitchhike back to Paris the next day, he looked shocked and told me in no uncertain terms that this was impossible. I told him that was how I had made it to Cannes, but he wouldn't hear of it. He insisted I take the train back and even forcefully pressed some francs in my hand—enough for a ticket—and I knew there was no point arguing. I took the money, thanked him for the advice, and hitchhiked anyway, at one point wondering if he'd been right when a stern-looking man in a Matra Simca Bagheera sports car that boasted three front seats picked me up after midnight and drove in complete silence at truly terrifying speeds for a couple of hours before dropping me off at an exit, having said neither a *hello* nor an *au revoir*.

The next morning a family—a couple and their young son—in an old Peugeot station wagon stopped and took me a good distance, pulling into a rest area for lunch at a picnic table and offering to share their food with me, albeit in total silence. The baguettes, butter, cheese, and raw onions offered to me with gestures, even though I spoke in French to them, was the most delicious meal I had had in a while, and one I remember every detail of still, almost fifty years later. An eighteen-wheeler took me on the final stretch to the suburbs of Paris, the driver telling me to say I was his cousin when we had to stop and be inspected, as I discovered it was illegal for trucks to pick up passengers. When I got back to Washington I gave my father, to his great surprise, some two hundred dollars left over from my stash, plus the money Farzaneh had given me for the train ride. I had spent a month on the French Riviera, bought a Cacharel sweater as a present for my little sister at a boutique in Cannes, and returned with a darker-than-ever tan.

Chapter 9

Ambitions

It was during this time—the mid-seventies—that I decided I would return to Iran after my studies, do my military service (which for college graduates was often teaching English somewhere in a government school), and then join the foreign ministry and follow in my father's footsteps. I'd have to learn to properly read and write Persian, but I thought that to be a minor detail. In some ways the future I imagined for myself was identifying with a homeland but not, I suppose, like my father, fully committing to it. My choice of an Iranian career would involve long absences in familiar places I grew up in—hedging between Tehran and the Anglophone West. I expected that after doing my time in Tehran I'd be sent to the United States, either to the embassy in D.C. or the consulates in Chicago, Houston, New York, or San Francisco, all of which appealed to me as places to live on assignment. I had been influenced by Zahedi, his parties and his lifestyle—dating Elizabeth Taylor included—and couldn't imagine a life more glamorous. Certainly not one spent in an engineering firm. How appropriate it would be, I imagined, to be posted to San Francisco some twenty-five years after my father had been, or even to London, where I had gone to school and often visited my father in his second-floor office in the embassy on Princes Gate.

It didn't matter that I was studying engineering, and in fact a degree in engineering would be viewed in Iran as proof of intelligence. A degree in political science or history or international relations, while more appropriate to diplomacy, would have had no advantage over being a *mohandes*, or engineer, and I would have to study for and pass the foreign-service exam anyway. (Zahedi's degree was in animal science from Utah State University.) My father had never expected one of his sons to want to live and work in Iran. He had left his village for good after school, only ever going back for a funeral or to visit a grave—he never took my mother or his children to his hometown (I am the only one who has ever been to both Ardakan and Yazd). He had purposefully discarded his regional accent soon after settling in Tehran, and having experienced both the upheaval in Iran in 1953 followed by a dictatorship, and the stability and democracy of the West, he actually hoped his children would choose to live there rather than in their home country. It never occurred to him that, like almost every one of his colleagues and friends, he should own a home in Iran. The first home he owned, an apartment on Campden Hill Road near Notting Hill Gate in London in 1976, became his, and my mother's and my sister's, lifeline when he sold it for multiples of what he had bought it for after he was dismissed from his position in the aftermath of the revolution of 1979.

When he was appointed ambassador to Japan in 1977, I was thrilled. Among some of my new Iranian friends, at least the snobbish ones, my status soared.

I was in awe of the fact that my dad would be meeting Emperor Hirohito, America's enemy in World War II and the ruler of Japan when it attacked Pearl Harbor. My brother Saman was now in graduate school at MIT, studying finance at the Sloan School of Management—he'd abandoned physics after receiving his degree (with a First) from Christchurch College, Oxford. I met him in Chicago and we flew to Japan on a Northwest Orient 747 via Seattle for the holidays.

Nasser Majd

Ambassador of His Imperial Majesty
The Shahanshah Aryamehr of Iran

01.

01.
The author's father's visiting card, engraved at Copenhaver, the Washington, D.C., stationers used by many diplomats

I sat in the back of the plane smoking Winston cigarettes (a popular foreign brand in Iran) most of the way. It was a habit I'd picked up from my new Iranian friends at our frequent poker games. One of the regulars, an older man in his thirties supposedly in D.C. pursuing a degree (with a suspiciously poor command of English), was thought by the others to be a SAVAK agent, sent to spy on them, and would insist I take one, almost daring me to refuse. He would also ask political questions as innocently as he could every now and then, and no one would answer, often just changing the subject, leading me to wonder why he was invited to the game in the first place. I realized later that it was precisely because they wanted him to report, if indeed he was SAVAK, that they were *not* anti-Shah or secret members of the Confederation—the Confederation of Iranian Students National Union—the main campus group active in Europe and the United States opposed to imperial rule.

Like many other Iranian men, I didn't smoke in front of my father, as I had learned that it was a sign of disrespect. I was shocked when I learned that my father had *never* smoked in front of *his* father, despite having acquired the habit in his young teens when he and his friends would pick up butts from the street and smoke whatever tobacco was still left. My paternal grandfather, who died from a heart attack when we were in India, himself smoked a *ghalyoun*, or hookah, as well as cigarettes and opium, but undoubtedly not in front of *his* grandfather, who had raised him from infancy after his own father died.

I have to think that my father could smell the tobacco on me, but he never said a word; he himself smoked a pipe in those days. (I finally admitted to smoking after the Islamic revolution—it was too stressful a time to follow cultural niceties—when he went into exile in London, and from then on did so in his presence; his only advice was to quit and start back up in my seventies, when it wouldn't matter to my health as much. I *do* have a carton of Camel straights—unfiltered cigarettes—that I've stashed away at the bottom of a drawer for the day when I turn seventy-plus, unsure of when exactly the "plus" should be.)

It was harder not to smoke in the summer of 1978 when I went back to Japan for a month and accompanied my parents to some of the diplomatic functions at other embassies and, of course, at the dinner parties they gave

01.

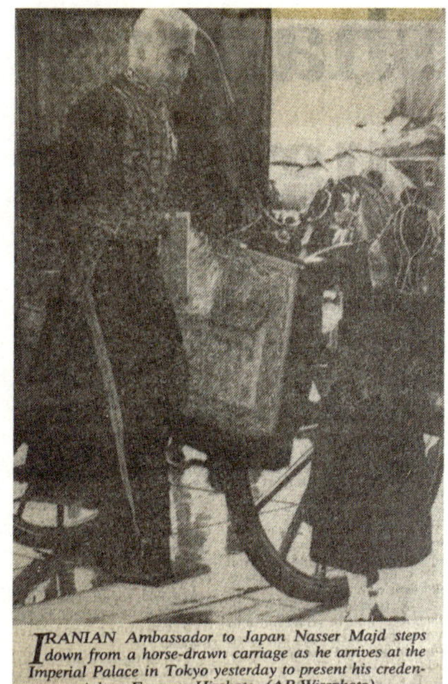

IRANIAN Ambassador to Japan Nasser Majd steps down from a horse-drawn carriage as he arrives at the Imperial Palace in Tokyo yesterday to present his credentials to Emperor Hirohoto. (AP Wirephoto)

02.

03.

01.
The author with his mother at the ambassador's residence in Tokyo, during a dinner party, 1978

02.
Newspaper clipping of the author's father descending from a carriage to present credentials to Emperor Hirohito of Japan

03.
Majd-ol-Olama, the author's great-great-grandfather, in Ardakan

at the residence. Everyone smoked, and at the *petites tables* my family would have small silver buckets filled with cigarettes—both full-nicotine and lights—and small silver ashtrays set in the middle of every table for anyone who needed a smoke between courses. One frequent guest, the Turkish ambassador's wife, was always pulling out her own pack of 100s from her purse and loudly declaring, "Must be *long!*" to guffaws from everyone at the table.

The Iranian Embassy compound in Tokyo was very grand: a three-story house behind gates in one of the most expensive neighborhoods, Minami Azabu, with a swimming pool and an expansive lawn that led to the chancery. I was thrilled to be staying there in the luxury and comfort I didn't enjoy in the same way in Washington; it couldn't be a home, but then again, nowhere was to me, not yet. Washington I had always thought of as temporary—the way a foreign diplomat or even a U.S. administration appointee might see it—and besides, any American city I might want to live in would be more sophisticated, such as New York or San Francisco. And while I planned to go "home" to Iran after my master's degree in operations research, on which I'd embarked as a sort of bridge between the arts and sciences, I certainly didn't know *that* home either.

I felt comfortable in Washington, although it seemed a cultural wasteland in the seventies when compared to London, Paris, or New York. My father's younger brother Masoud, a doctor, had studied there in the sixties and then moved there permanently, and he and his wife would invite me to lunch at their house almost every Sunday for a Persian meal—there were no Persian restaurants in Washington then—and when my cousins Mohammad Majd and Reza Sadighi came to study at George Washington, they would join us. Another cousin, Ali Ziaie, was studying for his master's there, and all of us came to live in the same apartment complex in Virginia across from the Pentagon.

After Ali finished his studies, he and his wife returned to Iran and yet another relative arrived to do postgraduate work. He was my cousins' first cousin but unrelated to me: his aunt and uncle had married one of my uncles and one of my aunts. His father was a well-known ayatollah from Ardakan, my father's birthplace, and was the prayer leader of the city of Yazd; one of his sons, Mohammad Khatami, would become the future president of

Iran. Ali Khatami, his brother who came to study in Washington, would become his chief of staff years later, but after returning to Iran before the revolution he married my first cousin Maryam Majd. Ali was, unsurprisingly, a practicing Muslim, and he moved in with *his* cousin Mohammad Majd. I wondered how he could pray every day and follow the religion faithfully while living with cousins who didn't—and seeing me regularly drinking. He wasn't dogmatic, though; he was peaceful, tolerant, and gentlemanly, and it was unsurprising to me that he ended up working for a brother who would become the most popular president in the Islamic Republic's short history, and the founder of the reform movement in Islamic Iran. (He, and his family, remain my friends to this day.) Still, I sensed that Washington wasn't a home for my family, and it couldn't be for me, either.

Chapter 10

Revolution

In the summer of 1978, while I was in Japan during school break, I was taken by an Iranian embassy staffer who had lived in Tokyo for years to discos almost every night. We drank and danced with European and American models at places like Castel, the local outpost of the famous Paris club, and then, in the early hours of the morning, went to a public bath along with drunk Japanese salarymen looking to sober up. I was blissfully unaware that a revolution was slowly brewing in Iran. In the fall, after I had returned to Washington, I heard about the Cinema Rex fire in Abadan, the southern city that serves Iran's oil industry, where hundreds of cinemagoers had perished after the doors were bolted shut, the building doused with gasoline and set ablaze. The nascent Islamic revolution—up until then merely an irritant to the Shah's regime—immediately blamed SAVAK for starting the fire. The Shah's regime in turn blamed the Shia revolutionaries, who people knew viewed cinemas as symbols of Western decadence and loose sexual mores, and which had been targeted by radical Islamists before. But at the time, the revolutionaries' argument that the Shah was only looking to gain sympathy for the existing order resonated among the public, at least among those who never trusted state propaganda to begin with. While it has never been proven that either the Shah's people or the revolutionaries were behind the act, at the time most Iranians accepted that the Shah's men had started the fire. It spoke to how cynically Iranians viewed their king; even many of those who had little time for Shia revolutionaries nonetheless believed the regime sufficiently corrupt, and even evil, to have burned civilians alive to preserve its power. I was beginning to see the Shah, despite my father's representing his regime, as less than someone to be admired.

I had dismissed some Iranian students' promises of one day overthrowing the Shah as mere pipe dreams, but the growing disturbances in the fall of 1978 were an awakening—not just for me, but for most other Iranians living abroad, students or otherwise (and students back then were the vast majority). An awakening that was exciting but terrifying, too, to those like me who wondered what would happen to the Iran that we knew—powerful, extremely rich, and, as important, Westernizing—and to our families who worked for the regime and benefited from precisely those features.

After immersing myself in Iranian culture in Washington, I had now begun to devour every bit of news I could find, reading *The Washington Post* and *Washington Star*, the now-defunct daily afternoon broadsheet. I spoke to friends who had family inside Iran, and asked my father on the phone what he thought. Being in Tokyo, he had little information, but he had no expectation that the fall of the regime was imminent. While he was no dyed-in-the-wool supporter of the Shah, and certainly not like the sycophants who surrounded the royal court, he was unconvinced that a band of mullahs could end two millennia of monarchy. As a staunchly secular, mostly Westernized man who paid little or no attention to the faith of his forefathers or contemporary fellow Iranians, he disdained any public exhibitions of religiosity and did not hold a high opinion of most clerics. He never prayed, drank alcohol his entire life, and thought most religious prohibitions ridiculous. One summer when we were staying at my grandfather's house in Tehran, he put a bottle of vodka, label removed, in the fridge (a religious authority's house could not under any circumstances have alcohol or pork, both *haram* in Islam). When he went to pour himself a drink after everyone had gone to bed one night, he noticed the bottle had lost some of its contents. I distinctly remember my parents talking about how my grandfather, who would wake up often, must've mistakenly believed the vodka to be water and poured himself a glass. True to his gentle character, though, he never said a word to either my father or his daughter, and to my surprise, my mother was less shocked; even a little amused.

As protests grew, the Shah tried to satisfy the demands of the population, even arresting a former long-serving prime minister, Amir Abbas Hoveyda, to deflect blame and anger from himself. My maternal uncle Nassir Assar had served with Hoveyda in Germany and Turkey when they were both junior diplomats, and they had become good friends. Some years after Hoveyda became prime minister in 1965, he asked my uncle to serve as head of the Oghaf—religious endowment—office in the ministry, responsible for redistribution of shrine-controlled lands and elimination of a revenue source for the ayatollahs. My grandfather urged his son to refuse the post, telling him, according to my mother, that he, an alemeh, knew the clerics, and it would not end well for him to go up against them. Nonetheless, my uncle took the job, but years later, having served as ambassador and in other governmental posts, he was fired by an angry Shah for giving an interview to a newspaper in which he disclosed Iranian policy in the Horn of Africa that the Shah was not prepared to make public. He remained sidelined for the few years leading up to the revolution and, like his friend Hoveyda, didn't leave Iran when he could have, believing that since he had fallen out of favor with the Shah, he would be left alone by the revolutionaries. Hoveyda was, of course, executed in the aftermath of the revolution after a trial with a predetermined outcome, and my uncle, a wanted man, dressed as a woman in full chador and escaped Iran by being smuggled over the border into Turkey. That the Shah, upon leaving Iran with enough baggage to fill two airplanes, didn't take his loyal prime minister with him into exile, leaving him at the mercy of the revolution, spoke volumes about his character.

Over Christmas and New Year in 1978–79 while it was my brother's turn to go to Japan, I went on Christmas vacation from college to London, staying with my friends Kaveh and Payman Bazargan in their flat on Kensington Park Road. Their parents had moved back to Iran when Dr.

Bazargan opened a private medical practice in his hometown of Mashhad, but both boys stayed in London to pursue graduate studies. The Shah had declared martial law, but protests against his rule continued unabated and many industries' workers were on strike. Ayatollah Khomeini had moved in October of that year from exile in Najaf, Iraq, to Neauphle-le-Château, a suburb of Paris, at the Shah's request of Saddam Hussein, who was now friendly with Imperial Iran after an accord had been reached on the territorial split of the Shatt-al-Arab waterway separating the two countries. I had personally witnessed the dramatic turnaround in relations between Saddam and the Shah when I was in Tokyo in the summer. My father invited the Iraqi ambassador and his wife to lunch one Saturday, and after a pleasant Persian meal of rice, crisped *tahdig*, and *ghormeh sabzi* stew cooked by my mother, the ambassador asked if they could have their photo taken under the large portrait of the Shah and the empress in the grand living room. They beamed in the photograph, of which I, unfortunately, do not have a copy.

My friends and I were very curious about Khomeini, an ayatollah (high cleric of the Shia faith) who had been exiled by the Shah for his opposition in the early sixties and until then had lived in Iraq, quietly communicating almost exclusively with his most ardent supporters. But he was in the news every day now that he was in a media-friendly location—a consequence the Shah had not considered—yet we, like many other young Iranians, had never heard of him until that year.

The Bazargan boys knew of their father's imprisonment by the Shah—Kaveh had been born during it—and they also knew of his family's left-wing and even Communist history. We, along with another friend, Farhad Emad, who had also grown up mostly in England, decided to drive to Paris to see the ayatollah. We drove to Dover in Kaveh's VW Golf to catch the ferry to Calais. On arrival in France, we showed our passports, but Kaveh's was held back by the immigration office. "*Refusé!*" the officer said, emphatically. The passport had expired. We tried to explain that Kaveh would go to the embassy in Paris and have it renewed before we left France, but the officer would have none of it. "*Refusé!*" he said, again and again, and led Kaveh away in handcuffs back to the ferry. Farhad sheepishly told us he wanted to go on to Neauphle-le-Château, but Payman and I couldn't leave Kaveh. Back in Dover, with a valid and unexpired student visa, Kaveh was allowed

01.

01.
Street in Tehran (mis)named after the revolution for the village Khomeini stayed in before his triumphant return to Iran

entry into the U.K., but we missed the opportunity to see the ayatollah. He applied for a passport renewal the next week.

I returned to Washington to continue my master's degree, and within days the Shah and his family left Iran in a Boeing 707 (an aircraft used by the Iranian government as late as 2011). Shapour Bakhtiar, an opposition politician and anti-authoritarian who was against clerical rule, whom the Shah had once imprisoned—and whose father the Shah's father had executed—had been appointed prime minister. His government lasted thirty-six days, until February 11, when he was forced into hiding when the military declared its neutrality, returned to barracks, and the Islamic revolution led by Khomeini, who had returned to Iran after the Shah fled, was declared victorious. Not much later, Bakhtiar surfaced in Paris, presumably having been smuggled out of Iran like my uncle. He was assassinated by a regime agent in 1991.

When the revolution triumphed, all I could think about was what was going to happen to my father, mother, and sister in Japan. In weekly phone calls (collect, to the ambassador's residence) my father assured me that all was okay with them, but that he had no idea what would happen to us as a family. I knew he must have removed the photographs of the royal family from the chancery and the residence, and I wondered how he felt doing so after a lifetime of living under and working for a king. Later, he told me a little more about his travails in Tokyo post-revolution. Under the stress of being away from Tehran and unsure of what was happening on the ground, he told me he received a phone call from Queen Farah's office a couple of weeks before the Shah and his family left Iran. "They wanted me to check and see if any galleries in Tokyo would be interested in an exhibition of modern art collected by the queen," he told me. "I asked if they were out of their minds. 'There's a revolution going on around you,' I said, 'and I will not even begin to entertain your request.'" He told me he hung up (but also said that he wasn't necessarily suggesting that the queen knew of the plan). Farah had spent millions of government dollars collecting modern art that still sits in the basement of the contemporary art museum in Tehran, and today would easily be valued in the billions. Had some of it been outside the country at the time of the revolution, it's hard to know who would have benefited from a sale.

In Washington the students who took over the Iranian Embassy on Massachusetts Avenue made a grand display of pouring all the bottles of liquor—including all of Zahedi's favorite, the magnums of Dom Perignon champagne and Royal Salute whisky—into the street with wide-eyed onlookers watching as the river of expensive alcohol flowed downhill, yet my father didn't destroy any of what he considered the "Iranian people's property." (In fact, when he left Tokyo he had his deputy walk through the residence with him and make an inventory of everything that belonged to the government, including all the tins of the special foreign-ministry caviar, so that he would not be accused of theft by the new regime.) Karim Sanjabi, a longtime opponent of the Shah's rule, was appointed foreign minister by the new provisional government of Mehdi Bazargan. Sanjabi replaced various ambassadors known to be close to the Shah, such as Ardeshir Zahedi in Washington and Parviz Radji in London. Other high-profile ambassadors were removed over time, leaving embassies to be run by a chargé d'affaires, many ambassadors choosing to go into exile rather than return to Tehran. It must've been an awkward time for people like my father, who had served the Shah their entire careers and now were unsure what their, and their country's, future held. When I called the residence in Tokyo, my father never let on if he was worried or under stress. He would say he was simply continuing to serve his country as Iran's representative, now representing the Provisional Revolutionary Government of Iran. I didn't know what to think, except I *was* nervous that the future would not favor my family given the revolutionary excesses—imprisonments, executions, and confiscations—that I was reading about in the papers. And indeed, a few months later, Ebrahim Yazdi was appointed foreign minister and removed all the remaining Shah-era ambassadors and deputies from their posts.

Chapter 11

The End of a Career

In early May 1979, not long after the referendum in April that created the Islamic Republic, my father and mother started packing up, ready to leave Tokyo. They were given a farewell dinner by the Japanese foreign minister, Sunao Sonoda, and in a sign of how little the rest of the world understood the new regime, the printed menu cards included the wines—now banned and illegal in Iran.

Many called to wish my father the best, including Mike Mansfield, the U.S. ambassador and former Democratic senator with whom my father had become friendly after inviting him to a dinner he hosted for Kirk Douglas in Tokyo in 1978. (Ardeshir Zahedi had introduced the actor and my father.)

After the execution of his friend and former foreign minister Khalatbari, who had appointed him to Tokyo, my father decided that it would be best not to return to Tehran immediately, as instructed by the foreign ministry; rather, he requested his vacation days and the family flew

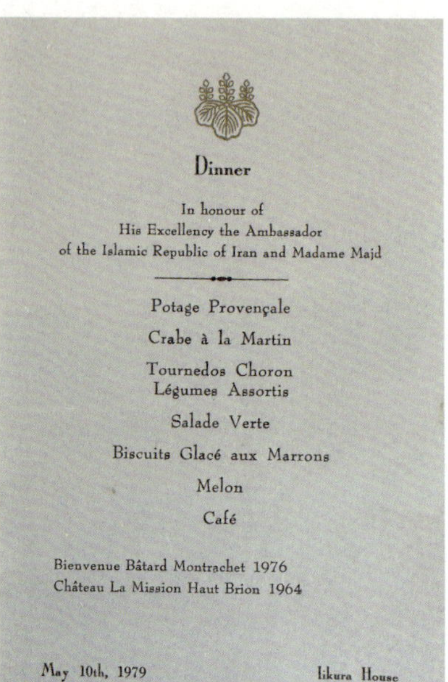

Dinner

In honour of
His Excellency the Ambassador
of the Islamic Republic of Iran and Madame Majd

Potage Provençale

Crabe à la Martin

Tournedos Choron
Légumes Assortis

Salade Verte

Biscuits Glacé aux Marrons

Melon

Café

Bienvenue Bâtard Montrachet 1976
Château La Mission Haut Brion 1964

May 10th, 1979 — Iikura House

01.

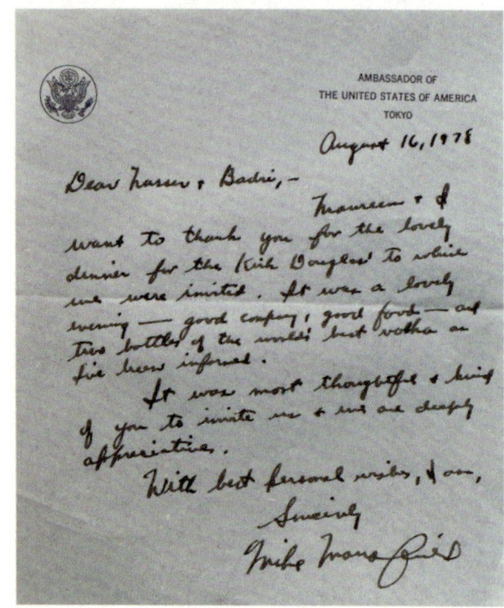

AMBASSADOR OF
THE UNITED STATES OF AMERICA
TOKYO

August 16, 1978

Dear Nasser & Badri,—

Maureen & I want to thank you for the lovely dinner for the Kirk Douglas' to which we were invited. It was a lovely evening — good company, good food — and two bottles of the world's best vodka as I've been informed.

It was most thoughtful & kind of you to invite us & we are deeply appreciative.

With best personal wishes, I am,

Sincerely

Mike Mansfield

02.

01.
Farewell dinner thrown for the author's parents by Japan's foreign minister. Only weeks after an Islamic republic was declared, foreign countries were not yet accustomed to alcohol-free and halal meals for Iranian diplomats.

02.
U.S. ambassador to Japan letter to the author's father

03.
Page from the author's father's diplomatic passport, canceled by himself when he was recalled to Tehran in 1979

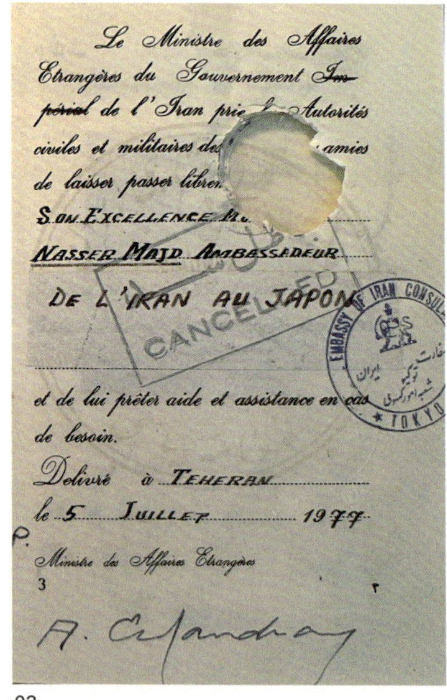

Le Ministre des Affaires Etrangères du Gouvernement ~~Impérial~~ de l'Iran prie [illegible] Autorités civiles et militaires des [illegible] amies de laisser passer libre[illegible]

SON EXCELLENCE M[illegible]
NASSER MAJD AMBASSADEUR
DE L'IRAN AU JAPON

et de lui prêter aide et assistance en cas de besoin.

Delivré à TEHERAN
le 5 JUILLET 1977

Ministre des Affaires Etrangères

3

A. Esfandiary

CANCELLED

EMBASSY OF IRAN CONSUL[illegible] TOKYO

03.

to London. His request was refused and he was ordered back to Tehran, but he ignored the demand, and on arrival in London he, my mother, and my sister were offered U.K. residency by the Home Office (presumably through the recommendation of the British ambassador to Tokyo, who was friendly with my father). After a few weeks of noncompliance, he was fired. Before leaving Japan, he had canceled his and his family's diplomatic passports and had the embassy issue civilian ones.

The next step was to secure British citizenship for my sister, who had been born in London. Even in countries with birthright citizenship, the privilege doesn't extend to children born to diplomats, due to the Vienna Convention on Diplomatic Relations, which sought to preclude the possibility that a hostile government could claim the children of foreign diplomats as its own citizens and prevent them from leaving the country. In the aftermath of the Islamic revolution, many children of Iranian diplomats born abroad were given exceptions, as their parents were in exile from the country they once represented, and, like my sister, were quietly issued passports. My brother and I were in the United States, still in college and on student visas but unsure of what our next steps would be once we finished our studies.

With no income now, my father informed my brother and me that he could no longer support us financially. My brother, pursuing a PhD in finance at MIT, could support himself through teaching, but I had few options aside from returning to Iran to begin serving in the military. I was concerned but not yet panicked, and flew to England in the summer to see my parents and sister in their small apartment on Campden Hill Road in West London. While I could have stayed with them indefinitely, I didn't want to live in Britain and missed being in America, and I returned to Washington after a few weeks to see what I could do to change my student visa. I had more than a semester left to finish my degree (plus the writing of a thesis).

I still had my studio apartment, rent paid for a month, the 1975 Toyota Corolla that my father had bought for me, and a few hundred dollars in the bank. I called the offices of Sylvan Marshall, who had been the Iranian embassy lawyer and had attended many a meal at my parents' house in Washington, to ask if he could represent me in an application for political

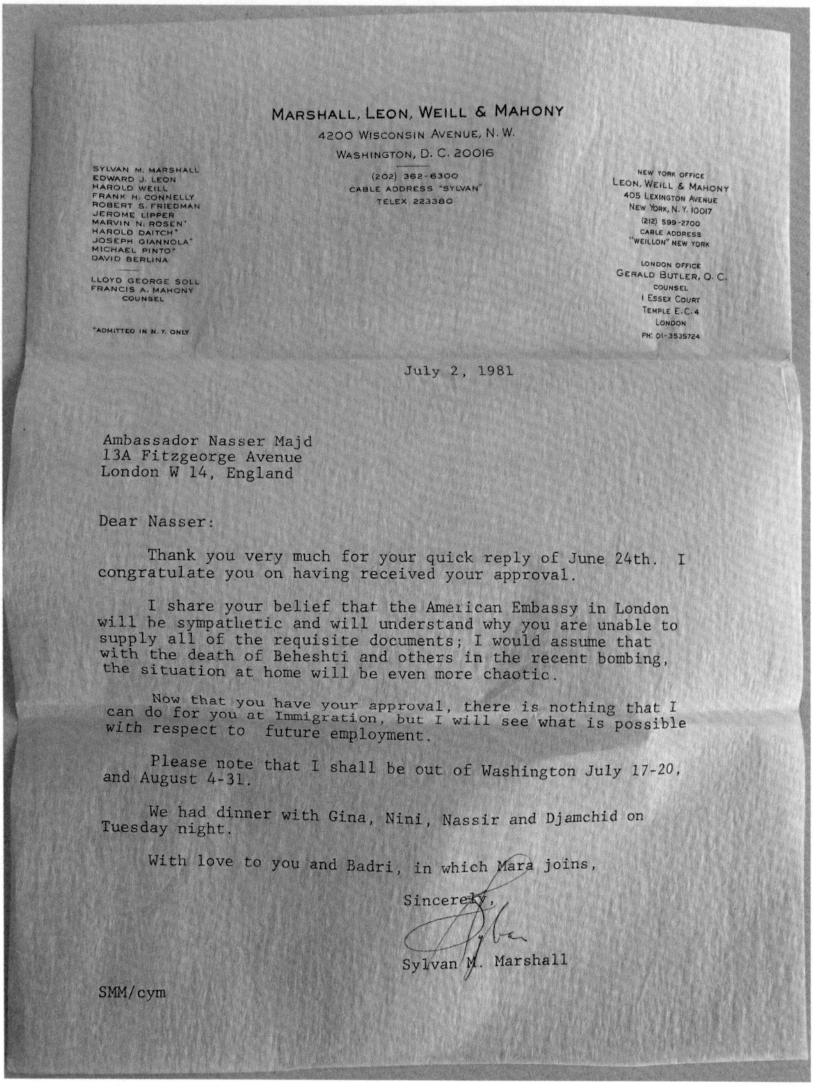

MARSHALL, LEON, WEILL & MAHONY
4200 WISCONSIN AVENUE, N. W.
WASHINGTON, D. C. 20016
(202) 362-6300
CABLE ADDRESS "SYLVAN"
TELEX 223380

SYLVAN M. MARSHALL
EDWARD J. LEON
HAROLD WEILL
FRANK H. CONNELLY
ROBERT S. FRIEDMAN
JEROME LIPPER
MARVIN N. ROSEN*
HAROLD DAITCH*
JOSEPH GIANNOLA*
MICHAEL PINTO*
DAVID BERLINA

LLOYD GEORGE SOLL
FRANCIS A. MAHONY
COUNSEL

*ADMITTED IN N. Y. ONLY

NEW YORK OFFICE
LEON, WEILL & MAHONY
405 LEXINGTON AVENUE
NEW YORK, N. Y. 10017
(212) 599-2700
CABLE ADDRESS
"WEILLON" NEW YORK

LONDON OFFICE
GERALD BUTLER, Q. C.
COUNSEL
1 ESSEX COURT
TEMPLE E.C.4
LONDON
PH: 01-3535724

July 2, 1981

Ambassador Nasser Majd
13A Fitzgeorge Avenue
London W 14, England

Dear Nasser:

Thank you very much for your quick reply of June 24th. I congratulate you on having received your approval.

I share your belief that the American Embassy in London will be sympathetic and will understand why you are unable to supply all of the requisite documents; I would assume that with the death of Beheshti and others in the recent bombing, the situation at home will be even more chaotic.

Now that you have your approval, there is nothing that I can do for you at Immigration, but I will see what is possible with respect to future employment.

Please note that I shall be out of Washington July 17-20, and August 4-31.

We had dinner with Gina, Nini, Nassir and Djamchid on Tuesday night.

With love to you and Badri, in which Mara joins,

Sincerely,

Sylvan

Sylvan M. Marshall

SMM/cym

01.

01.
Sylvan Marshall, formerly the Iranian embassy's lawyer, correspondence with my father

asylum. He not only refused, but told me that I shouldn't delude myself into thinking I deserved asylum, after American diplomats had been taken hostage by students at the U.S. Embassy in Tehran in November 1979, looking to force the Carter administration to return the Shah to face trial in Iran. (Pahlavi had been admitted to the States by Jimmy Carter, albeit reluctantly, for cancer treatment in New York.) The hostage crisis, which lasted the rest of Carter's presidential term (and probably contributed to his losing reelection to Ronald Reagan), was what led to a break in diplomatic relations between the USA and Iran and has led to almost half a century of antagonistic relations between my country of birth and my adoptive one. My father sent Marshall letters from London, asking if he had any leads on jobs or could help expedite a green card application for him and his family, but correspondence between them stopped soon after, as it became clear the Islamic regime was here to stay.

Chapter 12

Exile

Ignoring my new illegal immigrant status, I didn't register with the INS when President Jimmy Carter's administration required all Iranians in the United States to do so in the wake of the hostage crisis. Things were changing dramatically for most Iranians in the States. Every entry-level engineering job I applied for resulted in a rejection, although I can't be sure if it was because I was Iranian or because I wasn't particularly well qualified. I was terrified of running out of money, and I began looking for anything that would pay even an hourly wage. I saw some Iranian friends lose their apartments—becoming *truly* homeless—and Farzaneh Ehterami, one of the secretaries at the former embassy (and one who most vociferously disapproved of my choices in dating), asked if she could move in with me temporarily. She slept on the sofa in the studio, mere feet away from me on my bed. Some friends assumed that we were lovers, for she was a tall, beautiful woman (presumably why she was hired by the embassy in the first place, and invited to Zahedi's parties), but our relationship was strictly platonic.

My cousin Reza had begun driving for a limousine company soon after the revolution, and I thought that was something I could do, too. He recommended me to the limo service and I started driving right away; one of my first jobs was as a driver for the Jordanian entourage that accompanied King Hussein on a visit to Washington. It was ironic, I thought, that not long before it was I who'd been driven in Japan by a chauffeur who wore white gloves. I didn't mind the servile role the job demanded, though I expect the reason that few middle-class Iranians at the time thought of working as a waiter or bartender was that they couldn't imagine themselves, *yet*, as people who served other people.

I couldn't help but feel lost, like so many of my fellow Iranians in the States, but without a firm sense of home, I wasn't sure what it was I'd forfeited. My father had lost his job and sense of value, and I had lost the opportunity for the future I'd envisioned, but neither of us had lost a *home* in the common sense. My father had happily escaped his home and even his regional accent, and I never really had known one. Only my mother, in our family of five, knew she had lost her home. Picking up some members of the Jordanian delegation on the Andrews Air Force Base tarmac one day was surreal to me—only a few years prior, my father had received the Shah there on his state visit to the USA, and I had fully expected that one day *I* would be in a delegation from Iran invited to the White House. I simply couldn't imagine my future as a limo driver, but I had no idea what was next for me.

When driving assignments weren't coming in fast enough to make a living, I applied for a sales position advertised as lucrative in the *Washington Post* classifieds, income based on commission, for what turned out to be the door-to-door selling of high-resolution photographic prints of the kind you might see in a dental practice waiting area. I was desperate enough to give it a try. The recruiter would later remind me of Blake, the Alec Baldwin character in the *Glengarry Glen Ross* film: he would alternately motivate and tear you down for not making enough sales. Naturally, I focused on what I thought would be the most likely place to sell a print and knocked on as many dentists' doors as I could, including that of my own, Farshad Farhoumand, the onetime boyfriend of my ex-girlfriend's sister some years prior, and who had recently graduated from Georgetown and set up practice in Virginia. He would offer to work on my teeth for free, and in fact I still have, almost fifty years later, some of the fillings—in gold no less—that he put in. He happily bought a couple of framed prints of landscapes and seascapes. Hating the work and being naturally shy, I soon gave up knocking on doors.

Soon enough, I was forced to sell my car, which gave me a small cushion, but not enough to pay rent indefinitely. Now I was quite literally homeless, or more accurately "houseless." I was offered a couch to sleep on by my friends the Jalali brothers. Bahman, the elder, had started a construction company with a Chinese college acquaintance, with the idea of taking advantage of government contracts restricted to bids from minority-owned companies. Only a two-man operation, they would bid on a project and then act as general contractors if awarded the job, hiring another company to do the actual work. I helped out in the office in Dupont Circle—a tiny two-room affair above a store—writing weekly checks and doing office work. I even began sleeping at the office when I felt I was imposing too much on Bahman and Behzad by occupying their living room.

During this time, I was friendly with one of the former (nondiplomatic) employees at the embassy, who had managed to abscond with an official rubber seal when it closed. As in Tokyo, after the revolution embassies around the world used a razor to remove the word *Imperial* from "Imperial Embassy of Iran" encircling the lion-and-sword symbol, and used those stamps until the new regime could design and order new ones. All Iranian official documents—passports, birth certificates—had entries filled in by hand, and seals were simply rubber stamps. In the aftermath of the revolution, sending money abroad at the official bank rate became impossible for Iranians unless they had a document showing the funds were for children in college, but many were looking to send as much abroad as they could. The exchange rate on the black market was edging higher by the day, so a couple of those former local employees of the embassy were happy to provide the necessary document, stamped with the official seal, to anyone willing to pay for it.

They gave me some blank, stamped documents and I was able to sell a few to Iranians I knew. I pocketed enough money to leave Washington for California, where in my imagination there might be more opportunities for me than in politics-centric Washington. I left my friends behind and moved to Los Angeles, where I knew the Jalalis' friend Khosro Etemadi, who had just finished his degree at U.C. Irvine, and Shahin Zand, another of the former embassy secretaries, who before the revolution had married one of the diplomats, Nasser Zahedi, a close colleague of my father's and a cousin of the ambassador. After the revolution he had struggled, selling his gold coin collection and opening and then closing a roadside grill in Virginia, and the marriage crumbled. Shahin took her toddler son, Arya, to Los Angeles, where her older sister, once married to an American, lived and was a U.S. citizen, and she began working in retail sales while awaiting the green card her sister had petitioned for. She lived in an apartment in Beverly Hills with her mother, who had joined her from Tehran to help with Arya.

Chapter 13

California

When I arrived in California, I found a furnished studio in Costa Mesa, Orange County, near Khosro, and bought a beat-up Pontiac sedan for $500. Shahin, by now divorced from her husband, Nasser Zahedi, secured an interview for me at Gucci on Rodeo Drive, where she worked. I was hired right away and was back in sales, although this time I was on salary and able to survive, even as my daily commute was over an hour each way. I was placed in the watches-and-accessories department, dealing with small items such as key chains that basically sold themselves to anyone eager to buy a designer trinket. I gave up the apartment after a few months to save money and moved in with Khosro and his friend Masoud Seirafianpour, the son of an Isfahan businessman who had bought an entire three-story building for him in Costa Mesa. When I quit working at Gucci, which I came to realize was going to be a dead-end job unless I wanted a career in retail sales, and I sold my car, we had to rely on Masoud for transportation. Masoud insisted he had money to invest and might find something that Khosro and I could be a part of, but he wouldn't commit to anything other than buying more real estate and managing a handful of inexpensive apartments.

The unsettled life was beginning to be more than the aristocratic Khosro could take, and he soon announced that he would rather return to Iran than live like a pauper—and be reliant on the generosity of friends—in California. Having lost his father as a young boy, he wouldn't be obliged to do national service in the military—Iran was in a brutal war with Iraq then—and he could take care of his mother, who lived alone in their family compound.

I started to panic, fearing being alone, illegal, and with few prospects for gainful employment. Out of desperation, I called my old girlfriend in Washington, Pouran Jinchi, a fellow student at university whom I had dated briefly after the revolution and had broken up with on friendly terms when leaving for California, and suggested that she join me there and look for work. She was hesitant, but agreed to come if I would marry her. Déjà vu. I was torn but agreed. I wanted a partner, and she needed someone to help her get residency in the United States. I was applying for political asylum, finally, ignoring Sylvan Marshall's advice now that the Islamic Republic's reputation might make a more convincing case to an immigration judge, and I knew Pouran could apply as a spouse without having to show evidence of being in danger herself.

When I told my parents in London that I was going to marry, they showed little emotion, occupied as they were with trying to figure out their own lives and still suffering the trauma of losing their country and the life they were accustomed to. Neither warned against marrying someone older (Pouran was a year older than me), about the fact that I was only twenty-five, or, most important, about my not yet having a proper career. Like my smoking in front of my father, I think it was that they were still traumatized. I sensed my father felt somewhat emasculated by no longer being able to provide for his family in the way that he wanted to and believed he should. Had there been no revolution, my parents certainly would have tried to introduce my brother and me to the daughters of their friends, or daughters of the aristocracy or Persian elite (*khanevadeh-ye khoob*—or "good families"), but the only time I heard them express a hope that one of their children would marry into such a family was years later when my sister married an Englishman, a fellow medical student and one of no means.

When Pouran arrived in Los Angeles, I had a small apartment in South Beverly Hills on Olympic Boulevard, across from where Shahin lived, that I had found for only $400 a month. We were both nervous—not about getting married, to which I didn't give much thought with all the other worries on my mind, but for the future. Shahin, lonely and happy to have a friend nearby, offered to secure work for me through her sister: teaching English to newly arrived children in Beverly Hills, sons of wealthy Iranians, mostly Jewish, who had been able to transfer much of their wealth out of the country and into property and businesses there. (Los Angeles County was becoming a magnet for Iranians fleeing the revolution and its strictures. With its mixture of houses, villas, and small and large apartment buildings, its car culture, and its hills and valleys, Southern California reminded them physically of Tehran.) I was able to buy another clunker, one that barely could make it up the steep hill to Trousdale Estates, where many of the newly arrived Persian families lived in mid-century-modern houses that remarkably resembled those of Shemiran, the wealthy hilly neighborhood in the north of the city of Tehran, and where I taught their boys.

We got married by ourselves, casually dressed, in a civil ceremony at the courthouse in downtown Los Angeles. Neither of us was especially emotional; for me, it was another thing to cross off the list of duties before getting to the real business of securing incomes to pay for our lifestyle. Khosro, who came to drinks later at Shahin's apartment, was disappointed in my decision to marry, privately telling me that I was being rushed into something, and besides, "*behet nemeekhoreh*"—or "she doesn't suit you," implying that he thought her beneath my station. I ignored his warning, and Pouran began work at a Robinson's department store selling cosmetics. Iranian immigration to the USA was growing almost exponentially while the war with Iraq dragged on, and the cosmetics counter at many a department store in Los Angeles and Washington, D.C., became staffed by Iranian women, experts in makeup from a young age.

Apart from privately teaching English, I also found work at a Beverly Hills hotel, the Crescent, on—what else?—Crescent Drive, an old structure that another Iranian, "Fred" Hanassab, had bought when he had arrived from Tehran. He needed a weekend front-desk person for the 8 a.m. to 4 p.m. slot and I was happy to take the job, being paid in cash. The hotel was built in the 1920s and was by 1980 a decrepit two-story structure with mostly single rooms sharing a bathroom and shower down the hall. Beverly Hills, especially outside of the triangle of expensive shops and below Little Santa Monica Boulevard, was then still affordable, and the hotel was not unlike those in Hollywood that served struggling actors and unemployed and retired show-business folks who could afford the cheap rent. Hanassab was a kind man who, after he asked about my background, seemed almost embarrassed to hand me my wages, which he would put in an envelope and leave quietly on the desk beside me.

Shahin introduced me to a man she had started dating, Abbas Malakouti, the first since her divorce and a recent immigrant from Tehran who had studied at university in California in the sixties. A successful businessman in Iran, he and a friend of his, Fuad Sabbagh-Fard, opened an auto body shop on Beverly Boulevard and hired Mexicans and Armenian refugees who mostly worked on cars my new friends would buy at auction, fix up, and sell. Being close to Fairfax and a Hasidic neighborhood, Fuad's fluent Hebrew helped drum up some business from that community. Fuad was a Persian Jew whose family were originally from Baghdad, who had emigrated east to Iran in the 1920s when Jews were under attack in Iraq. He had studied at Technion in Israel, where he learned Hebrew, and on his return to Tehran had started an engineering firm with an Israeli partner.

During the Shah's time, Iran, of all the Muslim countries, had an especially unusual relationship with Israel. While Iran gave no official diplomatic recognition to the Jewish state, Israel had a diplomatic outpost in Tehran and Iran had one in Tel Aviv; Israelis worked and lived in Iran, and the Shah provided oil to Israel during its wars with its Arab neighbors. Other than with King Hussein of Jordan, the Shah's relationships with the Arab countries—and especially Egypt under Nasser and Iraq under Saddam Hussein—were fraught. Iran boasted the largest population of Jews in the Middle East outside of Israel (true to this day, albeit greatly diminished), and was less engaged—ideologically, religiously, or emotionally—with the Palestinian issue. The Shah maintained a delicate balancing act in relations with Israel, for he didn't want to inflame the passions of deeply religious Muslims who believed that Jerusalem, Islam's third-holiest site, should never fall under the control of a *kafar*, or unbeliever. (Ayatollah Khomeini was particularly disdainful of the Shah's coziness with Israel, and immediately on the success of the revolution he kicked the Israeli diplomats out and handed their mission to the PLO for a Palestinian embassy.) As an Iranian Jew who had an Israeli partner, Fuad was doubly suspicious of the new regime after the revolution and fled with his family first to Israel, and then to Los Angeles.

Some flights in the sixties and seventies from Tehran to Europe would stop over in Tel Aviv, making direct Tehran–Israel flights possible for Iranians and Israelis alike; I was on one as a child on our way to London, when for the only time in my life I spent a couple of hours on Israeli soil. When my father was director general for the Middle East—one of his posts in the foreign ministry for less than a year in the mid-seventies—he also visited Tel Aviv, both for business and to see one of his best friends, who was then the unofficial consul at the Iranian mission. My father, no Arabist, nonetheless was not keen on Iran's close relations with Israel, which he felt served the interests of the Jewish state (granting a certain legitimacy through what were very public relations with a Muslim country) without reciprocal benefit to Iran. He told me later that he also felt that the Israeli diplomats he was in contact with wouldn't (and didn't want to) recognize the sensitive position Iran was in with its Arab neighbors because of its ties with Israel.

I became fast friends with both Abbas and Fuad, his wife, Nasrin, and their two children, Arash and Arshia. I learned a lot about what life was like in Iran and how it felt to be at the center of a revolution from Fuad, one of the first entrepreneur businessmen from Iran whom I'd meet. He was, and is, passionately patriotic and even nationalistic—he told me that he, too, went onto the roof of his apartment building and shouted *Allah-hu-Akbar!* like so many of his fellow Iranians did during the revolution—and to this day keeps up with events back home. Nasrin's family started the Dr. Sapir Jewish Hospital in the early twentieth century in Tehran, still standing today; it was the only hospital in Iran that treated wounded revolutionaries during the Islamic revolution without informing the security services or SAVAK of their patients. I visited the hospital and its chief physician,

Siamak Moreh-Sedegh, who was also the sole Jewish member of the Iranian parliament, and wrote about the visit in my book *The Ayatollahs' Democracy*.

I would occasionally visit Fuad and Abbas's body shop, Intercars, and we'd eat sandwiches from Canter's Deli in the dusty office while the workers took their break in the covered garage. Masoud, with whom I had once shared an apartment, still lived in Orange County, but when I told him he could get a restored vintage Mercedes 280SL convertible from Fuad and Abbas, he jumped at the chance, paying cash. So, when my jalopy was on its last legs, Fuad and Abbas told me to use an older Toyota Celica they hadn't quite finished fixing up—it had Bondo on its panels but drove like a rocket—which I returned some years later when I could afford a new car. Eventually, the body shop closed and Fuad opened a dry cleaner near the same location, becoming successful again, while Abbas moved back to Iran to go into business there.

Chapter 14

"Beverly Hills, Where Rich People Live"

Early upon my spring arrival in Los Angeles I had called Kirk Douglas and his wife, Ann (they had told my parents that I should do so if ever in Los Angeles), and they invited me to dinner at their home on North Rexford Drive just south of Sunset Boulevard in Beverly Hills. Ann sounded genuinely pleased to be able to meet me. I arrived on the appointed day, a little nervous to meet a star I had been a fan of since childhood. To my amazement, before dinner and while we were having drinks in the living room, Ann brought out a bag full of matches from all over the world, telling me that she had seen my mother pocket matches at a restaurant in Tokyo despite not being a smoker, and had heard from her that I collected matchbooks. She said she'd been inspired to do the same, and thus ended up saving them for me.

Over dinner we talked about Iran, of course, and about Zahedi and my parents, and the Douglases showed great concern for their well-being. Kirk had written to my father when Iran was in the throes of revolution, saying he hoped "the Shah was doing everything he can to satisfy his people." I asked Kirk if he would give me a letter of recommendation for my political asylum application, which I still intended to file at some point, and he happily obliged. (Sadly, it didn't occur to me at the time to make copies of that letter and others like it). I also asked the Douglases if they knew of any opportunities for work, and Ann mentioned that she played tennis with Jon Douglas, a successful realtor (unrelated to Kirk, whose real last name was Danielovitch), and would be happy to put me in touch. I thanked her but didn't pursue the lead, as I hadn't yet envisioned that I could sell real estate, when all my sales jobs had ended unsuccessfully.

I enjoyed the California lifestyle in the early 1980s—the weather, the beaches, and the relaxed way of life—but I was frustrated about not having disposable income, money I could spend on anything we liked. I decided, having seen "for sale" signs show up all over Beverly Hills and then quickly disappear, that I might make good money selling real estate, despite my aversion to sales jobs and earlier reluctance. I went to the library and found books on the test, signed up for it, and within a couple of months, with license in hand, walked up Canon Drive to the corner of Brighton Way and the offices of Jon Douglas Realtors, remembering Ann Douglas mentioning him. I didn't call her, though, still a little shy and not wanting to impose, and thinking I would ask her for an introduction only if I was rejected at the Beverly Hills branch of the company. I didn't meet Kirk or Ann again until years later.

When I asked the receptionist who I should see about a job, she called the manager, Mike Higer. He took me back to his office and asked about me and why I wanted to sell real estate. I think he liked that I was college-educated, Persian (Iranians were flocking to the Los Angeles area then, often buying houses with cash), and that I admired his Mont Blanc Diplomat fountain pen—I told him my father was actually a diplomat and owned Mont Blanc pens, too. He hired me on the spot. He told me to talk to the secretary to arrange for business cards, and I left the office feeling somewhat positive about the future. Business cards! Little did I know at the time how hard it is to find clients—sellers or buyers—if you don't already have a circle of friends and acquaintances.

KIRK DOUGLAS

September 27, 1978

My dear Ambassador and Mrs. Majd,

We are finally back in the United States after a very exciting trip. I want to add my thanks to the letter that my wife sent to you and also to thank you for the wonderful photographs in the package. Of course, we thought about you during our visit to Iran and since then we certainly hope that conditions have improved. As I read the newspapers it seems the Shah is doing everything he can to satisfy his people. I hope he succeeds.

We really can't thank you enough for the courtesies you extended to us in Japan and, of course, I relayed our appreciation to Ardeshir as well.

I certainly hope we will have a chance to meet again here in the United States--Japan or maybe Iran. In the meantime, all our very warm wishes to you and your family.

With gratitude,

Kirk Douglas

The Honorable Nasser Majd and Mrs. Majd
Imperial Iranian Embassy
10-32 Minami-Azabu 3-Chome
Minato-Ku
Tokyo 106 Japan

01.

01.
Letter from Kirk Douglas
during the revolution

Mike had a law degree and was well-read and up on current events, and he showed serious interest in my background and in Iran. We would have lunch at least once a week. He had become friends with Jon Douglas, who hired him to manage the Beverly Hills office, which came with a salary and a percentage of the commissions brought in by the salespeople, but didn't require him to actually sell. Fortuitous, for he was the opposite of what one might envision as a high-performing salesman or aggressive motivator—and certainly not someone in David Mamet's imagination. Yet he didn't need to be: most of the agents working out of that office were high earners, self-starters who had plenty of contacts and leads. A few private offices with glass doors were reserved for the very highest earners—agents who managed to sell multimillion-dollar properties with astonishing regularity.

One such agent, Joan Leopold, took pity on me one day. She offered to share a listing on a house in Westwood owned by an Iranian investor, saying we'd split the commission if I would agree to hold the open houses on Sundays. Naturally, I assented. One Sunday as potential buyers and curious lookers walked in and out of the unfurnished home, an older couple walked in and we stared at each other for a moment. "*Hooman?*" the lady asked. "*Yola?*" I replied, and "*Dic?*" (which is how Richard Sigerson wrote his shortened name.) It was my schoolboy friend Davitt's parents, whom I had last seen in London more than a decade prior. Before the internet changed everything, losing contact with a friend made it extremely difficult to reconnect. I had tried once, sending a letter to Davitt care of *Rolling Stone*, imagining that somehow it would get to him since I knew he was a music writer and a producer. Of course it never did reach him, but here were his parents in California and they took my number. A day or so later Davitt called.

Davitt was now a music producer in L.A., I discovered, no longer writing much but instead making a good living producing pop and rock music. He was also recently married, to my surprise. I always imagined him in the entertainment world somehow, dating women, partying hard (but no drugs, as he was one of the few in school who had never tried marijuana or any other drug), and not settling down with a family until much older. But here he was, the New Yorker via London, now in California, and his parents had sold their duplex apartment in Chelsea and moved halfway across the world to be close to him. We reestablished our friendship, seeing each other often for Persian food at one of the restaurants on Westwood Avenue—Little Tehran, or "Tehrangeles," as the Iranians call it—and playing tennis, badly, in Roxbury Park across from my apartment on Olympic.

The house on Comstock sold after a while—the Sigersons had instead bought two apartments in a high-rise on Wilshire Avenue and combined them—and Mike Higer fell out with Jon Douglas and moved down the street to Mike Silverman & Associates, a boutique agency made famous by Mike Wallace's *60 Minutes* piece on Silverman as "realtor to the stars." He offered me a sales position there, introducing me to Silverman, a charming character who took a liking to me, imagining, I assume, that Iranian cash sales might soon be flowing into his coffers. Iranians, rich or otherwise, were indeed buying real estate—only not from me. I had few contacts in the business world of prerevolutionary Iran, so my lack of a home, so to speak, even hindered my potential as a real estate broker in Beverly Hills and Los Angeles.

I was getting frustrated with real estate sales. I was no match for brokers with long histories in the area or who were married to professionals and had access to their spouses' clients' long lists of contacts. I was surprised to find that many of the top brokers lived in Beverly Hills or Bel Air mansions themselves, and not a few would buy and sell their own houses, too. The Silverman brokerage was tiny; a true boutique that employed only a dozen or so agents, all top producers. Mike Silverman preferred to hire women; at the time, I was the only man in the office. He held court poolside at the Beverly Hills Hotel, had a house in Malibu on the beach, and spent summers on the French Riviera, drumming up yet more business.

One day I picked up a call from a man who wanted to know more about a house he had driven by in Trousdale. Arriving at our appointment, I saw a Rolls-Royce with a license plate that read CROWN. While that house wasn't to their liking, I did end up selling Mark and Marilyn Tenser a new home, as well as arranging the sale of their small one just off Mulholland Drive on the San Fernando Valley side. I also sold a vacant house in Brentwood that Marilyn had inherited from her father, and after they moved into their new home in Beverly Hills off Benedict, we became good friends. They were the owners of Crown International Pictures, a B-movie studio founded by Marilyn's father, Newton Jacobs; a lovely couple who never once failed to call me on my birthday in all the years that I knew them and who I enjoyed talking to about every aspect of the entertainment business as well as politics. The sales commissions I made from their business, plus a few other smaller deals (later including selling an apartment to Davitt and his wife, Ana-Rosa Aboitiz, and a small house to Michael Steele, bass player of the band the Bangles, whose new album Davitt was producing at the time) meant that I could buy a much-needed new car—nothing fancy, though.

Still I didn't think real estate sales could be a career for me. As I had always liked writing, from the time I was at St. Paul's and then at university, I thought that while still trying to make money in real estate, I should write a book about all the interesting Iranian characters I had met since the Islamic revolution. Living in the capital of motion pictures, I thought, perhaps I could even get a movie made about the diaspora—with its own mafia and crazy, traumatized characters—pouring from Tehran and every other city into America. (I did not anticipate that one day it would be on *television* that a cast of real-life Angeleno Iranians would be portrayed as they were in *The Shahs of Sunset*.) So in my spare time I started writing, with strong encouragement from Davitt, and a collection of stories about the Iranian diaspora took form.

Chapter 15

A Third Life

When I finished my collection of short stories in the mid-1980s, I showed it to Davitt first. He loved the stories—about exile, the trauma of losing a home, and fictionalized versions of people I had come across, including criminals. At this point Davitt, who already knew quite a bit about Iran and Iranians through our friendship at school, dove into the culture and was going to Westwood alone to eat Persian food—even at a hole in the wall that served *kaleh patcheh*, or a sheep's head and trotters stew that I wouldn't dream of trying. He told me he was going to send the book to his friend Michael Zilkha, the onetime owner of Ze Records—the label that Davitt had been signed to as a singer-songwriter after college.

I met with Michael the next time he visited Los Angeles to see his father, Selim, who lived in Bel Air and with whom Michael had started oil and gas exploration as the Zilkha Energy Company, based in Houston, where he had moved from New York after exiting the record business. He was taken with my stories and with my background, asking what I wanted to do with my life other than write books. I told him I wanted to get out of real estate and into a regular paying job, perhaps in the entertainment business—which was all anyone in L.A. seemed to want to talk about—and to continue to try to get published. Michael immediately thought to send my stories to Chris Blackwell, owner of Island Records (which had distributed Ze) and Island Pictures, both of which I knew well—some of my favorite artists, like Cat Stevens, Steve Winwood, and Bob Marley, had been signed to Island, and I'd seen the film company's logo and credit in indie films such as *Bagdad Café* and *Kiss of the Spider Woman*.

Davitt was a bit doubtful about Island. He told me that Blackwell had a reputation for falling out with people he worked with and dropping talent he no longer felt would be productive. Nevertheless, I received a message from Chris a few weeks afterward asking me to see him at the offices of Island Pictures in a nondescript office building on Sunset Boulevard. I went into the meeting unsure of what to say, but Chris was charming. I knew he was a creative type, but I was a little surprised that a man with his success was wearing a T-shirt, jeans, and flip-flops to the office where I assumed he met with agents, producers, and film distributors. He admitted that he hadn't read my collection of stories, but said, "If Zilkha likes them I'm sure they're great." He said that he had kept the manuscript at his house in Nassau and promised to read it when he got a chance. "I had a Persian friend in London in the fifties," he added.

It turned out that Blackwell had been a young professional gambler, and he and this friend plied their so-called trade as backgammon players in London's private gambling clubs, taking money off unsuspecting patrons. When we got to talking about what I wanted to do with my life, I used one of Davitt's explanations for our education at St. Paul's: that English public school had really taught me only how to be a good dinner guest, but that I was confident I had skills that could be applied to either of his businesses. Chris, himself a boarding school alumnus, laughed, and told me to meet him in a couple of months at the same office. I left excited: finally I might be on a path that would give me some stability in my so far peripatetic life.

When I met Chris again, he offered me a job but said he still had no idea what it would entail—he was sure I'd find my place soon enough. He told Dan Genetti, the Island Pictures office manager of sorts as well as a production executive, to put me on the payroll at $40,000 per year. (By now my political asylum case had been approved, with my green card on the way, and I was no longer illegal.) Davitt was encouraging and pleased to see me employed, and no longer whispered warnings to me about Chris. But his original doubt remained at the back of my mind. I was determined to not fall victim to my new boss's reputed fickleness even as I wondered if I could be successful when so many before me had not been.

Mark Burg, the young new president of Island Pictures, started dumping script after script on my desk and telling me to write "coverage." That, I thought, I could do quite easily. Chris would call every now and then from wherever in the world he was—one time he showed me his calendar, and he had taken more than 150 flights in a year—and ask me how things were going, about what was happening or hot in Los Angeles, and if I thought any of the scripts were any good. I was enjoying the job and the benefits that came with it: health insurance, a steady income, and as many music albums from any label that I wanted. My new Island Entertainment Group business card allowed me to be a part of all three distinct Island properties—records, film, and music publishing. I felt I might have found a home, or at least a *work* home.

I saw Chris whenever he was in L.A. for a few days, and I would drive him around, even joining him occasionally for lunch with a fellow music or film business executive. One such lunch at a West Hollywood restaurant was with Lionel Conway, head of Island Music (publishing), and Peter Paterno, a powerful music business figure who was then Guns N' Roses' lawyer but later became the president of Hollywood Records, Disney's foray into the business. I didn't say a word at lunch, and they must have wondered what I was doing there, as Paterno regaled us with stories about Guns N' Roses and Axl Rose. Chris had started calling me his "minister without portfolio"—a nod, he said, to my diplomatic background, which he found interesting—which confused the other employees at Island even more. I, however, rather liked being able to straddle the different worlds of entertainment, and the reference to diplomacy and politics in my title was, I thought, fitting. I also found it liberating to be able to become whatever person was necessary at the time—Chris himself seemed to me to be a sort of portfolio-less boss who would straddle different disciplines, and even arts, depending on necessity or mood.

Chris started asking me to go to New York to see him there, where the record company was based on the second floor of a building on Fourth Street and Broadway that housed Tower Records on the ground floor. I was spending more time on the record side of Island, being an assistant of sorts for Blackwell and often translating his thoughts on marketing and strategy for other employees, and I was getting to know the A&R people and the radio promotion people on both coasts. Lou Maglia, a veteran music business executive, was the president of Island at the time, and he didn't seem particularly concerned about me, or even the fact that Chris decided, on the spur of the moment, to move my employment to the record company roster and bump up my pay by 50 percent, to $60,000 per year, a decent-enough salary for someone who hadn't been in the business very long. Lou was charming, even asking me to come along with Chris on an East River cruise on his yacht one day, but he never asked me to listen to music demos or Island CDs and offer my opinion.

I told Chris that now that I was at the record company, I would need new business cards, but I couldn't really put "minister without portfolio" as my title. Chris had no opinion to offer and so I had no title at all on my cards, which I think kept people off guard as they couldn't be sure whether I had real power. Soon, Island employees who couldn't (or didn't want to) reach Chris himself started coming to me with messages for him or to ask what Chris might think of something, and Chris started telling people that I ran the L.A. office. I didn't change my business cards, but it sounded good to me.

In 1989, Blackwell was looking to sell Island Records, having been solicited by more than one conglomerate and realizing that it was worth far more than he could have ever dreamed. One day he asked me if I could place a rumor in *Variety*, the Hollywood entertainment daily that most people in the industry read religiously *before* the *Los Angeles Times* every morning. He wanted me to suggest that Island, which was in play publicly by then, favored a sale to Fujisankei, Japan's largest media group. Japanese companies such as Sony were looking to expand into Anglophone entertainment, either to provide "content," as it were, for their hardware or to expand their horizons beyond Japan.

Sony, I later realized, would have been too obvious and easy to fact-check; few people, however, knew Fujisankei in the States. Chris had no intention of selling to a Japanese company—he told me he would find it hard to communicate with the executives—and was leaning toward selling to Polygram, a subsidiary of the Dutch Philips Electronics, which already owned Polydor Records, Mercury Records, the classical label Deutsche Grammophon, and the jazz label Verve. The new head of North America for Polygram was Alain Levy, a French former executive who headed CBS France and then Polygram France. He intended to broaden Polygram's presence—then trailing Warner Music, Sony, BMG, EMI, and MCA (Universal)—by acquiring independent record labels to expand his market share and back catalog, ripe for exploitation in the CD age. The bigger independent labels were A&M, Geffen, Island, and Virgin, and Levy first had his sights on Island.

It's impossible to know if Chris's rumors had any effect on Levy or on his bosses, David Fine, president and CEO of Polygram in London, and Jan Timmer, the new president of the parent company, Philips. Chris knew Timmer, saying to me, as he was about to do the deal with Levy, "I like the Dutch." Levy was a corporate soldier through and through, a "suit" in a business where executives wore shorts, and it seemed odd that he would find Chris sympathetic to his management style. Chris had always done things his own way, for some thirty years—he told me he survived "*by my wits*"—and he didn't care what people might think as long as he was confident of his own opinion. He dressed as he pleased, generally in jeans and T-shirt, in flip-flops in the city and barefoot in the islands. I don't think he owned any socks.

As the deal with Polygram was nearing completion, I was in New York with Chris one afternoon, at one of his two one-bedroom apartments at the Essex House hotel on Central Park South. He was getting ready to go out and have dinner with Levy and Tom Hayes, Blackwell's longtime number two in London and chief business affairs executive, when he looked down at my loafers and asked what size shoes I wore. He thought for a second that perhaps he should wear actual shoes to dinner, but his feet were larger than mine and so he went ahead and met Levy in his jeans, T-shirt, and ragged flip-flops. It didn't affect the sale, though, and Island sold for $300 million (later reduced somewhat, after Polygram performed due diligence). Chris did not net the rumored $270 million, as he had silent investors, and the band U2 had once accepted 10 percent of the company in lieu of royalties Island couldn't pay at the time. Nonetheless, Chris was now a multimillionaire and cash rich, able to pursue other projects.

Over Christmas of 1989, I came to understand Island Records and the way Chris saw his role in bringing music to the world. Davitt Sigerson and Bob Thiele, Jr., had put together a band of sorts, the Royal Macadamians, and recorded an album as a lark, *Experiments in Terror*, to give to friends as a present. I gave a copy to Chris, who knew Davitt from the Ze Records days, and he took it with him to the Bahamas, where he was going to spend the holidays. He called me one day and said that he had started to play the cassette in a boombox on his boat, and his friends pleaded with him to shut it off. But, he said, if it elicited that kind of reaction, we should put it out. And so Island released the record on CD and cassette to some good notices but few sales, and with surprising enthusiasm from most of the staff. They knew there was no expectation for this record, but they could at least have fun with it.

Chapter 16

Passports & Polygram

In 1990, Chris wanted me to travel internationally—to Britain, where Island had been based before opening offices in the United States, and to Jamaica, the spiritual home of Island Records, where he had grown up and was always most comfortable—but my Shah-era passport had long expired. The Iranian government was under no obligation to provide me with another; since I was resident in the States through political asylum with category AS6 on my green card. Almost as if to prove I'd be in danger if I returned to the country of my birth, I could get only a *laissez-passer* that would be good for a one-way trip to Iran. The Islamic government was especially scornful of asylees.

At this time, Iranians who once had green cards were gaining citizenship in the USA or in various EU countries if they had been resident long enough. Meanwhile, the Iranian passport had morphed from one of the best for visa-free travel across the globe into one of the very worst. Most countries Iranians wanted to travel to were less and less accommodating of visa requests by Iranian passport holders. In the USA, many Iranian Americans who wanted to maintain the ability to travel to and from Iran would, before naturalization, report their green card missing and apply for a replacement. Once the replacement was in hand, they would surrender that card upon gaining citizenship (which one had to do), keeping the old card to show the Iranian consular officials. (After the severing of diplomatic relations with the United States in the aftermath of the hostage crisis, Iran kept an "Interests Section" at the Pakistan embassy to handle consular affairs, such as passport renewals, with the Swiss embassy in Tehran representing U.S. interests there).

In a twisted and complicated dance, Iranian Americans traveling to Iran would then take their U.S. passport and their Islamic Iranian passport to a U.K. or other European consulate and ask for a visa to be stamped in the Iranian one. Then they would fly to a European capital with their U.S. passport, leave their American passport with friends or family, and fly to Iran with their Iranian passport and U.S. green card, leaving Iranian authorities in the dark about that second citizenship—illegal and not recognized under Iranian law (pre-dating the Islamic regime). Then, on return to the States from Tehran, they would show the airline their visa for the European country, and leave Iran with their Iranian passport, picking up the American one at the layover in Europe.

I had by this time resigned myself to the fact that I wouldn't be able to travel to Iran anytime soon, whether with a green card and Iranian passport or a hidden U.S. one. In fact, I would often dream of being in Iran and not being allowed to leave—a premonition of what was to come years later. But since the late 1990s, no complicated passport dance has been necessary, as Iran today turns a blind eye to dual citizens—unless, that is, the authorities decide to take them hostage. The Shah, even more than the ayatollahs, was contemptuous of any Iranian who wanted to adopt a second nationality, and if anyone relinquished their Iranian citizenship, they were banned from ever visiting Iran again.

Blackwell himself had three passports—Jamaican, British, and Irish (through his father)—and was somewhat bemused when I told him I had to get a visa on my U.S. State Department–issued laissez-passer (for asylees) in order to travel internationally. The Jamaican and Bahamian consuls in New York who issued me visas were even more bemused by a document they'd not seen, and the Jamaican immigration officers in Kingston or Montego Bay would inevitably cross out the citizenship entry on my landing card, where I had written "stateless," and write "U.S." instead, presumably because of the eagle symbol and U.S. State Department wording on the cover. I didn't bother to argue with them. Despite the complications, having Island Records as my employer allowed me to leave the United States for work and even for pleasure. To me, Island was becoming my passport, my citizenship, and my identity.

When the Polygram sale was completed, Mike Bone took over from Lou Maglia as president. He was a radio promotion man who had worked his way up to the presidency of Chrysalis Records, as Alain Levy believed that promotion or marketing people should be in charge of the record labels, not A&R (artists and repertoire) people or the "creative" types, who should instead focus on acquiring talent. Chris didn't want to argue with the new owners of his company, and he welcomed Mike to Island, giving him wide latitude to run the label. Mike, a straight shooter, didn't understand my role at the company, but he left me alone. Polygram had yearly conferences, gathering the presidents and managing directors of its labels worldwide for a four- or five-day set of meetings in which each label would present its new acts and upcoming records and give a rundown of its performance over the past year. In 1990, after its purchase of Island and A&M Records (which Levy bought for $500 million less than a year after buying Island), the conference was to be in Nassau, Bahamas, where Chris conveniently had a home, a famous recording studio, and a yacht.

Chris called me and said that I should meet him in Nassau in time for the conference, but when I told Bone I was headed there, his response was *You're not invited!* I tried to explain that Blackwell had specifically instructed me to go, but he just repeated emphatically that I wasn't invited. I told Chris, but he just said in response that he'd see me in Nassau. And so I went, going directly to Chris's house where I was to stay, as all the *invited* Polygram executives were staying at a hotel resort on the beach where the conference was held. Being in Nassau at Chris's house made me feel even more at home in my special role at Island.

To what I presume was the dismay of Mike Bone, and I'm sure Alain Levy, too, Chris asked me to go with him to the conference on the days that he was scheduled to speak. One panel was on Philips Electronics' latest music product, the DCC, or digital compact cassette, soon to be introduced to the world. It was Philips's idea—as the inventor of the hugely popular and successful analog cassette around which Sony later built its Walkman—that in the digital age of CDs, which it had co-invented with Sony, the cassette format, portable and even pocketable, would still be viable if the sound was pristine like a CD's. As the rest of the panel *oohed* and *aahed*, Chris fumbled with the cassette in his hands, head down. When asked what he thought of the product, he replied, "Well, I don't think much of it at all." The room fell silent, and the panelists moved on.

Chris was known as a music impresario, whose creative instincts and marketing chops were legendary—he had successfully marketed Bob Marley as a rock act, not a reggae singer, after all. And here he was dismissing his new parent company's hope for a hit consumer electronics product. As much as Alain Levy and Jan Timmer may have respected Chris's taste in music, I expect they put his dismissal of the DCC down to a lack of understanding of hardware. But I was a little shocked. When I asked him later if it wouldn't have been better to hedge on the cassette, he shrugged his shoulders and said it was a silly product that no one would buy. He was proven right, although I doubt Levy or Timmer remembered his verdict as the DCC players and prerecorded Polygram albums on DCC languished in warehouses unsold. (I reminded Chris of his pronouncement in Nassau years later when he was in a conflict with Alain Levy over what he wanted to do in the audiovisual realm with the advent of the DVD, which Chris thought was the future of entertainment. No one, of course, could have predicted streaming.)

In Nassau, Chris hosted a party at his house for some of the conference attendees—mostly the executives he knew and the A&M contingent. Chris had a history with A&M and Jerry Moss, the co-founder of the label, which once distributed Island acts in the States. We took the A&M executives on a cruise on Chris's fishing yacht—a modest affair, but I worried that we must be annoying the top executives of Polygram by acting like the cool guys among a group of suits and nerds. Included on the cruise (but presumably uninvited to the conference) was A&M's legendary radio promotion man Charlie Minor, who made our cruise off the coast of Nassau a nonstop party. He was known in the business as a flamboyant, vivacious character who reveled in the "sex, drugs, and rock and roll" repute of the industry, and music executives were in shock a few years later when he was shot to death by an ex-girlfriend.

01.

01.
Chris Blackwell driving his speedboat in Nassau; photo by the author riding shotgun

OB MARL
WAILERS
KIN'
ES
ffer inna the ghetto . . .
e live a Ghost Town
ush it down . . ."

Chapter 17

The Jamaicans

When Chris and I left Nassau, I returned to Los Angeles briefly before going to Miami to rerecord "Electric Boogie" with Marcia Griffiths, one of the I-Threes—Bob Marley's backing singers. "Electric Boogie" was a song written and recorded originally by Bunny Wailer (of the original Wailers band) and later covered in the early eighties by Marcia Griffiths for Mango, a sublabel of Island that released Jamaican and other "world music." The single didn't make a particularly big splash in the pop market in 1983, but in 1990 it became a phenomenon when the U.S. Black community set a line dance to it called the Electric Slide, and it quickly spread to mainstream pop culture, played as a dance track at weddings and parties. Marcia Griffiths had called Chris a few times to tell him Island should rerelease the single and put marketing muscle behind it. Chris asked me to investigate further, and to talk to the Jerks, a Miami production trio—Joe Galdo, Lawrence Dermer, and Rafael Vigil—behind Gloria Estefan and the Miami Sound

01.

01.
With David Byrne in
Cartagena, 1990

Machine. Joe, a Cuban American who had left Havana as a child, was a musician himself and led the team. Joe told me the song definitely needed a remix, though Chris wanted Marcia to rerecord it instead.

I arranged to have Marcia fly to Miami from Kingston, put her up in a hotel, and flew there myself. As we rerecorded the song in a couple of days, I became friends with Joe, who was a gracious host, taking me to Cuban restaurants and showing me around South Beach, which Chris had once told me would soon be *the* American Riviera, despite the dilapidated art deco hotels in which senior citizens spent their days on the porches and verandas with pastel-colored paint peeling all around them. Later, with money from the sale of Island, Chris bought up some of those old hotels, remodeled and refurbished them, and in a self-fulfilling prophecy, created an American Riviera that other hip hoteliers and conglomerates alike rushed into. Chris believed that hotels should be marketed like acts—each should have a personality that would appeal to a certain segment of the market—and he eventually became a hotelier almost above all else. The first of his numerous properties on Ocean Drive was the Marlin, where he kept the top floor as an apartment for himself and converted the basement to South Beach Studios. Under the name Island Outpost, he expanded the hotel business to the Bahamas and Jamaica, where today he still operates Goldeneye—Ian Fleming's old estate—and three other properties (two of them for sale as of this writing) as luxury resorts.

Joe Galdo, now a friend and colleague, asked me to attend a music festival with him in Cartagena, Colombia, at a time when no U.S. airline would fly to the country and the drug cartels were in full force. I agreed, knowing that Mango was soon to release a Colombian label's music in the U.K. We arrived in Cartagena on a special Avianca flight from Miami, and the Americans were all pulled aside for questioning while I breezed through immigration with my UN-approved document, making it the first time I was happy to be stateless. We stayed at a sixteenth-century mansion owned by Sam Green, an art dealer who had once hosted Greta Garbo, and went to concerts in the stadium every night with David Byrne, who would dance the night away to cumbia music.

Later that year, trying to board a Pan Am flight from Miami to London, I was denied a boarding pass due to my place of birth, listed on my travel document: Tehran. The agent and then her manager explained that in the aftermath of the Pan Am 103 bombing over Lockerbie, Pan Am had instituted a policy that no Iranians could fly on their planes. I tried to explain that discrimination on the basis of national origin was illegal in the United States, and that I had a valid visa for the United Kingdom and a legal travel document. Still denied boarding, I called Galdo's wife, who worked for Pan Am in the Miami offices, and I had my boarding pass in hand moments later.

Island Records arranged a rush release of "Electric Boogie." We quickly shot a video on Commerce and Barrow Streets in Manhattan's West Village featuring the line dance, and the record reached the middle of Billboard's Top 100 pop singles without, unfortunately, any play on MTV—at the time the most important promotion a record could get. Marcia was an easygoing person with a beautiful voice, who was never anything but gracious and understanding. I worked with her again a few years later when Chris asked me to go to Tuff Gong Studios in Kingston to oversee the recording of Bob Marley songs covered by the I-Threes—Marcia, Rita Marley, and Judy Mowatt. (We didn't release the record in the States, but it was picked up by the Japanese and German Polygram companies, and Rita released a vinyl version in Jamaica.)

Blackwell had recently been given personal managerial control of the Bob Marley estate, with the full approval of his widow, Rita, and the family, and we were embarking on a project to expand Bob's profile across the world even as his records were selling in the millions every year. Chris asked me to go to London and pull the tapes of Bob Marley and the Wailers' live performance at San Francisco's KSAN radio station, which he told me was perhaps the best raw performance of the band. His idea was to splice an interview of Bob by Dermot Hussey, famed Jamaican journalist, into the recording at intervals, to show the world who Bob was with words and music.

Marley held a special place in Chris's heart. He was touring when he met Chris in London, broke and unable to pay for flights back to Jamaica. Seeing something special in him, Chris gave Bob the money for the trip as well as an advance payment for a record. The rest is history, but for the rest of Bob's career (and short life), his relationship with Chris was as close as that between any artist and their producer can be, made especially so because of their Jamaican background and mutual love of the country. (Sadly, Bob died of cancer in early 1981 before I met Chris or worked at Island.)

Chris told me to look through the archives and include unreleased studio tracks or other live recordings that would fit the album and the concept. In London I met up with Suzette Newman, Chris's longtime right-hand person in Britain (and a dear friend to this day) at the offices in St. Peter's Square. I worked with Trevor Wyatt, in-house Island producer and engineer almost since the label's inception, who knew the archives inside out. This "new" Bob Marley album would be released on the Tuff Gong label, Marley's own imprint that he had founded in the seventies for releasing Jamaican music. Chris wanted the cover of the album to reflect the rawness of the recordings. We asked Neville Garrick, Bob's collaborator on art direction, and Adrian Boot, a British photographer who worked in the art department in London, to come up with an image that we then manipulated to be imperfect, almost like a painting instead of a photograph.

Around this time Chris asked me to meet him in Jamaica, and I dutifully flew down to Montego Bay, rented a car, and drove to Goldeneye in Oracabessa on the north coast, near Ocho Rios. Chris had once told Bob that he should buy the house when it came up for sale by Ian Fleming's estate, but Bob didn't think it suited him, so Chris bought it himself. Chris had visited it as a child with his mother, Blanche, who was a good friend—with *benefits*, Chris told me—of the creator of James Bond.

When I went to Goldeneye the first time, it was a one-story, three-bedroom house on a bluff surrounded by lush tropical acreage overlooking the Caribbean at the spot where, in the first Bond film, *Dr. No*, Ursula Andress emerges from the water in a white bikini with a large knife strapped to a belt. It had no telephone, and if I wanted to contact anyone I had to drive to the Island office in Ocho Rios, twenty or twenty-five minutes away. At the time, Goldeneye was exactly as Ian Fleming had left it, including his desk and all the furniture. I had been a huge fan of James Bond novels and films from when I first saw *Dr. No* in the early sixties, and it was thrilling to sit at the author's desk and sleep in his bed.

I met Denise Mills, an Englishwoman who was Chris's right-hand

01.

02.

03.

01.
Bob Marley *Talkin' Blues*
album cover

02.
Dinner at Goldeneye with
Chris, Ursula Andress, and
Grace Jones, Bond girls both

03.
Chris Blackwell with Diane
Jobson at Goldeneye, photo
by the author

person in Jamaica, for a delicious Jamaican dinner of jerk chicken and rice and peas at the house cooked by one of the longtime chefs. Chris was delayed in Nassau, Denise told me, but he wanted me to go up to Nine Mile, Bob Marley's birthplace in the mountains, to see Mrs. Booker, Bob's mother. Denise, a no-nonsense woman not given to idle chitchat and hardened by life in a misogynistic work environment, gave me pre-GPS directions of a sort, telling me to just drive toward Montego Bay, get off the main coastal road at Runaway Bay, and head toward Browns Town. From there, she advised, it would be best to ask. I did manage to make it there (this was well before it had become a tourist destination), and although Cedella Booker wasn't expecting me, she was gracious, welcoming, and interested to hear about Island Records' and Chris's plans to expand Bob's reach, popularity, and influence worldwide. Bob's mother had adopted his Rastafarian faith and dreadlocked style, and despite having lived in America for years, had a thick Jamaican accent that she moderated somewhat for the stranger appearing at her door. Cedella didn't live in Nine Mile; rather, she had a home in Miami but would visit the hamlet in Jamaica where her son was born and buried.

As part of making peace with his Jamaican detractors—there were a good number both in Jamaica and in Europe and America—Chris instructed me to refuse licensing for anything that smacked of exploitation, and I turned down all sorts of offers that flowed into our offices, such as matchbooks, rolling papers, bongs, and the like. Diane Jobson, one of Bob's Jamaican lawyers (the Rastafarian sister of Chris's boyhood friend Dickie Jobson) who at one time was estranged from Chris and on the detractors' side, was from then on part of the crowd hanging out at Goldeneye whenever Chris was on the Island.

Chris gave me a more delicate task: seek out Roger Steffens, a fan of Marley in the true sense of the word *fanatic*, who had amassed the largest collection of Marley memorabilia and recordings in the world, bootlegs included. Roger was perhaps the most vociferous of Blackwell's critics and detractors, believing that the White Jamaican had exploited Black Jamaicans while personally profiting mightily from their toils. He also decried the fact that no other Jamaican or African act received the same marketing push by Island as Bob did, who was marketed as a rock act (and whose biggest audience was white). Steffens hosted a reggae show on the Los Angeles radio station KCRW and was well known in the reggae community, and it was important to plead with him to not disparage Chris or Island as we took over managing the estate, releasing not just a new record but marketing the entire Marley catalog remastered on CD. Steffens had worked in promotion at Island in the early eighties, and his distrust of Blackwell was partly due to the lack of promotion or marketing for acts Steffens championed and believed deserved a bigger push, such as King Sunny Ade. It was going to be an uphill battle, but Chris decided my ministerial, or diplomatic, talents could be helpful.

Steffens was polite and welcoming when I visited him at his home in Los Angeles, and he happily showed me his massive collection of Marley tapes and memorabilia. I told him about Island's plans for the Wailers and the Marley catalog, and about Chris's plans—endorsed by the family—for the estate, which was to become a foundation based out of the Island Trading offices and run by Doreen Crujeiras, who had moved over from the finance department at Island Records. I left him somewhat mollified, I thought, and for the next few years, at least, there were no more rants about Blackwell on reggae shows on the radio or in the music press. He never changed his mind about Chris, though, as evidenced by his comments over the ensuing years, but there can be no denying, and Chris never did, that Roger was a fan of the first order who contributed much to the understanding of and promotion of reggae in America.

Carlos Santana, influenced by Steffens, also believed that Chris had exploited Black artists. He was keen on African music as well as reggae and was especially dismissive of Chris's lack of commercial success with the African artists we signed to the Mango imprint. The Malian artist Salif Keita wanted his 1990 album on Mango to be produced by the jazz musician Joe Zawinul, and he wanted to meet Santana in the hopes that he might agree to perform with him on the record. Chris asked me to fly up to San Francisco, where I was met by Carlos himself, who drove me in his black Citroën SM—one of the coolest French cars, a collaboration with Maserati—to his sprawling modern home in Sausalito to show me *his* collection of Bob Marley tapes, an impressively massive quantity of live recordings and bootlegs that almost rivaled Steffens's. He was perfectly happy to see Salif and appear on the album, called *Amen*, which was also to feature Wayne Shorter, but was less convinced of Chris's sincerity in wanting to promote African music to the mainstream culture. I'm not sure what he made of me, Chris's "minister without portfolio" and envoy, but later I would end up working with Carlos and his team twice more, at two different labels, but that's a different story.

Chapter 18

On Leave

In 1991, after Alain Levy had bought Island and A&M for Polygram, he wanted to expand its U.S. operations and grow market share while simultaneously cutting costs and overlapping functions. He formed a new company, the Polygram Label Group (PLG), based in New York, which would serve as the marketing, promotion, and sales arm for multiple labels, including Island and London Records. At a dinner in New York he offered the presidency of the Polydor label (moribund in the States) to Davitt, who would be free to sign acts and release international Polydor artists' records in America. We had become even closer, seeing each other every week, as we did when schoolboys, to discuss and argue about new records, films, and the politics of the day. Davitt was excited to move back to his hometown of New York, and he asked me to join him there at Polydor.

I was enthused with the idea of working with my best friend, though I knew I would miss Chris and his cohort: his girlfriend Mary Vinson, his ex-girlfriend Nathalie Delon, and the various characters in their lives, such as Suzette Newman, her assistant Cathy Snipper, Dickie Jobson, and a slew of Jamaicans including Perry Henzell, director of *The Harder They Come*, and his wife, Sally. I also was a little concerned with leaving a home I knew to join a company I knew nothing about, but I trusted Davitt and thought if I was to have a proper career in the music business, leaving behind the ambiguous "minister without portfolio" title would be an advantage. After Davitt asked to poach me, Chris surprised me, saying, "It's a good idea; you can work inside the corporate structure for a couple of years, get to know the ins-and-outs, and then come back to Island with inside knowledge of the behemoth." Chris still viewed Island as an independent company, and he believed that my experience inside the beast would be valuable. *Canny Chris*, I thought to myself. *He could be right*.

In the meantime, Chris was busy with his newly created Island Outpost hotels and Island Trading Company, a retail outfit run by Mary Vinson, and he was still in the film business with Island Pictures. And so I joined Davitt in New York in the spring of 1991. Pouran, who had moved from cosmetics sales to window dressing at Saks, secured a transfer to the flagship Saks store on Fifth Avenue in Manhattan, and we settled in an apartment on Second Avenue at Seventeenth Street that cost four times the rent of our place in Beverly Hills. Like most other Island Records spouses—and the music business generally—Pouran didn't get involved in my work at all. She was fine with moving to New York and happy to be friends with Davitt and his wife, who was now pregnant and soon to deliver their first daughter. Pouran and I were relieved that my career seemed to be providing stability, an ever-increasing salary, and a good future. She wasn't especially interested in the business, and although she was a film buff she was much less of a music fan.

Once ensconced at the Eighth Avenue Polygram headquarters, my presence at Polydor was a mystery to Alain Levy and Rick Dobbis, the newly installed president of PLG, who saw me every day and was quite dismissive of my role. He knew of my close relationship with Blackwell, as did some of his staff, and there was also the rumor, I was told by a friendly staffer, that I was really there to spy on Dobbis and PLG for Chris.

I wasn't bothered by any of that, but I was shocked to discover that while Polydor could sign whatever act we wanted, we had no say over how

01.

01.
With Perry and Sally Henzell at their beautiful eighteenth-century house in Jamaica, one that they lived in without electricity, and that Chris and I would visit on occasion

they'd be marketed and promoted. All decisions were made by Rick, who was in reality the president of the labels he marketed and distributed. Rick clearly understood this, which was made awkward by the fact that label heads didn't. And so there was a sort of dance, where Davitt and I, and also Peter Koepke of London Records and the Island staff, had to schmooze Dobbis and others in charge of ensuring our acts' successes, while convincing our acts that we had a real say over their careers.

Chris, meanwhile, with Island artists such as U2 and Melissa Etheridge overshadowing any act Polydor or London would sign, wasn't especially worried that PLG wouldn't prioritize Island, the *famous* label. He was generally dismissive of Rick and the notion that a marketer rather than a creative executive should be in charge of developing an artist's career. By his reasoning, the person who signed an act should know who the fans would be and therefore know how to market to them.

Davitt, too, came to realize that he had wide latitude to do as he pleased but had little say in promoting his artists. As time went by and frustration grew, Davitt, Peter Koepke, and I bemoaned the fact that we often couldn't get the PLG staff excited to work with our artists, and I tried to get Chris, as the most influential label head, to force some changes within the structure. Roger Ames, part owner of London Records, one of the labels and, unusually (and in what most would consider a conflict of interest), also a Polygram employee running the U.K. operations, didn't want to challenge his boss Levy. In one meeting at Ames's Hammersmith office, he told me, in so many words, to shut up with the grumbling and get on with my work, whatever that was. It was not an auspicious beginning to a necessary relationship. Roger, a fellow Caribbean native, had a contentious relationship with Chris, whom he had nicknamed "the crocodile," and my closeness to Chris made him instantly distrust me. Later, he would call me "the terrorist"—because of my being Iranian, but perhaps he believed me capable of wanton destruction on Chris's behalf. I once yelled at him—technically my boss after he became the head of Polygram U.S.—at a restaurant in Manhattan, warning him to never call me that in public again, which may have reinforced his belief that it was, after all, an appropriate moniker.

Levy also picked up on the terrorist label and once, according to those who heard him, said he believed I was capable of an *actual* terrorist act. Everyone else saw me as another executive, and in fact one day at a meeting with some staffers at Polygram, I made a pointed comment about something happening in the Middle East, and another staffer jumped in and asked me, "How would you know?" I replied, "Because I'm Iranian—where did you think I was from?" He shrugged his shoulders and said, "I don't know—California?" But no, I was *not* the son of hippie parents who had found the name Hooman in a book of Eastern philosophy or religion sometime in the sixties.

Levy had started a management-training program for executives, and at Davitt's recommendation, I was sent to one such training—an MBA program of sorts—over a long weekend in Tarrytown, a suburb of New York. We were assigned a game in which groups of four were pitted against each other and had to come up with strategies and tactics. Alain Levy himself drove up to the hotel, listened to our presentations, and then launched into a critique that was not just harsh, but denigrating and dismissive. I could understand management training for the business affairs and finance people, but no training was going to make for a better A&R person or even someone in marketing and promotion.

You weren't going to get a better radio-promotions man than Johnny Barbis, who was the head of radio promotion at PLG, or a better A&R man than Denny Cordell, even if you "trained" them in game theory. It was about instinct, an ear for talent, and a nose for star quality. It was how Chris, who never finished school, found and promoted Bob Marley, Steve Winwood, Traffic, Cat Stevens, Robert Palmer, Grace Jones, and so many others. (Chris once told me that when Robert Palmer's record "Addicted to Love" was finished, he knew he had a hit on his hand but was worried about the finances at Island. When he saw the video, though, the one with Palmer in a suit and tie and models in heavy makeup simulating playing guitars surrounding him, he instructed the Island staff to go all out and spend whatever they needed to promote it. The record was indeed a huge hit, putting Island back in the black.) Nonetheless, Levy would send top executives—but thankfully not me—to Harvard Business School for executive training seminars, too.

Dobbis's disapproval of me was cemented when, with Davitt's enthusiastic support, I signed X Clan, a hip-hop group from Crown Heights, Brooklyn, who asked to leave Island and the 4th & Broadway imprint and come to Polydor with me. Island wasn't especially known for hip-hop—Eric B. & Rakim was its biggest hip-hop act—but had had some success with X Clan, who were notorious for their leather outfits in Black liberation colors, their nose rings, and their militant activism. Lumumba Carson, known as Professor X, the leader of the group and the Blackwatch Movement, a Crown Heights–based Black activist organization, was in my office at least two or three times a week. He often showed up unannounced with his group, an intimidating presence for their outfits and custom leather hats adorned with symbols, nose rings (uncommon at the time), and the carved wooden staffs they carried. Sonny Carson, Lumumba's father and group manager, who had a wonderful sense of humor and was a master hustler, would sometimes accompany them (usually when money was involved), and we'd have long meetings in Davitt's office.

Dobbis, however, believed that Sonny, the group, and the movement itself were anti-Semitic (this was a time of the Crown Heights riots that pitted the Black community against the Hasidic) and he refused to have anything to do with them. As such, they were handled almost exclusively by the PLG R&B marketing and promotion department and had no chance of breaking through to a more mainstream audience. Sonny Carson, an ex-convict and a well-known and controversial community organizer and Black activist (and subject of the 1974 film *The Education of Sonny Carson*), had indeed been accused by his critics of being anti-Semitic, to which he had responded that he wasn't "anti" only one group of people; he was anti-*white*. Sonny and Lumumba would call me *hooomaahn* and both loudly gave the Muslim salutation, *Salaam aleikum*, when meeting me, which may have fed certain notions that people had of them (and of me). But after one record, *Xodus* (which sold around half a million copies), the group broke up and Polydor was no longer in the Sonny Carson business. Lumumba was fond of Iranians and even had an Iranian girlfriend in London with whom he had a child, but after Sonny's death, I lost contact with the movement he started. Later, I would work with Jason Hunter, or Brother J of the group, also known as Grand Verbalizer, or Grand Verbalizer Funkin' Lesson Brother J, on his solo career.

Much of Polydor's roster was inherited from European and U.K. signings, such as Van Morrison and the Moody Blues, and we had very little to do with them other than dutifully showing up at concerts and gigs. An exception was Vanessa Paradis, signed to Marc Lumbroso's Remark Records in France (distributed by Polydor) at the age of sixteen and now a huge star. Marc wanted her to record an album in English, and Davitt thought Lenny Kravitz would be the ideal producer. She came to New York and recorded with him; her manager uncle, the French film actor Didier Pain, accompanied her everywhere she went. The record was successful worldwide, albeit not a *smash* hit in the States, and she went on to have greater success as an artist, actress, and model, and later notoriety as Mrs. Johnny Depp.

Davitt only once felt obliged to sign an artist that Dobbis and Johnny Barbis heavily promoted to him: Steve Miller, of the Steve Miller Band, who was a friend of Johnny's. Davitt was under no obligation to take A&R advice from PLG executives, but he liked Johnny, and it wasn't a difficult favor to do for him—with the proviso that he would not listen to the record. Levy asked him why, and Davitt replied that if he listened he would have to have an opinion of it, and if he had an opinion, he would have to express it if asked. Davitt told me that Levy's response was a friendly "you fuck." Dobbis decided to pull out all the stops and do a live broadcast to radio and sales reps across the country announcing the signing. It was going to be live from Steve's home in Sun Valley, Idaho, and Davitt asked me to fly there and be the face of Polydor Records. I did, forcing myself to say, on camera with a straight face, a few words about how happy we were to have the band on our label. It was a miserable experience; not just because I wasn't a fan of Miller, but because having to fake enthusiasm along with our distinct lack of power to control our destinies was not how I thought my career should go.

While we did our diplomatic duty with Steve Miller, we were especially proud when Davitt signed Carlos Santana, who was looking for a new home for his own label, Guts & Grace. That's when I first worked with John Meneilly, who went on to manage Jay Z, and with Phil Sarna, who later started his own business management firm, PSB, focusing on the music business; and who has been my accountant for more than twenty-five years now. I was thrilled to be working with Santana, of whom I'd been a fan since I first saw the movie *Woodstock*, and of his brother Jorge, whose album *Malo Dos* was one of my favorites as a teenager. I loved the idea that a Mexican playing Latin-tinged rock music could be as successful as Carlos

01.

01.
Steve Miller in 1993, flanked by Jon Birge, marketing head, and Joe Riccitelli, pop promotions, and with other PLG staff. Dobbis far left, Sky Daniels, rock promotion, with arm around my shoulder.

was, but the music was unique and infectious on its own. Live, the band was riveting to watch.

On his debut album on Polydor, *Milagro*, Carlos covered Marvin Gaye's "Right On" with vocals by Larry Graham, and it was decided that that should be the song to promote the record. There had to be a radio edit of the song and a video to get to MTV, or—if their executives, in their obsession with appealing exclusively to high school and college kids, decided Santana was old news—on the sister station VH-1, where "softer," or "adult contemporary" artists (known as AC in radio lingo) landed. We made plans to film Carlos playing a concert for the first time in the town where he grew up, Tijuana, Mexico, at the bullring, and to shoot other footage in and around the town.

Peter Nydrle, the Czech-born director and cinematographer who was hired for the project, hit it off with Carlos and would later film his concert in Mexico City for the live album and video *Sacred Fire*. Davitt and I flew to San Diego to witness what was to be a historic homecoming for Santana. When we drove across the border on the day of the shoot, we were met by the Mexican Policía Federal, or Federales, who gave us a motorcycle escort to the bullring by the sea, visibly thrilled to be seeing native son Santana, but still solemn enough to refuse Davitt's offer to trade his baseball cap for one of their much more impressive ones.

The performance was electric, not least for the thousands of screaming fans, on their feet, ecstatic to see the hometown superstar. The last time I had seen Santana in concert was in London in the early seventies, when I was fifteen and he was already a star, and now in Tijuana I was on the stage, behind the band and the equipment, to hear him again in my thirties, sounding exactly like I remembered. I drove back across the border that night with Carlos and the band in their van, my green card at the ready, and I was relieved when we weren't stopped or questioned at the U.S. border.

In 1991 Island Records, through PLG, had a massive success with U2's *Achtung Baby* and later with Melissa Etheridge's breakthrough album, *Yes I Am*. Island's surprise new hit act in 1993 was the Cranberries, with their album *Everybody Else Is Doing It, So Why Can't We?*, and the single "Linger" and their extensive touring turned the band into superstars in a very short time. Chris didn't particularly like the music (pop rock didn't appeal to him, and even less so as he became more focused on African and Jamaican music), although he fully supported promoting the act. Meanwhile, frustration with the PLG structure was building, and Chris grew annoyed at its lack of success with any other Island artists and the handcuffing of Island independent artists relegated to independent record distribution outside Polygram. In 1994 while still on the board of Polygram, he began putting pressure on Alain Levy and Eric Kronfeld, the company's head of business affairs and COO, to change the structure to Island's benefit. If Island was the main provider of revenue to PLG, he argued, then shouldn't it be *Island* that ran the show, not PLG, and Island that distributed other Polygram labels?

In 1994 I finally became a U.S. citizen, along with Pouran, and no longer had to explain to consulates why, as a U.S. record company executive, I had to get a visa for every overseas trip. There was a ceremony in front of a judge who assured all the immigrants present that we were now no different from him, which was indeed moving, but it seemed, after all these years of American schooling and living in America that it was somehow perfunctory. The little booklet—we got U.S. passports the same day—was more exciting to me than the actual citizenship. The first time I returned to the States from abroad with the passport, the immigration officer's saying "welcome home" after stamping it made me pause and wonder how confident I was that it was true.

Ironically, as Pouran received her American citizenship—a reason for our marriage in the first place—we were growing apart. She had decided not long after arriving in New York and working at Saks that she wanted to be an artist and study at the Art Students League, and I was supportive of her quitting work and focusing on art. She had, in California, dabbled in painting, but hadn't thought to pursue it as a career until my drastically improved financial situation obviated the necessity of her income to support us. As happy as I was to be able to support her financially, we both knew by then that happiness was not going to be found in our marriage. Our life together had become dull, and we had fewer and fewer mutual interests. I had known this for a long time, and occasionally I cursed myself for agreeing to a marriage in the first place, not having appreciated the seriousness of the institution at the time.

In truth, we'd become more like good friends than lovers. We had never fought—not once—though Davitt postulated at the time of our separation that when two people love each other, there must also be moments when they absolutely hate each other. It is likely that had Pouran and I simply reverted to being more boyfriend and girlfriend, and just as our relationship ended abruptly when I had first moved to California, we probably would have broken up much earlier if either of us had taken the initiative. Not long after our separation and subsequent divorce, Pouran, using her maiden name, Jinchi, achieved some success with her paintings at galleries and at auctions, and remarried happily.

The second half of 1994 was also when Chris finally decided to confront Levy and demand that the PLG experiment end. Davitt was in agreement with Chris, but he and I kept our conversations secret from Polygram and PLG. Chris asked Davitt and me to come to Nassau to discuss how the new Island structure would work. We were picked up in a speedboat at a dock across from his private island and whisked across the bay to meet with him. If Levy could be persuaded—and Chris was fully confident that he would get his way—Davitt would take over as president of Island, I would be the executive vice president and GM, and the Island and PLG staffs would be combined, with layoffs coming from the PLG side. Chris had never *not* been in control of his destiny, and he still believed his destiny was tied to Island. He was not going to let a Harvard Business School graduate dictate his destiny, and I was just as confident as he that Levy would fold. I not only admired Chris, my first real boss, but viewed him as almost superhuman in his ability to do whatever it was that he wanted.

When Chris was back in New York a few days later, we had dinner with Davitt and Michael Zilkha at Basta Pasta on Seventeenth Street—Michael's favorite, the New York branch of a Tokyo Italian restaurant that was run by a Japanese chef and staff. (Davitt commented that the concept was at least better than an *Italian sushi* restaurant.) Michael said he wanted to make sure that I was protected in the new system that was being devised for Island and Polygram, and both Davitt and Chris reassured him that that would be the case.

Later, Chris did get his way: Island Records would be a full-service label within Polygram, just like Mercury and A&M. There would be no central marketing group—as PLG had been—and Island would take over the Polydor signings that were made under Davitt and the distribution of London Records. Davitt later received a call from Chris, who, in his inimitable way, said that he hoped Davitt "wasn't hung up on titles." This meant, of course, that Davitt would not be president of Island; rather, he would be head of A&R. The new president, Alain Levy had insisted to Chris, must be Johnny Barbis, the legendary head of radio promotions. Chris was forced—not quite reluctantly—to agree, for Barbis would still have to report to him. Davitt, meanwhile, felt that if he accepted the job he would be exactly where he was with PLG, only with a different label name, and he would again have little say in how any of the acts he signed would be marketed. He left Polygram and was hired by Charles Koppelman, chairman of EMI Records Group, to be the president of the EMI label. I stayed on, back at Island—not exactly two, as Chris had uncannily predicted, but almost three years later.

Chapter 19

Back to Island

Chris told me that I'd be in charge of the creative side of Island, while Johnny Barbis would look after sales and promotion, but that I should coordinate with him on marketing plans for our artists and acts. In reality, I was to be the conduit between Chris—the real creative head—and his president. Larry Mestel, Island's CFO, was moved to Polygram at Worldwide Plaza and became CFO and head of business affairs of the "new" Island Records. Johnny had no problem with the new structure—he had the *title* he craved. The Island A&R husband-and-wife team James Dowdall and Rose Noone, brought to Eighth Avenue to join Polydor's A&R man, Joe Bosso, would report to me, as would the publicity and marketing departments, which combined PLG and Island staffers. While Chris had wanted the revived Island to be located at the loft downtown on Fourth and Broadway, Levy insisted that it be at Polygram headquarters, presumably so he could keep a closer eye on it for the times he traveled to New York from the world headquarters in London.

Chris of course hated the Polygram offices, thinking them too corporate and completely soulless, and didn't want an office for himself, even as chairman. He preferred staying downtown, where Mary Vinson and Island Trading took offices on Lafayette and Fourth Streets, and used my new corner office when he needed a place to work when visiting Eighth Avenue. Polygram subsequently sold the loft that had been Island's home in the United States for years, as well as its apartment on Queens Gate in London next to the Iraqi embassy—Chris's in-town flat where I stayed occasionally when visiting London when I first joined Island. I bemoaned the loss of the apartment in South Kensington, which I thought Chris should have found a way to exclude from the sale.

Now separated from Pouran (who stayed in our apartment), I moved to number 2711 in Essex House, one of two condos in the hotel that Chris owned. I took the "disco" apartment with shag carpeting and a sunken living room, leaving the more contemporary number 2411 to be rented without embarrassment at the tired decor. I wasn't saddened by the separation, but once again I felt unmoored, looking to start a new life. The difference, of course, was that I didn't have to worry about money. Soon the year was up and Chris asked me to spend Christmas in Jamaica with him and Mary—and, of course, a multitude of other guests, including Tatia Blackwell, Chris's adult daughter whom a former girlfriend had never told him about, and whom he officially recognized as his after a DNA test proved positive. I flew with Chris and Mary on his private jet, a smaller Cessna Citation that could nonetheless make the nonstop trip to Kingston. Suzette Newman met us there, as did Marianne Faithful, whose assigned villa at Strawberry Hill, Chris's new hotel in the Blue Mountains above Kingston, was next to mine.

Marianne was a longtime Island artist, albeit with slow record sales. She had an air of dissatisfaction with her lot in life—her being the famous onetime girlfriend of Mick Jagger, being an artist in her own right, and her modest lifestyle in Ireland notwithstanding. I enjoyed being her neighbor, and we had a few good laughs. We spent New Year's Eve there, with Marianne serenading us with an a cappella "Danny Boy" at midnight and the girlfriend of Simply Red's Mick Hucknall passing out (for a moment Suzette and I really panicked and thought she was dead) from too much

02.

01.

03.

01.
Chris on the wing of his jet, grabbing a cup of coffee before takeoff, photo by the author

02. & 03.
With Chris at Strawberry Hill, in Jamaica

drink and possibly excess ganja. We then helicoptered to Goldeneye, on the other side of the island, where we spent a few days by the sea before returning to New York.

I immersed myself in Island Records and in Chris's world, making them my home, and Chris relied on me to be his eyes and ears at the label. Johnny and I became closer, extending our friendship to dinners at his house with his wife, Edwina. We would discuss almost every aspect of a record's release, and he liked the fact that I would be the one to deal several times a day with Chris, who could be mercurial and demanding. Alain Levy seemed to prefer Johnny's company over that of any other Polygram employee, which was understandable: few music executives were as fun to socialize with as Barbis was. With his sense of humor and love of life, Johnny was one of the most gregarious and loyal people I had ever met. He wanted to make sure that everyone he was involved with was okay and that any job we were tasked with should be fun, too. He had the constitution of an ox and could go toe to toe with anyone in a night—and there were many—of drinking. With Johnny as head promotion man, any manager, act, or independent label looking for marketing and distribution would be happy to land at Island.

Once I was a bachelor in all but name, Chris and Mary became my surrogate older brother and sister. Mary, a Black woman from southern Virginia, had made her way to New York and the fashion and design world; she had great style and was a talented designer. She wasn't really a smoker, but she'd bum my cigarettes and we'd talk about how ridiculous everything was to her, from the new restrictions on smoking to politics and Chris's wardrobe choices.

I was too busy, I suppose, to miss being married and having a "normal" life, but I stayed in touch with Pouran, supporting her—and putting the down payment on an apartment in the Village that she wanted—while she stayed busy with her paintings and trying to get noticed by galleries. She seemed happy to move on with life and career. I found a rental apartment in a condo building on Fourth Avenue near Union Square, but I was hardly ever there, and when the owner decided to sell it, I moved to a studio apartment in London Terrace in Chelsea I bought for the grand sum of $120,000, a third of what my rental had been asking. My mortgage and maintenance cost a total of $800 a month, what today might be closer to the rent for a parking spot in Manhattan.

Many a Thursday or Friday, Chris would call and ask me what I was doing for the weekend, and invite me to Jamaica or his island in Nassau with him and Mary. The private jet made it rather too simple to get away, especially to somewhere warm in the winter, and I never refused. Chris had a smaller single-propellor plane in the islands, piloted by his cousin David Lindo, who would meet us at the airport in Jamaica and fly us to Oracabessa, a few minutes from Goldeneye but with a runway that couldn't accommodate a jet, no matter how small.

The more time I spent with Chris, the more I came to realize that we viewed the world in much the same way. He was the product of being raised in Jamaica—of the "third world," or global south—from a Sephardic family of converts to Christianity and an Irishman father, all of whom embraced British upper-class values, and was at home in both worlds. I, too, had been at home in my Anglo-American world and my Iranian one, and admired Chris's ease in slipping into incomprehensible patois with Black Jamaicans whenever the occasion arose. To me, it was the equivalent of my knowing "street Persian" (or Farsi), having picked it up from college friends, which indicated a knowledge and *understanding* of culture that merely learning another language—no matter how fluently—could not match. Chris also had two "homes" he could live in, and I longed for my second.

Not long after Chris regained control of Island Records, Mary Vinson started having severe back pains that wouldn't go away. At first we thought it might be from the WaveRunner and Jet Ski excursions we'd make off the Jamaican coast at Goldeneye—her Yamaha a smaller, faster, and more maneuverable machine—and the waves we'd jump over enthusiastically, sometimes crashing down hard, especially at Galina Point, where the waves were *always* high. Chris and I had become Jet Ski fanatics, taking them out a few times a day at Goldeneye or at the island off Nassau, and Mary liked them too, albeit without overdoing it as we did. (Chris once surreptitiously took a photo of me disembarking a WaveRunner, had it made into a postcard, and sent it to me at the office. He and Suzette had started jokingly calling me "Almost," for I had used the word a few too many times in conversation about our records—"we're *almost* done with the marketing plan," etc.—and I took the ribbing without complaint.

As Mary's pain worsened, doctors were sought out and it was discovered that she had multiple myeloma, a cancer of the plasma cells that was generally incurable. Chris, never one to give up hope, set about finding out as much as he could about the cancer and the available treatments. They tried everything from a macrobiotic diet to employing a Chinese medicine practitioner who was also a medical doctor and cancer specialist who melded the ancient tradition with modern medicine; we'd pick up the Chinese herbs he prescribed in New York's Chinatown. Mary would often get better only to get worse again. Chris wanted her to spend as much time as she could in the islands, and our weekend getaways became more frequent. (Once, in Jamaica, Mary's Chinese American doctor asked to feel my arm, and after a few minutes of poking, declared that I suffered from a weak kidney and should take the herbs, boiled in water, that he wrote out in Chinese characters to be picked up at the Chinatown herbalist's store that we used. He hadn't known that I had had to have surgery to remove a massive stone from my left kidney in 1991, so naturally I dutifully took the herbs for a year or so, and to this day have not had any further issues with my kidneys.)

For the first time in his life, Chris, who rarely spent more than a day or two in any one place, was forced to spend days at a time in New York for Mary's treatments and doctor appointments. We'd have lunch at Barbetta near the New York office—courtesy of the "light bulb people" (as Chris referred to Philips, owner of Polygram), since I would put it on my expense account, which Chris lacked under his contract—and sometimes dinner, too. Or he would call me on my cell phone out of the blue and say we should have a drink somewhere.

Chris was a heavy user of mobile phones from the time they became reasonably practical to carry around, and in the '90s he and I both became obsessed with the Motorola models that shrank in size by the year. Chris, Mary, and I had the StarTAC when it came out, and my monthly bill was never less than $2,000. When the less-expensive gray StarTAC phones were released, Chris insisted, to the dismay of Larry Mestel and the Polygram accountants to whom he had to justify our budgets, that every employee

01.

02.

01.
The author standing by Chris Blackwell's smaller prop plane in Jamaica, with the Island Trading logo on its tail

02.
Postcard from Chris Blackwell teasing the author

of Island should be issued one. We may have been one of the first fully cell-phone-equipped companies at a time when mobile phones were not yet ubiquitous. Mobile communication was crucial for me in Jamaica and Nassau, where there were no phones in the villas or rooms I'd stay in, and finding me on a seventeen-acre property dotted with huts, or out riding a Jet Ski with Chris (with phone in a waterproof bag), would be impractical.

He called to have me meet him at the Temple Bar on Lafayette once when Mary was in hospital having an especially hard time, and we spoke about everything except music and Island. It was a difficult time for him; dealing with a sick loved one who needed care, which he'd never had to do in his peripatetic life. It was the first time I saw tears in his eyes. He was sad and constantly worried during Mary's most difficult days, and I think he was surprised at his own soft-heartedness. I felt closer to him than ever, and the idea of him as superhuman faded away. In hindsight, it was perhaps my mistake to allow myself to forget the warnings about his capricious personality, but I can't regret the deep friendship that ignoring the advice allowed to develop.

Chapter 20

Successes (And *Almost*)

One day I received a call from Julian Schnabel, the painter, who told me that after trying to reach Chris, he'd been sent a message telling him to call me at Island. Julian said he had made a record and wanted me to hear it with the aim of releasing it. He showed up at my office with his brother in tow and played me the record, which he had titled *Every Silver Lining Has a Cloud*, on cassette. It featured some well-known names in the music business, having been produced by Bill Laswell (whom I knew from his label with Island, Axiom) and featuring the musicians Bernie Worrell of Parliament-Funkadelic, Nicky Skopelitis, and the underground favorite Buckethead. I thought the record interesting and obviously professional but had no idea to whom it might appeal. Schnabel was famous, of course, but I didn't think art lovers were rushing to buy music from artists they admired.

Julian was polite, warm, and gracious to someone he didn't know at all, but I was hesitant. I called Chris, who asked me what I thought about the record, and I was honest: it wasn't bad at all—not *great*, though, and hard to categorize—though we'd likely get some criticism for releasing what some would call a vanity project. *Exactly* the kind of record Chris thought Island should release, I realized as I said it, especially if it featured musicians he admired such as Laswell and Bernie Worrell. I asked him if he wanted to be in the Julian Schnabel business, and he said sure, I should go ahead. He didn't ask to listen to the album, and I can confidently say that to this day he's never heard a single song from it.

Julian, seemingly intent on being a renaissance man, also made a semi-fictional film on the life of Jean-Michel Basquiat. His producer Jon Kilik came with him to my office, as did Peter Brant, the industrialist art collector who was financing the film, but I had no authority over Island Pictures in Los Angeles, and the film was sold to Harvey Weinstein at Miramax. I was, however, interested enough to sign and release the soundtrack, which had a number of great songs on it that we licensed for the album.

At around this time, the record company head of marketing, Matt Stringer, requested a leave of absence for personal reasons, and I was left shorthanded. When I happened to tell Michael Zilkha that we were looking for someone to hire, he told me I should talk to Glenn O'Brien, who was creative director at Barney's, then the hippest department store in New York. When he came to my office, wearing a beautifully tailored gray suit and Belgian loafers, we hit it off. Anyone with that much style, I thought, on top of his reputation and background in the downtown music scene, would be a great addition to Island. Glenn didn't want a job, per se, but he agreed to be a marketing consultant and come into the office from time to time. Within weeks, we became best friends, and on weekends (when I wasn't in the Caribbean with Chris and Mary), I was inevitably at his house in Bridgehampton with his girlfriend and later wife, Gina Nanni. I rarely dated at this time, being preoccupied with my work (and plus-ones were often not especially welcome in Chris's world), but one Halloween night I was having drinks with Glenn, and I met Karri, a bartender at the very empty Le Colonial Restaurant on 57th Street. She soon became my girlfriend and subsequently my wife.

Glenn, known as an art critic and collector himself, had a contentious relationship with Julian Schnabel, not being enamored of his plate paintings

01.

02.

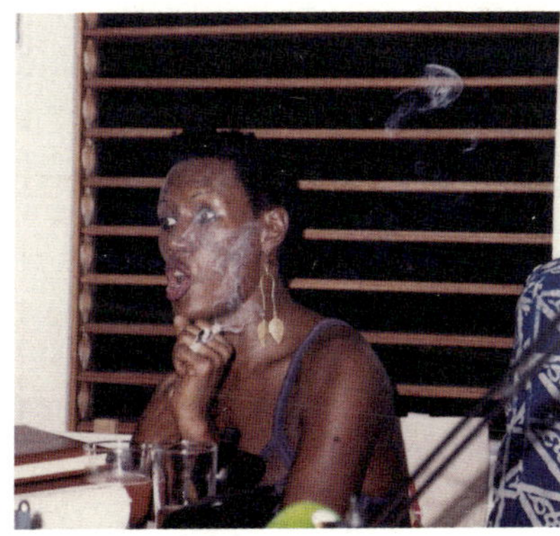

03.

01.
Julian Schnabel, Johnny Barbis (right), and the author at a record release party, 1995

02.
Glenn at Ian Fleming's desk at Goldeneye, Jamaica, photo by the author

03.
Grace Jones in Chris's office at Goldeneye, captured by the author

(and Julian knew it). But he especially resented the movie *Basquiat* for what he considered Julian's extreme stretching of the truth—especially regarding his own portrayal by Gary Oldman, when it came to his relationship with Jean-Michel. Glenn had been a close friend of the artist, working with him on his New York City public access cable show *TV Party* and writing the screenplay for the film starring Jean-Michel, *Downtown 81*, and knew him better than Julian or even Andy Warhol did. Ultimately the soundtrack was one of those records that was neither a failure—since it wasn't expensive to acquire—nor a smash. Glenn was, however, unfailingly fair in his critiques of everyone and everything—later he would say how wonderful the subsequent movies Julian directed were.

Glenn soon became an unofficial advisor to Mary Vinson and her retail line, too, since Mary knew him through Grace Jones, who had first introduced her to Chris. Glenn and Gina would accompany me to Goldeneye every now and then and came to love staying there or at Bolt House, Blanche Blackwell's onetime Jamaican home up the road that Chris had kept after his mother moved to London. The couple became fixtures at Blackwell gatherings, in Jamaica and in New York.

When Chris signed Willie Nelson to Island, Glenn got involved with the marketing of Willie's Island debut, *Spirit*, and came with me to Atlantic City to see Willie perform live at Caesar's. We visited him inside his custom touring bus parked outside the casino, which was perpetually filled with marijuana smoke. His album performed as well as Willie Nelson albums always did, and it received good notices, but we were unable to expand his audience beyond his core base. Willie was also a big fan of reggae and had talked to Chris about making a reggae record. He started working on the album while with Island, but it wasn't released until years later, titled *Countryman*, also the title of Chris's first film production, a movie directed and shot in Jamaica by his old friend Dickie Jobson.

There was a tradition at Goldeneye before it became a resort hotel, started in the 1950s when Ian Fleming lived there, to have guests plant a tree on the seventeen-acre property, usually along a path somewhere with a sign indicating who planted it and the date. I'm not especially superstitious, but I was always wary of having my name on a tree—what if it died, or bloomed bigger than all the others? In either case, could it prove a harbinger of my early death?—but Glenn and his wife, Gina, went ahead and planted trees. Anthony Eden, the British prime minister in the 1950s, had planted a tree and it looked healthy fifty years later. So did River Phoenix's ackee tree, planted in 1988 and doing very well after his death, but other trees didn't. Neither Chris nor I have trees at Goldeneye.

Our greatest success in this new era of Island was a smash-hit record by the Cranberries, *No Need to Argue*, which featured the hit "Zombie." There was little that Chris or I had to do with the success; it was entirely radio-, video-, and touring-driven, and Johnny's team did a terrific job of promoting the record, establishing the band as new rock and pop stars across the world. Melissa Etheridge's fifth album for Island, *Your Little Secret*, became her breakthrough record, establishing her as a pop and rock star and selling more than two million copies in America. A sore point for Etheridge and her manager, Bill Leopold, was her lackluster international sales; especially disappointing was that our U.K. sister label, of which Chris was chairman, couldn't come close to her American success. The argument was that her music was "too American," to which I would often reply that so was Bruce Springsteen's (to whom she had often been compared). Chris, who had personally signed Melissa after seeing her perform at a club in Long Beach, California, was thrilled with her success but was less thrilled with the complete lack of attention for the world music acts weakly promoted by Johnny and his team. (To be fair, it would have been preposterous for radio promotion men to be pushing the unfamiliar rhythms of music and songs in unheard foreign languages to American pop radio.)

In 1994 Polygram had made a deal with Sony to buy its stake in Def Jam Records, with distribution by Island, and by 1995 Chris was already feeling that the marketing and promotion of Def Jam acts was hoarding too much attention. (The owners Russell Simmons and Lyor Cohen's relationship with Sony had deteriorated to the point that when Lyor first asked to meet me as the sale was going through, it had to be at the St. Regis Hotel around the corner from Sony, as he was not allowed in the building.) Lyor was omnipresent and (most of the time) welcome on the twenty-fourth floor of Worldwide Plaza, where Johnny and I had our offices. Lyor must have heard from people that I was "Chris's man" at Island—his minister, yes, but now with a portfolio. It was paramount for him to ensure that Chris be satisfied with Def Jam at his label, as Russell Simmons, who at one time lived in a loft in the same building as Island on Fourth Street, was barely present.

Johnny, through his close friendship with Elton John, had also brought Elton's Rocket Records to Island, and while Chris respected Elton as an artist (though he'd turned down signing him years before, a sore point for Elton), he had no time for Elton's signings or even his own (and ultimately only) record for Island, *Made in England*. John Reid, Elton's longtime manager, had an office on our floor and I would often see him in Johnny's office. Like Johnny, he was fun to be around and generous to a fault. The music business—one that so many wanted to be a part of—was *supposed* to be fun, and characters such as Reid and Barbis made it so despite the stress that could accompany a career in music. But as time went on, Chris grew more and more unhappy with the direction of Island Records and with its president, thinking that Johnny's ways were simply not *Island* ways. It didn't help that Larry Mestel, the former accountant and now CFO whom Chris trusted, often complained to Chris about Johnny's profligate spending—Johnny ran out of his first yearly T&E (travel and entertainment) budget before the end of February—and would make his dislike of Johnny obvious in meetings.

While Chris liked success, he hated the idea of having to use people who made millions to "ensure" that success: the independent promotion men (and sometimes women) record companies used to avoid charges of payola. If we paid an indie promotion person a sum of money to promote a single to radio, what he did with that money was none of our business; nor did we want to know how he got radio play, just that he *did*. When Johnny took over Island, we were closer than ever with Dennis Lavinthal and Lenny Beer at *HITS*, a gossipy promotions magazine that we and every other label subscribed to for astronomical figures, and Johnny's friend Michael Klenfner (whose contributions to the success of our records Chris was suspicious of) was on a consultancy. I liked Klenfner—at least, when he was with Johnny he could be amusing—but also didn't understand his value. Klenfner had been a record executive for years before creating his own consultancy. He knew everyone in the business, and most were willing clients of his, but Island acts were not benefiting from his advice, and Chris wouldn't have dreamed of asking his opinion on any of our records.

I met one infamous independent record promoter, Fred DiSipio, who had a long and close relationship with Charles Koppelman, Davitt's boss at EMI. Davitt introduced me to him and I found him a fascinating character, having known of his mob connections, including with John Gotti and the Gambino crime family. The promotion-and-distribution end of the record business had always been rumored to be heavily involved with organized crime, especially the Mafia, and was detailed in Frederic Dannen's book *Hit Men*, in 1991. DiSipio was exhibit number one, but I confess I thoroughly enjoyed the one or two lunches I had with him at an Italian restaurant in midtown Manhattan on his visits up from his house in Philadelphia where, rumor had it, he had millions in cash buried in the backyard.

Unhappy with Johnny and what Island Records looked like now, Chris asked me to set up a dinner with him and Larry Mestel at Seryna, a Japanese restaurant in Midtown we favored. I was conceited enough to think that I might be able to somehow ensure an entente between the two—to convince Johnny to rein in some of his impulses and Larry to be less combative. Johnny, though, was expecting some kind of dressing-down. While he and I waited in the courtyard of our office building for Chris's car to arrive, he complained to me, grumpily, that Chris wanted to clip his wings, and how *dare* he when it was *he* who was running Island more successfully than ever while Chris was off gallivanting in the islands. And how dare Chris be late for a meeting—as he nearly always was—which Johnny, punctual himself, took as being disrespectful.

I had a bad feeling in the car going to the restaurant. Larry's presence at the dinner would make the possibility of the evening ending well even more remote. But still I was unprepared for what came next: from the moment we sat down at our table, Johnny took a belligerent tone with Chris, even insulting him, and eventually storming out of the restaurant in a huff. Chris was taken aback. Back at his apartment, Chris told me, "That's it; Johnny has to go. Levy has to do it." I knew, really, that there was no way back for Johnny—Chris could take a ribbing, but not being insulted or his acumen being questioned. *This is going to be messy*, I thought, and I said that Johnny had been drunk and perhaps would apologize. The next day, however, Johnny shut himself in his office and didn't call me, as he usually would multiple times a day, not even once. Chris, true to his word, told me he called Levy and said he couldn't work with Johnny and that he simply had to go—and he didn't care where.

In the meantime, Carlos Santana was unhappy to be at Island, which had released his Guts & Grace albums, because he felt Chris was uninterested in him. Though he admired Carlos, it's true that Chris wasn't a huge fan of his music, and he thought it only right that we let him leave the label if he wasn't happy. Davitt pursued him at EMI, but Carlos eventually decided to go back with Clive Davis—who had signed him at Columbia decades ago—and his Arista Records. I had told both Carlos and his brother Jorge how much I loved their music, and we departed on good terms.

Chris was determined that if an artist or act didn't like what he or she had at Island, they should go somewhere they'd be *happier*. He also once told me that when Harrow, the prestigious English boarding school to which he had been sent as a child and where he quickly became the supplier of alcohol and cigarettes to the student body, the headmaster told Blanche, his mother, "Perhaps Christopher would be *happier* elsewhere." And indeed he was.

When Chris essentially told Alain Levy that it was either Barbis or him, he put Levy in an awkward position. He didn't want Chris's dissatisfaction to become public, but he also disagreed with him. Who, he asked, did Chris intend to appoint as president? Chris told me that Levy firmly said, "Hooman cannot be president," to which Chris replied that then he would take over those duties. Levy couldn't very well say no to Chris Blackwell, one of the legendary music men, becoming both the chairman and CEO of the label he had bought from him for $300 million. And so, Johnny Barbis left Island without a word and moved to Los Angeles, where Levy created A&M Associated Labels for him, making him president of a company that had Rocket Records, Nick Gatfield's Atlas Records, and Polydor Records under its wings.

I became executive vice president of Island, once again the "minister without portfolio," irking Levy and other Polygram honchos who saw me as an enabler of Chris's worst instincts. Larry Mestel remained as CFO and head of business affairs (legal department), and Pat Monaco, a longtime Island employee who had started in sales, became the general manager. We, perhaps naively, thought the structure could work, despite the misgivings of Levy and Roger Ames, who had been appointed head of Polygram in the United States.

01.

02.

01.
Suzette Newman, Carlos Santana (wearing a shirt of his own design), and the author, Hammersmith Odeon, London, when Island inherited Santana from Polydor

02.
The Author backstage with Carlos Santana (wearing another shirt of his own design) and band before he left Island Records

Levy by this time was more focused on film, having kickstarted Polygram's movie business, Polygram Filmed Entertainment, or PFE, headed by the British executive Michael Kuhn, which acted as a parent company and distributor of "labels" such as Propaganda Films, Working Title, and Island Pictures, which Polygram finally bought in 1994 and quickly shuttered in 1997, leaving Chris and John Heyman (father of David, the producer of the Harry Potter films), his partner in the film business, free of the burden of managing a Hollywood production company long-distance.

Nevertheless, many in the industry seemed to think that Chris was not only still in the movie business, but that he could greenlight a picture or make an acquisition for distribution. I had signed up the soundtrack for Sling Blade, Billy Bob Thornton's directorial debut, after being invited to a screening before Island Pictures closed, and strongly suggested that Island pick up the film for distribution, too, but Burg wasn't interested (although Kuhn was, albeit too late, as Harvey Weinstein of Miramax jumped right on it). I was especially keen on a screenplay my friend the director Jeff Stein had written, an adaptation of James Ellroy's short story "Dick Contino Blues." A fictionalized story about a real-life character, an accordion player famous for a moment in the 1950s, the screenplay lent itself to a great soundtrack featuring bands like the Brian Setzer Orchestra or Stray Cats or David Johansen as Buster Poindexter, and it had the backing of the British film producer Jeremy Thomas, who'd become a friend. Chris, of course, didn't read the script, but he loved the idea when I spoke to him about it and told me to push Mark Burg to commit to it. Mark, however, wasn't interested at all, and so "Dick Contino's Blues" remained a short story, as Jeff's option on it ran out.

Chapter 21

A Third Island Records

With Johnny Barbis gone as head of Island, our successful acts were anxious about their future. Bill Leopold, Melissa Etheridge's manager, voiced his concerns but was mollified by Chris's and my assurances. The Cranberries had switched their management to Allen Kovac and his Left Bank Management company, the lead singer, Delores O'Riordan, having married Duran Duran's tour manager, Don Burton, who brought the band to Allen's company and effectively became their day-to-day manager. They were touring and should have been basking in the limelight, but Delores was annoyed that she hadn't met Chris Blackwell, who was closely associated with the *other* Irish group on Island, U2. She hadn't met that band, either, her fellow Irish superstars, and felt like an orphan—albeit a mightily rich one—at Island Records.

It became my diplomatic job to correct one complaint or the other—or both, if possible. I told Chris he really should invite Delores and the band down to Goldeneye, and while he didn't or couldn't disagree, he maintained that he just wouldn't be the ideal host. "I don't know them and I just can't pretend to like their music," he explained. Delores, however, was well aware of various U2 members' time in Jamaica, and of the celebrities who visited there and who often appeared in the *New York Post*'s Page Six. Chris also operated Firefly, Noel Coward's hilltop estate overlooking the sea where he is buried, a few minutes away from Goldeneye, as a museum of sorts. He enjoyed taking guests up to the property in the evening to watch the sunset at least once during their stays, and the famous and not-so-famous friends—Dennis Hopper, Adam Clayton, and Michael Caine to name just a few I saw and accompanied on Chris's plane down from New York—would mingle until dark before heading back down the hill.

Paul McGuinness, U2's manager, was especially worried about Barbis's departure. The band was getting close to releasing a new album and starting a world tour, and he felt that Island without Johnny wouldn't do as good a job as PLG had with *Achtung Baby* or *Zooropa*. Paul and I were friendly and became closer friends later, but he took out his frustration on me—like others in the business he partly blamed me, or my existence, for Johnny's ouster—when their album *Pop* did not achieve the success of the band's previous albums, nor did it meet the expectations of Paul and the band themselves. In coming up with *Pop*, the band had misread their audience, the culture of the moment, and everything about the promotion of the record—though Island had little say over it, as the band paid for and made their own videos and chose virtually every aspect of a release—from introducing the record to the public at a Kmart store in downtown Manhattan to the video for the first single, "Discothèque," which was out of character, awkward, and to many even embarrassing.

The band and Paul being who they were, and because of their importance to Island, I decided that it should be me who submitted the first single's video to MTV—a crucial outlet for the success of a record—instead of the video-promotion team. I called Andy Schuon, then MTV's head of music programming, and made an appointment. When I handed him the video on a U-matic cassette and we watched it in silence, he was clearly unimpressed. He wouldn't commit to playing the video in heavy rotation (multiple times a day) and added that he thought the

01.

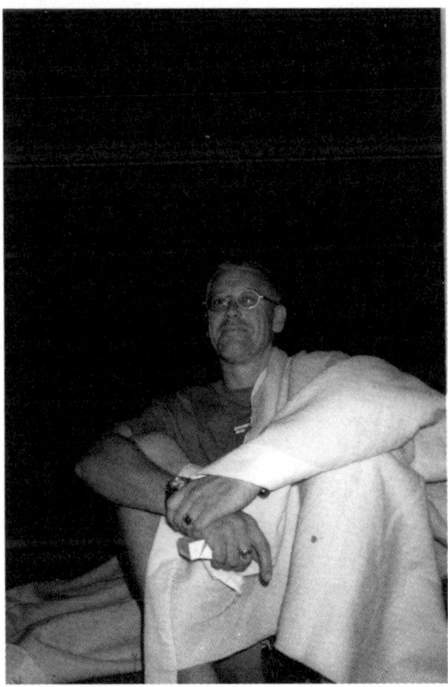
02.

01.
Dennis Hopper, photographed by the author taking his picture with the same model of camera at Firefly, Jamaica

02.
U2's Adam Clayton at Firefly, Jamaica, photo by the author

band was entering "Rolling Stones territory"—and he didn't mean it as a compliment. The Rolling Stones hardly ever had a video on MTV, despite touring to huge stadium audiences, and most in the industry believed that their hit-making days were over. To youth-oriented MTV, U2 was no longer relevant, especially not in this incarnation with them trying to appear "cool."

I wasn't surprised. The tour, PopMart, which started in Las Vegas (almost half the label staff had flown there and we booked up the Hard Rock Hotel) only six weeks after the album release, was an over-the-top production that was successful at the box office (although well below what the concert promoter, Michael Cohl, had anticipated after paying a $100 million advance) but was less well received by critics and, in some U.S. markets, failed to sell out stadiums—a first for U2 in many years. The record sold very well at first, but sales dropped precipitously week after week. The band was annoyed by the seeming lack of enthusiasm for their new record and the direction they were taking musically, and it became my thankless job to tell them just how bad things were, usually at off-hours.

After talking to both Chris and Paul, I took Chris's plane up to Boston to see the band at their hotel and tell them that we were having trouble generating any enthusiasm for *Pop*, and that they should probably remake their videos in a more traditional format—not try to be clever as they had with a Village People parody for "Discothéque"—if we wanted to get MTV on board. I knew Bono and Adam best, having seen them more often than Larry Mullen and the Edge, but I directed my talk to Larry, aware that Paul was paying close attention sitting to the side. Chris had long ago said to me, "You know, Hooman, it's Larry's band"—it wasn't Bono's—so I tried to make sure that Larry understood what I was saying, while being as diplomatic as possible. The band were polite, listening but not saying much, although their faces, sullen, betrayed their disappointment. Larry barely said a word.

I flew back to New York the same afternoon, thinking the band probably hated me, but in reality, as they confessed later, they knew all along that the album wasn't up to their own standards. Their misreading of the culture—with the irony and the "pop music" and "disco" concept of the record and the tour—was harder to swallow and spoke to a sort of mid-life crisis for an act. I had one Hail Mary pass to try with MTV, which was to take Andy Schuon on Chris's jet to a U2 show outside the big markets, where the band would be more accessible backstage and less occupied with friends and celebrities in attendance. I decided on Madison, Wisconsin, where the band was to play at the University of Wisconsin football stadium, and Andy was up for it. I met him at Teterboro Airport in suburban New Jersey and we flew to Madison, the pilots having arranged for a car to take us to the venue. Andy enjoyed himself, I think, standing in the VIP section and chatting with the band (whom he'd never met) after the show. Bono, ever the charmer, suggested that we go with them after the show to Chicago, where they would have their postconcert party, and offered us a ride on their tour plane. I told him that I had my *own* plane (he knew I meant Chris's) but that, sure, we would meet them there.

After the concert we headed to the airport in four or five limousines that the tour had booked, with a police motorcycle escort (Andy was duly impressed, I'm sure), and we boarded our two planes parked next to each other; U2's tour jet dwarfing Chris's Citation. I told the pilots our plans had changed: we were going to Chicago (a thirty-minute-or-so flight) and we'd probably not return to New York until the early hours of the morning. I also told them that whatever they did, they had to land ahead of U2's plane, as I had said to Bono that I bet him we could beat them to Chicago. And we did, *just*.

We hung out at the hotel with the band and their friends, drinking and talking, and Andy decided he wanted to stay the night. I said my goodbyes not too long after midnight, headed to the airport, flew back to Teterboro, and was back at the office by 9 a.m. From then on MTV played U2 with a little more regularity, but not in heavy rotation.

I experienced another example of Bono's star power a year later, when I was staying at the Hotel du Cap in Antibes with Karri, who was then my new girlfriend, for a week's holiday. It was the first time we went away together and alone, and we were getting to know each other. Paul McGuinness had told me that Bono and his family were staying on Paul Allen's (of Microsoft) yacht nearby and I should see them while we all were in the South of France.

01.

01.
U2 laminates had photos and codes on the front and back for exactly how much access one would have, and were difficult to forge

Bono called me one morning, suggesting we join them for lunch on the yacht. A very short while later, before we left our room at Eden Roc (the seaside building), the phone rang again and it was Bono, asking if he and his family could come to the hotel instead, as they had never been there. I said of course, the children should bring bathing suits, and I'd book a table for lunch.

I asked the concierge for a table away from the crowds, if possible, and overlooking the sea. "Of course," he replied, and then said, "May I ask you a question? Was that *Bono* who just called you?" When I said yes, he asked, "Bono from *U2*?" (He'd either been listening in on the call or Bono introduced himself when asking for my room by name.) I said yes again, and we walked to the pool, prepared to take our usual spots in the third tier away from the pool itself, the closer chairs and lounges being reserved for more *deserving* clients, or just more famous. The pool attendant, however, took us to two choice lounge chairs right by the pool's edge, and said, "For the rest of your stay, *these* are your spots." When Bono, his wife, Ali, and his daughters arrived, I asked the attendant if the children could swim in the pool, which was ordinarily restricted to hotel guests. "Of course!" he replied. While the kids played in the pool the rest of the afternoon, Bono held forth on numerous subjects—music, film, entertainment, politics—and the lunch went on for hours.

The next day, we found that we indeed had kept our new spots at the pool. A few days after that, I rented a scooter to take us to dinner with Marc Lumbroso and his family at their summer vacation house in the hills. On a twisting turn, I skidded in what I thought was dirt and crashed the scooter, falling on one side and bleeding profusely from one leg. Karri, who was riding on the back, was fine, though shocked. Someone called an ambulance, and I was taken to a small clinic down the hill where several injured people were waiting to be treated. A harried doctor came out into the waiting room and asked to see the various patients' admission forms, and when he saw mine, took me straightaway back to his examination room and spoke to me in Farsi. A Persian doctor, here in the French Riviera, where I had spent a summer as a teenager. Witness to the power of celebrity and the power of kinship, all in one week. Lumbroso came to pick us up at the clinic, we had dinner with him and his family, and I, bandaged up, sat on a lounge chair right by the pool for the next few days, unable to take the short steps into the water. I haven't been back to the Hotel du Cap Eden Roc since.

Chapter 22

The Irish

In 1996 I still hadn't resolved Delores O'Riordan's issues—neither with Chris, whom she still hadn't met, nor with U2. She had become more intransigent in terms of access for the Polygram labels worldwide, who needed to speak to her about interviews, promotions, etc. At one point David Munns, Polygram's head of international based in London, called me about some requests that were being funneled through his office, as it appeared the only person at Polygram anywhere in the world she would talk to was me. (I once called her in Spain when she had decided at the last moment that she wouldn't attend a photo shoot for a planned magazine feature and begged her to reconsider, promising I would send our head of publicity from New York, John Vlautin, to Madrid to ensure that everything went smoothly. John got on a plane a few hours later.) I had gone on a pub crawl with her and Don in Dublin once, and attended her brother's wedding in Limerick—a grand affair she presumably paid for now that she was both famous and rich—and we got along well. She always complained about Chris, though, saying things like "When am I going to meet Chris?" or "Is Chris coming to the show?" And I knew her feelings about the "favorite" Irish band on Island.

An opportunity for rapprochement arose when Bono and the Edge were finishing the refurbishment of a Dublin hotel they had bought, the Clarence. I flew to Dublin to see Delores, and after asking Bono if he would meet with her, I invited her to dinner with the two of us at the hotel. Bono was his usual gregarious self, and by the end of dinner and with great grace he had Delores relaxed and happy—two Irish singers together with similar political views, both hugely successful, both recording their next albums in Ireland and on Island, one no longer resentful of the other. Chris didn't have to host her band at Goldeneye, after all—probably for the best, as Chris could never hide his feelings about a person, a band, or a song. When Delores left after dinner, Bono took me to a nightclub around the corner. There—and I'm sure he has done this with so many people that he wouldn't remember it specifically with me—he danced, alone, with other patrons, and, after some urging, with me. It was as if, in this little corner of Dublin, he wasn't Bono, but rather just another fun-seeking Irishman out for a night on the town.

Delores came across to many as an innocent waif, and in the music business some believed she was dominated by her husband. I found her to be genuinely in love with Don and very smart, astute, and mature for someone in her mid-twenties. She displayed a surprising canniness to me on that trip, too, when she asked me to accompany her to the gala opening of the first Virgin Cinemas in Ireland—a party with a guest list of Irish celebrities. When we arrived, flashbulbs popped as we got out of the car. A Virgin publicist approached and said that Richard Branson wanted to meet her, and he greeted her with a big hug. She said to Branson, "This is Hooman, from *Island* Records." He shook my hand with a pained grin and said to her, "Come, let's have our photo taken!" She followed him to a sofa and said to me, "Come here," to the obvious dismay of Branson. She wasn't going to let Branson, who had founded Virgin Records, associate himself *musically* with one of the biggest bands in the world at the time, not after she had satisfied herself that Island, and Bono, cared about her. In the pre-social-media era, I have to assume Virgin publicists cropped me out of the photo. I left Ireland the next day without seeing a newspaper.

Chapter 23

Impending Clouds

Island was having trouble with new artists. I signed Brother J from X-Clan to a solo deal, releasing a hip-hop album called *Seeds of Evolution* by his act the Dark Sun Riders. When it was only nominally successful, I wondered if Island could break R&B or hip-hop records at all, while Def Jam, which we distributed, continued to succeed with its acts, new and veteran. Island had had success with hip-hop in the past, in label deals such as with Jon Baker's Gee Street Records or Delicious Vinyl, as well as direct signings, but had misfires, too, such as with Mobb Deep's *Juvenile Hell* in 1993, and the label dropped the act before its later hits.

Chris developed an idea to separate the mainstream Island label from R&B and start a label called Island Black Music, and hired Hiriam Hicks, an executive known in the business for his work with successful Black artists. Levy was not fully on board with a new division for Island—he had bought Motown for Polygram in 1994 and installed Andre Harrell, founder of

Uptown Records and mentor of Sean Coombs (or Puff Daddy and Diddy as he later became known), as its president. With Motown and Def Jam already in the Polygram family, a separate Black label within Island made no sense to him, but he didn't try to stop Chris. Before the contract with Hiriam was signed, though, Chris told me that under no circumstances should I say anything to Lyor Cohen, whom he knew I saw often, about Hiriam or Island Black Music, worried that Lyor could very well sabotage the whole thing to prevent any internal competition with his acts.

When rumors were flying about in the music business that Hiriam was going to go to Island and start a new Black music label, Lyor did in fact come to my office and ask me if it was true. I was very friendly with Lyor, and I think he liked and respected me, too. But I was also loyal to Island and to its chairman and founder, my friend, and I said, *no*, that we were not creating a Black music division and no, Hiriam was *not* coming to Island. I was both troubled and uncomfortable with my lie, and yet I had said it. I justified the lie in my mind on the basis that if our positions were reversed, he would have done the same. When, a few days later, Hiriam's contract was signed and his hiring became public, Lyor stormed into my office. "You *lied* to me!" he yelled, and told me he couldn't forgive me. "You were my *friend*," he shouted, a little hyperbolically. As time went by, we became collegial again, though I continued to find myself a little embarrassed whenever I was in his presence.

Hiriam in the meantime busied himself with separating Island Black Music from Island, forbidding his staff from even socializing with the mainstream staff, wanting his own fiefdom. He signed Dru Hill, a Baltimore quartet that sold well, but Hiriam's relationship—a very controlling one—with the members was so contentious that they asked for an appointment to see me, along with their attorney, Londell McMillan, and manager, Keith Ingram. They wanted off Island Black Music and wanted to come to my division, what the act members themselves called "Island White Music." I explained that there was no such thing as Island "White" music, and that they should try to sort out their differences with Hiriam, whose division was doing a good job of selling their debut album.

Sadly, things got worse. At an Atlanta nightclub, Hiriam was accused of beating Ingram with a pool cue and watching his brother—not an Island employee—beat both Ingram and McMillan. (Their lawsuit led to an embarrassing moment for Polygram when Eric Kronfeld, the COO of the parent music company, was asked under oath in a deposition why a convicted criminal, Hiriam's brother, would be employed by Island as a bodyguard. He replied, "If every African American male in the United States was disqualified from pursuing a livelihood . . . because of his criminal records, then there would be no, or virtually no, African American employees in our society or in our industry." There were, quite naturally, cries of racism from artists and others, and Kronfeld not only was forced to apologize, but was demoted from his lofty position.)

Chris neither backed Hiriam nor supported him beyond giving him the space to sign and develop acts. Lyor and Russell Simmons, meanwhile, felt that he had created Island Black Music not just to compete with Def Jam, but to find a way to overshadow it, which may have been partially true. At any rate, going into the fall of 1997, Chris was getting more unhappy with Polygram and felt that Levy wasn't giving him latitude—he wanted to start an audiovisual department and focus on the new DVD format, which he thought could replace CDs because it could play music along with *visuals*. Levy said an emphatic *no* to that and told Chris he should concentrate on Island's record business, which at that time wasn't especially successful, rather than trying to come up with new and expensive ideas. It wasn't a good idea for Levy to talk down to Chris, I thought, and I was sure Chris wouldn't forget it.

Chris and I had instituted regular dinners with Jerry Moss, legendary co-founder of A&M Records, who also had his issues with Levy. Although he was no longer involved in the day-to-day business of A&M, he had disagreed with Levy's decision to make Al Cafaro, the head of radio promotions, the president of the label. Moss felt an attachment to the label he had co-founded in a garage, and like Chris couldn't stand the corporate structure Levy had imposed; we commiserated at dinners at Seryna, in a private room on the second floor of the restaurant. It was difficult, if not impossible, for entrepreneurial music men to abide by rules, not when for decades they had played only by their own. Chris, in anticipation of celebrating Island Records' fortieth anniversary in 1999, wanted Jerry to be involved, as he had been an early distributor of Island signings (such as Cat Stevens) in the States. Our dinners often degenerated into a mutual grumbling party about the evils of corporate entertainment run by businesspeople and not entrepreneurs.

When I called Chris in August 2023 to tell him that Jerry Moss had just died, he was saddened and told me he had *just* seen him in London in the summer when he'd accompanied Jerry to a Herb Alpert show at Ronnie Scott's, the famous jazz club. Herb's playing, he said, was fantastic. Music men to the end.

Chapter 24

The Iran Connection

Especially in the years since my return to Island, both with Johnny and then without, I had been so immersed in the business and so enmeshed in the Blackwell universe that Iran was rarely, if ever, a preoccupation. My career and my friends were now my home—it was Jamaica, the Bahamas, New York, London, and Los Angeles—and my identity was tied up in all those people, companies, and places. I spoke to my parents once a week, in Farsi, chatting about how they were doing, and they would inevitably ask me when I would next visit them in London. They were happy I had found stability and a good income, but didn't really understand what exactly it was that I did. I often tried to explain to my father that it was not really that dissimilar to what *he* had done, except with music and music artists, but he couldn't reconcile that. Despite my having an expense account and staying in expensive London hotels, both my parents wished—as Persian culture dictates—that I would stay with them and have most of my meals at home.

We had given up speaking about change in Iran, as my father no longer believed change would come in his lifetime. With my sister, who had lived in England from childhood, and my brother, who had been recruited from Salomon Brothers in New York to join Deutsche Bank as vice chairman of asset management in London, I spoke in English, not least because my brother's wife, Kathleen, was an American from Long Island and his boys spoke only English. My parents had resigned themselves to a life of exile and limited means: my brother bought an apartment in Chiswick for them so that they could sell their studio flat in Kensington and use the proceeds for general living expenses. (My mother had taken a job at a patisserie on Church Street in the early years after the revolution, over my father's objection—in much the same way he had objected to my brother and me working as salesmen when at St. Paul's—but gave that up after the move to Chiswick. She was able to buy my sister a small car with the money she had saved, as well as put a small down payment on a house in Chiswick for her after she finished medical school and began working as a pediatrician for the National Health Service.

In the mid-nineties, President Hashemi Rafsanjani had slowly opened Iran to the West after a decade and a half of revolutionary isolation, and my father decided to return to Iran and clear his name. He felt he had done nothing wrong as a civil servant, had served his country as duty required, and had been fired and deemed counterrevolutionary unfairly for not having returned to Iran from Japan when ordered. He had a passport issued by the Islamic regime from the Iranian consulate in Kensington, and since he had never been an asylee but rather a permanent resident in Britain, there was never a question that he should be able to travel to Iran, only that he might not be given permission to leave once there.

Nonetheless, he decided he had to go. He had a large extended family in Iran—sisters, nephews, and nieces—and many friends from the private sector whose careers had not been as affected by the revolution as his was. We also had family connections to the regime that replaced the monarchy; my father's nephew Hossein, younger son of his eldest sister, Aghdas, and a revolutionary in 1979, was married to President Rafsanjani's niece and was already a well-known eye surgeon. The risk that my father would be detained was low, given his age and his not having joined any opposition or monarchist group in exile. (Later, when Mohammad Khatami succeeded Rafsanjani as president in 1997, the risk became zero, as Khatami's aunt and uncle were married to my father's brother and sister.)

In Tehran, the foreign ministry put my father on trial (a foreign ministry inquisition, not a judicial trial). He was accused of having served alcohol at the embassy in Japan, to which his response was yes, as it was not only not illegal at the time in Iran but was also expected of his station as ambassador. The second accusation rested on his handwritten notes relating to Persian Gulf affairs that revolutionaries had found in the Shah's desk after ransacking the palace. My father responded that he didn't know why his notes, which he had addressed to Foreign Minister Khalatbary, ended up in the Shah's possession, but he surmised that Khalatbary—his friend and fellow career diplomat who would meet the Shah once a week—would, instead of trying to curry favor with the monarch by aggrandizing himself in summarizing various foreign policy issues, hand over notes from trusted colleagues like my father, letting the notes speak for themselves.

His answers satisfied the ministry enough to merely fire him (he had never been officially fired), depriving him of any pension he'd receive if he had returned to Iran, but they did not refer him to the judiciary for a trial. He was free to leave Iran, and come and go as he pleased, but his name was never properly cleared. (During Khatami's presidency, my cousins told him to retain counsel and sue the ministry for wrongful termination, as other diplomats had done, but my father refused to "beg" the ministry or to use family connections—*partee bazee* in Farsi—to receive his rightful due. I didn't discuss the matter with him until years later, when I chimed in with my cousins, pleading with him to pursue his pension and back pay (which would have by then amounted to seven figures, in dollars), to no avail.

In the mid-nineties, I met Maryam Malakpour, an Iranian fashion stylist in Los Angeles who worked on a music video of ours. She was well known in the business, I discovered, and a friend of Jeff Stein's. The Iranian diaspora wasn't as big yet or as influential as it is today, and the children of Iranian immigrants who would grow up to be tech billionaires or CEOs of major corporations (such as eBay or Uber) were still in school. I had not come across a single other Iranian in the music business, and it was refreshing to see a countrywoman successful in her career. It turned out her mentee was an old friend I had met in Los Angeles after the revolution: Mojgan Sangi, or Moji to her friends, was also a stylist, and we rekindled our friendship. She still traveled back and forth to Iran as her father lived there, and when we'd first lost contact she had become Neusha Farrahi's brother's girlfriend. I had met Neusha and his younger brother, Nima, in Los Angeles in the early eighties—Neusha was a firebrand leftist, anti-Khomeini *and* anti-Shah, but sincere and smart. I was shocked when, in 1987, I heard that he had set himself on fire outside the Federal Building in Westwood to protest the regime in Iran, Ayatollah Khomeini, and then-president (and now supreme leader) Khamenei. Out of curiosity I had often attended rallies outside the building where Iranians, mostly monarchists, gathered from time to time to protest the regime back home. I wasn't there when Neusha self-immolated, but I discovered years later that my friend Porochista Khakpour, who was a child and recent immigrant, had been. Porochista went on to have a career as a successful writer and novelist, and her first book, *Sons and Other Flammable Objects*, she told me, resulted from her childhood experience of seeing Neusha set himself alight.

Moji had since broken up with Nima and had dated the actor Fisher Stevens for several years and was close to Matt Dillon, who years later hired her to be the costume designer for his film *City of Ghosts*. I would see Moji and Maryam whenever they were in New York or I was in L.A. After her first trip to Tehran in years, I met Maryam for drinks at a bar in Worldwide Plaza. She showed me dozens of photographs she had taken in Iran and was gushing about how great it was and how I, too, should visit. For a moment I was jealous. Why should I not be able to go to Iran, and why was it so complicated for me? And why did I have both a sense of Iran not being my homeland *and* it being my home, simultaneously, while I lived and worked in a very Anglo-American world?

Moji called me one day in the late nineties and asked if I would be willing to meet a friend of hers who was lonely in New York and didn't really know any Iranian men. Leila Pahlavi was the younger daughter of the former Shah. Leila would sometimes stay with her aunt, Princess Ashraf (the Shah's twin), when visiting Manhattan, at Ashraf's town house on Beekman Place, and we met a few times for drinks or dinner at the Four Seasons Hotel on 57th Street. She seemed a terribly sad person but very bright, sharp, and a good conversationalist. She was, I thought, way too thin to be healthy; she would order lots of food but eat almost none of it. I wondered why her family—her brother Reza, the onetime crown prince and, to monarchists in exile, their Shah, or her mother, Queen Farah, or even her aunt—didn't intervene with her, for surely I couldn't be the only one who could recognize something was wrong. I told Moji of my concerns, but she didn't know what she could do long-distance from Los Angeles. Leila died of a drug overdose in a hotel room in 2001, after we had lost contact with each other. I was both saddened for her and angry at her family.

When her brother Ali Reza committed suicide in 2011, I was again dismayed by the family—why had they not recognized *his* depression, and if they had, why had they not done anything to help him? Queen Farah and Reza Pahlavi had foolishly severed their relationship with Ambassador Ardeshir Zahedi soon after the Shah died in Cairo, when he was the one person they could have relied on as a friend and consigliere, someone who might have helped ease their adjustment to civilian life in exile, and even intervened in solving family troubles. I understood the royal family's trauma—we all were traumatized by the revolution and the sudden loss of possessions, a home, and, most important, identity—but Leila's death was unnecessary and Ali Reza's perhaps even more so.

When Moji died suddenly in 2016, I was more deeply saddened than I could have imagined. She had been a friend—an honest, loyal, fun, and funny person with a positive outlook on life despite it being unfulfilled romantically. (Moji and I and Matt Dillon once had had a wild night together dancing at the Copacabana on the west side of Manhattan, followed by drinks at his stylishly decorated apartment on the Upper West Side until the early hours of the morning.) I happened to run into Fisher Stevens at Goldeneye in 2017—Moji had introduced us long after they had broken up, and they remained friends—and we commiserated on the loss of such a good person.

I was often in London on business to visit Island UK on St. Peter's Square. Sitting in the British Airways lounge in Heathrow's Terminal 4—or, if I was lucky, in the Concorde lounge—I would see the announcements for the BA flight to Tehran and wonder what it would be like to be on that flight, heading east instead of west. When I saw an Iran Air 747 taxiing to the runway, I would feel close to Iran, even if I knew I wouldn't be heading there anytime soon. I would be momentarily jealous of the passengers of those flights, and of Maryam and Moji, who seemingly so easily could fly between Tehran and Europe, which seemed almost unimaginable to me.

Another Iranian who entered my life when I was at Island was Farhad Azima, who owned an airline leasing company that Air Jamaica (now defunct) leased its planes from. When I first met him with Chris Blackwell, I found Farhad to be an interesting character, and I discovered his intriguing past—he had been known to have leased aircraft to the CIA and was rumored to have been involved in Iran-Contra. Chris was also friendly with Gordon "Butch" Stewart, the Jamaican who owned the Sandals resorts and numerous other local businesses and was the largest private shareholder in and chairman of Air Jamaica, and through this Jamaican connection, Chris had met Farhad.

I met Butch, who had a house on the beach near Ocho Rios, later, when he invited Chris to tea one day when we were both at Goldeneye. Chris asked me to go with him—on the Jet Skis instead of driving. We set off in the afternoon and pulled our Jet Skis up on the sand when we arrived, took stairs up from the beach to Butch's house, and were with him for an hour or so while Chris and he talked Jamaican business. I watched the sea to check on the tide. What started to alarm me, though, as the two men chatted away, was the approaching dusk. I knew it would take a good twenty to twenty-five minutes to ski back to Goldeneye, and while one could follow the lights on the coast, maneuvering back into the lagoon along a trench between the rocks and coral reef would be virtually impossible in the dark. I warned Chris, who looked out the window and said, "Oh, shit."

We begged apologies to Butch and ran down to get our Jet Skis. We set off as fast as we could and went far out to sea to be sure to avoid the reef, but darkness fell rather suddenly, and we knew we were still a good fifteen minutes from home. There was no moon that night, and we were soon in complete darkness, the sea a deep black. Chris shouted at me to cut my engine, and we both drifted for a while, wondering what we should do next. The reef wasn't our only problem: we couldn't see each other if we separated and were in danger of crashing into each other. We decided to go slowly, and started our engines, gently gunning them so that we could be within sight and sound of each other. But a few minutes later, when I went over a wave, I could no longer see Chris on the other side. We found each other after a while, still trying to navigate far from shore according to landmarks we could recognize. We lost and found each other a few times, once because Chris came swooping in front of me, almost crashing into my Jet Ski.

Meanwhile, back at Goldeneye, Mary, who hadn't wanted us to take the Jet Skis in the first place, was deeply worried. She sent Roger Brown, the project manager at Goldeneye at the time (as villas and huts were being built) to search for us with the Jet Ski maintenance boys, equipped with flashlights. Eventually, as we made out the lights at Goldeneye, we saw Roger zoom up next to us, and with the two other escorts beaming light on the water, we slowly drove back into the lagoon. Mary was standing at the top of the cliff, ready to let us have it. I slinked away back to my room after getting off the Jet Ski by Chris's office, but not before Mary gave us both a thorough tongue thrashing.

It was the second time she had berated Chris and me for being reckless. The other time we were at Chris's house outside Nassau and she was meeting us at the dock across from their small private island a short distance away by car. Chris thought we should go on his speedboat, but within minutes of leaving the dock, a storm came through and we were in very rough seas. Chris didn't seem to mind—at one point he even asked a horrified me to take the wheel while he urinated over the side—but when we reached Mary, she was furious at us for driving a boat through open sea to meet her.

Chris and Farhad Azima became good friends, not least because of Butch Stewart, with Farhad a regular guest at Chris's apartment in New York and at his properties in Jamaica. I enjoyed his company and our endless games of backgammon, but he never joined us on a Jet Ski ride. Farhad was a big donor to both Clintons' political campaigns and to the DNC; he'd had coffee at the White House with Bill and later hosted Hillary at his home in Kansas City for fundraising dinners. In 1997 he invited Chris to an event at the White House. Chris bought a navy-blue suit (his first in years, if ever), and I helped him with a tie while Mary watched with obvious pleasure. He looked good, wearing socks probably for the first time since boarding school at Harrow, but this time he didn't need to ask me what size shoe I wore, as he had his own quite decent-looking pair on his feet.

Chapter 25

Turmoil

Throughout 1997, Chris's frustration with Levy, Polygram, and the corporate world was growing. As he had said to me many times, he liked to live "by his wits," and his work life was not allowing him to. He would talk to Larry Mestel and me behind closed doors, and at one point, worried that Polygram brass had gotten wind of his discontent, he asked us to leave our offices for a few minutes so that he could have them swept for listening devices.

Chris told me one day, after attending the Allen & Company conference in Sun Valley, Idaho, that summer, that Herbert ("Herb") Allen himself had told him that if Chris could get out of his contract with Polygram, he could raise at least $400 million to start a new company. Levy, meanwhile, had been incensed that Chris—his employee now—had been invited to and attending the famous and exclusive media and finance conference since the sale of Island, years before Alain himself was first invited. Chris had also met Ted Waitt, co-founder of Gateway computers, at the Sun Valley conference, and Ted was especially interested in the entertainment business after having built a major corporation out of an office in his father's cattle ranch in Iowa. Anyone with the slightest interest in the music business knew Island Records and knew Chris Blackwell, and Chris was adept at collecting groupies.

With the intriguing notion of Herb Allen's promise and Ted Waitt's indication to Chris that he was interested in whatever he was planning in the entertainment field, Chris had one problem: how to get out of his contract with Polygram. He thought that the best way might be to publicly criticize Polygram, and especially target Alain Levy, via an interview with a respected music writer for a major media outlet (this was years before social media, blogs, and YouTube offered everyone a platform). I thought Neil Strauss, music critic at *The New York Times*, might be a good person to conduct an interview, but he was young then and I was wary after he had given a poor review to U2's *Pop* and gently mocked their tour announcement fete at Kmart. I spoke to our publicity head, John Vlautin, and he recommended Chuck Philips of the *Los Angeles Times*, who was a highly respected music journalist and wrote for Hollywood's hometown paper, after all.

John called me first, while I was having a late breakfast with Chris at his hut on the lagoon at Goldeneye, giving me warning that Chuck would call any minute now. When he did, I handed the phone to Chris, who stood up, coughed, and walked away with the phone to his ear. I sat there for a long time, drinking coffee and smoking cigarettes. Chris finally returned, phone in hand, and sat down. "Well," he said, "I did it." He told me that he had come down extremely hard on Levy and the way he ran the record business. He said he couldn't see how Levy would be able to ignore the article, and that he was sure this was the end of his formal association with Island Records and Polygram. He called Tom Hayes and Larry Mestel—who as business affairs executives on either side of the Atlantic would have to deal with Levy's fury and any legal consequences that would follow—and told them to start preparing for what might be an ugly divorce. I told John in New York to expect an absolute *shitshow* the day the article was published, and he should also expect that Dawn Bridges, head of publicity for the parent company, would be calling him. Chris and I braced ourselves, for what, we didn't exactly know, but it was going to be an interesting week.

As we predicted, when Chuck's article hit the newsstand in the last days of October, the music industry was abuzz, and Levy was furious. He let it be known to Chris that he could not stay at Polygram any longer, and so the divorce process, which Chris had hoped for, began. But although Polygram was going to let Chris out of contract with non-compete and trademark-protection clauses, it also wanted him to take me and Larry Mestel with him, without paying off our contracts, even though they would be firing us *without* cause (which made me all the more appreciate Chris's sweeping of my office for bugs). Paying us off, it seemed, would have added insult to injury in the mind of Alain, who actively disliked me and begrudgingly tolerated Larry, who he at least respected as a finance executive.

It was a testament to Levy's ego, I thought at the time, that he believed the best option moving forward for Polygram was to be rid of one of the most respected creative executives in the business rather than figure out how to make it work with him, but Levy was more focused on the film business by this time and, as Chris said to me dismissively, was "busier reading bloody scripts than running a music company properly." Chris, of course, had no intention of paying off our contracts himself, as Levy had maintained should happen, and he told me to just hang on and eventually Polygram would give in and fire me, and I would join him in his new venture, which he was going to call Palm Pictures, Polygram trademarks be damned. (Palm wasn't an Island Records trademark, but the logo—a palm tree that Island had almost always featured—would make Polygram try to stop its use.)

Starting in November, with Chris gone, I was essentially locked out of any decisions being made and had no real work to do. I would dutifully show up for work every day but spent most of the day in my office. It was near the end of the year, and we had no major Christmas releases planned, so the label was in maintenance mode until the holiday break anyway. Some Island staff came to see me to ask if I knew what was going to happen at the label, but I told them I had no idea, and I *really* didn't. Chris told me, in the lobby of his apartment building in New York across from the Museum of Natural History, that when free from Polygram I could join Palm Pictures either with the same salary or take a 40 percent cut in exchange for 3 percent equity in the company. I told him that naturally I would put money where my mouth was, so to speak, and take the equity.

I spent the holidays in Jamaica, taking Karri with me to Goldeneye for her first visit there and her first time meeting Chris. Chris never liked taking the master bedroom in the main house (perhaps because his mother and Ian Fleming had their assignations there, or because he preferred being in the background), and before he built huts and villas he would sleep in one of the two back bedrooms. Karri was excited and loved the house and the Jamaican food the cook made, and found Chris to be charming, as almost everyone did who met him for the first time. Karri took to Jamaica and Goldeneye right away, and is at home there as much as I am, a testament to her ease with foreign cultures and her curiosity about the world beyond the heartland of America.

That Christmas we had the run of the house, which Chris had had remodeled over the years in a Balinese style while he and Mary stayed in their hut by his office on the lagoon. We didn't talk business very much, but I knew that Allen & Company were the bankers putting together Palm Pictures' "book" and that Chris had secured a commitment from Ted Waitt for an investment of $25 million. After the holidays and after Chris's divorce from Polygram was finalized, he took offices a few blocks away from Island on the corner of 58th Street and Eighth Avenue, and Larry Mestel, newly released by Polygram, followed him there as CFO of the new company.

I was stuck at Island—neither Chris, who was in no hurry to have me start, nor Polygram, which didn't want to fire me and pay me the six figures they'd have to—made a move regarding my future. Roger Ames and Alain Levy were now looking to change the structure of Island entirely. I was seeing Davitt more regularly for lunch since he had left EMI after it shuttered its doors as a fully staffed label—both of us underemployed—and I talked about my frustration with having a job that required me to do nothing. I couldn't understand why Polygram was trying to avoid a payout that, while significant for me, was a drop in the bucket for them. Davitt was close to Roger, and he told me that Roger had been talking to him about going to Island and running it with Johnny Barbis, who Alain wanted to bring back to New York. As things got closer to an agreement with Davitt and Johnny—with Davitt becoming chairman and Johnny president of Island—Davitt finally told Roger that he needed to do the right thing and put me out of my misery *and* pay out my contract. Roger agreed, and by the end of February I was free, and had some money in my bank account to cover for the financial hit I was going to take by moving to Palm. Alimony payments alone were going to take a good chunk of my yearly income, and my hope was that I would end up with a piece—small to be sure—of a successful company that might be worth something substantial in the future.

Chapter 26

Palm Pictures

My job was head of music and film, although I began by focusing on filmed entertainment and let Faisel Durrani, who came with us from Island, where he oversaw international marketing, run the day-to-day music side. Kathy Reynolds, my longtime assistant, now married and going by Kathy Salt, agreed to come with me to Palm (for her same salary). We convinced Sarah Weinstein-Dennison, one of the publicists at Island, to join us as head of publicity, and Michael Seltzer, a lawyer at Island, as head of business affairs. With Ted Waitt's investment, Tom Grueskin, who had been an early employee of Gateway, joined Palm, working on digital applications. He brought with him David Beal, a drummer friend of his, eager to get into the digital entertainment world. Chris also made an informal production deal with Mark Burg and his new partner, Oren Koules, formerly of Paramount Pictures, who had started a management and production company in Los Angeles, Evolution Entertainment—to bring film projects to Palm.

Mark called me one day very early in my time at Palm and asked if I'd be interested in a new James Toback project. Toback, an indie film director and Oscar-nominated screenwriter (for *Bugsy*), had made the tiny-budgeted *Two Girls and a Guy*, which received good notices, especially for Robert Downey, Jr.'s performance (his first since his release from jail). The idea of an extremely low-budget film by an accomplished director appealed to me, and to Chris, too. After meeting the producers, I met Toback for lunch at one of his favorite spots, E.A.T. on Madison Avenue, and was immediately charmed by him, a raconteur of the first degree who was also very confident and even persuasive that his film would be a hit. He said he wanted to make a movie about Black and white cultures colliding—white kids who wanted to act Black, and Black kids whose records sold to white teenagers in the millions. Known as a screenwriter—he had also written the semi-autobiographical script for the film *The Gambler*, starring James Caan as Toback—he nonetheless wanted to rely only on notes and an outline for the film he was going to call, quite simply, *Black and White*. After all, his last film had been mostly improvised, and he said he felt that with the subject matter, this one lent itself even more to improv. He told me that Downey (a friend of his who had been in another Toback film, *The Pickup Artist*) had already committed to doing the film for SAG low-budget scale, which meant virtually no money at all, and that he was going to get other stars, including Ben Stiller, who had come off the smash comedy *There's Something About Mary*. Ben Stiller, Robert Downey, Jr., and a cast filled with other names, directed by James Toback, all for a million dollars? I was in. We made the deal with the producers, Ron Rotholz and his partners Dan Bigel and Michael Mailer, and with Jeff Berg, Toback's agent and president of the ICM talent agency.

We established low-budget-scale salaries across the board and a thirty-day low-budget union shoot. Ron had introduced Toback to Oliver Grant, known as "Power," an associate of the Wu Tang Clan, whose members he had grown up with in Staten Island and who launched their clothing line Wu Wear, and he agreed to play a role in the movie and get members of Wu Tang to act, too. As news got out—no doubt fed by the producers to the trades—other actors wanted to be involved. Ron told me that Brooke Shields's agent had called him, and so he had her call *me*. I explained that there was no budget to fly Brooke out to New York, or to put her up in a hotel for a month, and her agent assured me that Brooke would cover those costs herself. So she signed on as Downey's wife in the movie. At a cast-and-crew preshoot dinner at Joe Allen, when time came to pay for the burgers and martinis, I was told that Brooke had already covered the tab. She was, apart from her generosity, a gracious and calm presence on what became at times a very chaotic set. Especially when Mike Tyson, with whom Toback was friends and had agreed to be in the movie playing himself, physically (but actually gently) attacked Downey in an improvisational performance when Downey, playing a gay man (his own decision), tries to come on to the boxer.

As the shooting went over schedule, so did the budget. It was incremental, and I'd be faced almost every other day with yet another budget shortfall, and frustration on the set. I was stressed beyond usual—this wasn't the "light bulb people's" money anymore. But to Chris's credit, he supported me as the budget ballooned, telling me that we would sell the film to a major and hopefully make money, or at least break even. At the end of shooting, the budget had reached $5 million, but I felt reasonably confident that after editing we'd be able to sell the film off for distribution. From Palm's inception, Chris was really only interested in the DVD rights and wanted to avoid the theatrical distribution business, so he authorized me to retain Jeff Berg and ICM to be our agents in selling the film once I had a print to show.

While spending my days in the office and almost every evening visiting the set, I was able to greenlight another film, which wouldn't require my presence as it was going to be shot in northern India. The British producer Jeremy Thomas called me one day and said he had a script that would be perfect for Palm—a film written and directed by Khyentse Norbu (full name Dzongsar Jamyang Khyentse Rinpoche, known simply as Rinpoche), a Bhutanese Buddhist high lama, who based his script on a true story of children in a monastery in the mountains near Dharamshala in India, desperate to find a way to watch the World Cup on a television they didn't have. The actors would be the actual children, and the monks in charge of the monastery, the actual monks. Jeremy had met Rinpoche on the set of *Little Buddha*, the Bernardo Bertolucci film he had produced. One of the producers, Mal Watson, an Australian follower of Rinpoche, told me he had come up with a budget of about half a million dollars—and with him knowing Dharamshala well, it looked accurate—so I told Chris I was going to greenlight it and he was happy for us to be in business with his friend Jeremy, especially at that price.

In 1998 Mary Vinson's cancer was in remission, and we had many quiet times in Jamaica, relaxing and swimming or going for walks, and doing almost nothing on the tiny private island in the Bahamas—often just Chris, Mary, and me there, as there were only two or three huts to stay in anyway. With Mary back to her old form, full of pep and optimism for the future, Chris announced that they would finally be getting married, with a wedding at Pantrepant, his cattle farm in the mountains above Montego Bay. Dickie Jobson, Chris's oldest friend, would be his best man, and Naomi Campbell, who had become close to Chris and Mary, would be maid of honor. Naomi had taken to calling Chris "Dad," which I don't think Chris necessarily liked, but didn't object to.

The guests at the wedding were to stay at Goldeneye, which now had more huts and a few villas, and make the trek to Pantrepant—a two-hour-plus journey, the last half hour up an unpaved mountain road—in vans. There was also a small helicopter—the island's only charter—which would take off from the tennis court and land right by the main house at the farm ten minutes later. I was grateful to get a ride in the latter, so I wouldn't have to suffer in my suit and tie on a two-hour, bumpy car ride. I'm pretty sure that I was one of the last to go to bed the night before the wedding after Chris's bachelor party, which featured young Jamaican dancers and lots of booze, and I overslept in the morning, something I hardly ever did. Tom Hayes came into my bedroom and shouted that the helicopter was leaving in ten minutes, and if I wanted to be on it . . . I jumped out of bed, into the shower, dressed quickly, and ran to the tennis court, getting on the helicopter as its blades were spinning. The wedding, no surprise, was a lovely, relaxed affair, with guests mingling and exploring the gorgeous landscape of the farm, eating delicious, fresh Jamaican food prepared by longtime Blackwell cooks, and I was happy to see Mary not just well, but at her happiest. And I knew that she was the true love of Chris's life, even as he had loved many other women in that life.

01.

01.
Mary Vinson at her hut on the private island in the Bahamas, photo by the author

I spent Thanksgiving 1998 at Goldeneye with Karri. Glenn and Gina had taken Bolt House for a week's vacation, and we'd see them every day for lunch or for dinner. And Chris's friend Jean Pigozzi, who had a huge oceangoing yacht that he was sailing around the world, was anchored off Goldeneye. Chris and I had gone to see the yacht for the first time in the Bahamas; it was impressive—it was painted a military gray and looked like a working ship, yet was very luxurious inside, with only a handful of staterooms but with a large crew and a kitchen that could serve meals for six months without stopping in any port. Pigozzi, heir to the Simca automobile fortune and an art collector, was heading to Santiago de Cuba, and he invited Chris and Mary on the trip. Chris asked me if Karri and I would want to join them, and we jumped at the opportunity. So one evening we took a tender out to the yacht, were shown to our cabins, and set sail for Cuba. It was dark soon and the sea was a dead calm, so we stood on the deck watching the lights of Jamaica fade away, with only the moon dancing on the shimmering surface of the water.

After a restful night, we arrived in Cuba and anchored in the Santiago harbor, as Pigozzi's yacht was too big to dock. We were met by Cuban immigration officials who arrived on a tender and took our passports, with instructions to (please) not stamp the Americans'—Mary's, Karri's, and mine. We had breakfast on board: croissants, baguettes, and butter and jam from the boat's last time in France, and coffee and other pastries. Our passports were returned, and we prepared to go ashore in the yacht's tender and explore. I was taken aback when two hardy young Australian men brought a huge cooler aboard the tender—it took two men to carry it, and it was filled with assorted sandwiches and drinks. (Pigozzi later quipped that when he visited coastal India on his yacht he didn't have a single meal, Indian or otherwise, on land.)

We had a small van, driver, and guide waiting for us at the dock, and we spent the day roaming about, seeing various sites—the cathedral, public squares, government buildings, even a department store—in Cuba's second-largest city, close to Guantánamo Bay. In the afternoon Mary, Karri, and I went to a hotel for a drink, but when we walked up the stairs, Mary was stopped by a guard. "No Cubans," he said, assuming that she was one—perhaps even a paid escort—and I quickly explained that she was

American and with us, while she just laughed. She *was* wearing the skimpiest of dresses—it was exceptionally hot that day—and she could easily have passed, with her slim, athletic body, as a native. We had our drinks and returned to the yacht later with Chris and Pigozzi.

The next day Karri was seasick, which was strange given that we were in the harbor. But she stayed in our cabin while we went back to town, visiting tourist spots, Mary looking for Cuban furniture and home goods. (Karri recovered quickly, however, and took up her regular routine of yoga on the yacht's deck, basking in the weather and the scenery in the bay, looking at the city in the distance.) Mary managed to buy a couple of carved wooden chairs, and we returned to Jamaica all in one piece. Pigozzi dropped us off and left for his next destination as he sailed around the world, and I next saw him the following year when he invited me to a party at his villa by the sea in Antibes during the Cannes Film Festival. I had my Nikon camera with me, but I regret that I was too slow to capture the photographer Peter Beard picking up another guest by the pool, both laughing hard before he put him down.

As word was out in Hollywood in 1998 that Palm was financing low-budget films, another acquaintance of Chris's from the film business, Peter Frankfurt, producer of the English director Steven Norrington's hit film *Blade* starring Wesley Snipes, told him that Norrington had a script for a movie he wanted to make for about a million dollars, set in London, called *The Last Minute*. Chris had him send me the script, and then sent the producer, Matthew Justice, to see me. I thought Norrington talented, and the story was fascinating, wondering if in his imagination it was about him and his fears, for it was about a person in an unidentified business who is touted as "the next big thing" by the media but then crashes and burns and is neither famous nor employable any longer. I wondered how he could pull it off for the money, but Matthew, also English and a real professional, assured me that they had done their research. Chris was fine with financing it if I really liked the screenplay.

After a few days of shooting in the summer of 1999, Matthew called me from London and said the budget simply wouldn't work, and that he and Steven were happy to shut the film down if I didn't want to come up

01.

02.

03.

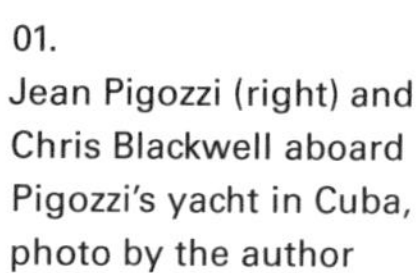

01.
Jean Pigozzi (right) and Chris Blackwell aboard Pigozzi's yacht in Cuba, photo by the author

02.
Karri aboard Jean Pigozzi's yacht, Cuba 1998 (Pigozzi standing in background), photo by the author

03.
With the star of the film *The Cup*, in Cannes, 1999

with what it would *really* cost. Now I had another film that was going two or three times over its projected budget, but again, Chris supported me if I thought it could be a good title for Palm. I visited the set in London and thought what Norrington was shooting was terrific—one sequence I watched with Jason Isaacs, where he is on the hunt, underground, for a Fagin-like character, was especially good, and another, where his character, Percy, sings "I've Got You Under My Skin," was both well done and funny—so we went ahead with the shoot.

The stress, however, of juggling a number of films and worrying about costs while trying to keep an eye on the music side was a little overwhelming. Mark Burg and Oren Koules brought another project in—Master P, the rapper from New Orleans, had a script that his No Limit label wanted to produce, and Chris had always thought we should be in the genre business. I read the script and thought it was a typical prison movie, but with Master P, a big star in hip-hop then, I thought it could sell. I now had another set to visit—an abandoned state prison in New Mexico—in the heat of summer, taking frantic phone calls from Jim Toback telling me *his* picture was out of sync. It had to get it fixed quickly as I was taking the film to the Telluride Film Festival in August, then having ICM arrange screenings in Los Angeles with distributors, and then taking it to the Toronto Film Festival in September. *The Cup* was, fortunately, now finished at close to budget, and had been accepted as an official selection in the Cannes Film Festival's "Directors Fortnight" in May 1999. It would be my first Cannes, and we arranged to have Rinpoche, a few of the monks, and the main child protagonist come to Cannes, where I hoped we would sell it to a distributor in short order.

Meanwhile, Suzette had been helpful in London on the music side, signing deals, but one DVD music project with Sly and Robbie that I had Jeff Stein direct was one I felt I had to be on top of, and I visited the set in Los Angeles. Michael Zilkha also brought us a record by Ned Sublette—a master in fusing Latin and Country musical styles—that Chris and I thought was great, and we signed him and released *Cowboy Rumba* to critical acclaim.

My sister, Marjan, was getting married in London in the summer of 1999, which my brother was paying for, at a venue in Kensington and at his house in Notting Hill. She had been dating her soon-to-be husband, Justin Lee, a fellow medical school attendee, quietly so as to not get into arguments with my parents about the appropriateness of her choice in boyfriends and, of course, the worry over their daughter having premarital sex. My mother arranged a second Shia Muslim ceremony with a mullah that Justin willingly participated in at Saman's house, probably unaware that any Shia faithful would consider him converted to (Shia) Islam. Marjan loved our mother and was happy to indulge her this one request, even though she'd become thoroughly British in her outlook on life, which to her meant relinquishing her "Persianness" and certainly her faith (if she had any to begin with) outside of her relationship with her parents. Karri and my family got along well—my parents were happy to see me in a relationship and liked Karri for her charm, the interest she showed in them, and her modest behavior. Karri liked them and my siblings very much—seeing a side of me she was curious about.

Amid film, family, the wedding of my baby sister, and on top of it all worrying about the slow pace of getting investors (we so far only had Ted Waitt), I had no time or energy to think about anything other than what was now, in my early forties, my *fifth* career. Why had I not, I wondered, at least *tried* to become a banker like my brother, who had a nice house big enough to host a wedding, a chalet in Chamonix, France, and two children in private school? Still, I thought about Iran and, once in a while, woke up from a bad dream where I was in Tehran but terrified about whether I'd be allowed to leave.

Chris was stressed, too, as was Larry. We had no real money coming in, and Chris couldn't understand why Allen & Company had not been able to secure a *single* investment. It was a little embarrassing to talk to Ted Waitt, too; we took the plane once to San Diego to have a meeting with him and try to reassure him that we still believed that our plan was achievable. Allen & Company, though, didn't like our book. Chris had included his hotels—at this point he had quite a few, in Miami, Jamaica, and the Bahamas, now including the Pink Sands resort on Harbour Island, refurbished with décor by Barbara Hulanicki and linens by Mary Vinson—in the prospectus, something the bankers said no entertainment investor would understand.

But Chris was adamant: hotels *were* the entertainment business, and each hotel was, to Chris, one of our *acts*. Once again, he was ahead of his time.

Ian Schrager and Steve Rubell, co-owners of the infamous disco Studio 54 in New York, had known it with their hotels the Royalton, Paramount, and Morgan in Manhattan; Chris was among the first of the boutique hoteliers who understood how each hotel he owned had to have its own, unique character and appeal to a certain clientele, especially in vacation spots like Miami or the Caribbean. (Today many of the newer and more popular hotels in major cities are exactly what Chris said they should be, rather than staid classic luxury or mid-level accommodations.)

Pink Sands had become, along with the Compass Point hotel on the beach across from the recording studio, another of the destinations I would visit with Chris, but I don't recall any banker ever even thinking of visiting any of the hotels in order to understand what it was that Palm, and Island Outpost, wanted to be. Glenn O'Brien—whose contract at Island had been terminated by Davitt and Johnny—was advising Chris and Mary on the Island Trading retail line, and I took him to Pink Sands with me once. When he saw the Adirondack chairs in bright pastel colors, ever quick with a bon mot, he proclaimed a new style: "Afro-Adirondack." Glenn went on to rename Island Trading as Royal Hut, and to design the logo, a silhouette of Mary Vinson that lives on in linens at the hotels in Jamaica that Chris still owns.

The banker at Allen & Company in charge of the Palm Pictures file, Richard Fields, was someone I liked, but even after the prospectus had been massaged multiple times to his, and to Chris's, reluctant satisfaction, there still was no infusion of cash into Palm other than Chris's own funds. I took *Black and White* to Los Angeles, and ICM set up screenings with the major distributors and their art house divisions, as well as a screening at the Sony Pictures lot in Culver City for the chairman, John Calley. Miramax, whose young acquisition executive Jason Blum had followed the film from when it started shooting and with whom I had a long lunch at the Chelsea bistro La Luncheonette, and whose co-founder Bob Weinstein came to dinner with me and Toback in New York, didn't attend any of the screenings, and Harvey Weinstein, who was in L.A. at the time and demanded a private screening, was a no-show when I invited him to one at the William Morris Agency's screening room. I didn't mind, as I knew, from both reputation and from Mark Burg, that Harvey was notoriously difficult to deal with,

01.

01.
With Chris at Pink Sands—
showing off how buff he had
become; photo by the author

especially when it came to getting him to write a check. (Jason Blum left Miramax and went on to form his own production company, becoming hugely successful with low-budget horror films.)

When John Calley saw the film, he told Jeff Berg he wanted to buy it, and that Jeff needn't show it to anyone else. I took Jim Toback to the Sony lot in Los Angeles to meet Calley, a prolific film producer and highly regarded executive with decades of experience. He had recently been brought back to the business and made chairman and CEO of Sony, with a gargantuan office in the architecturally and decoratively impressive Irving Thalberg Building, the *California moderne* onetime headquarters of the MGM studio. He greeted us warmly, making chitchat and commenting that he hated the computer monitor on his desk, as he was sure that "the Japs are listening in on me," meaning his bosses in Tokyo, who, if they were, were probably not amused by the language of an American of his generation—teenagers during World War II when "Jap" was what people called the enemy that had bombed Pearl Harbor. He said he wanted the picture for Screen Gems, a division of Sony, and that he wanted to do more than just this one film with him: he wanted Sony to be in "the Toback business." He said Toback could make any movie he wanted to for a budget of up to $20 million, and it would be automatically greenlit. Jim was very happy to hear this, of course, and told me later that after signing his contract that he received an advance of $750,000 from the studio against his salary for the next film. He never made another film for Sony, though, and his contract was canceled. He did not return the advance.

Jeff Berg called me after our meeting at Sony and told me Calley had made an offer of $10 million to buy the film. I was ecstatic: even after the ICM commission, we were still almost doubling what the film had cost us. I called Chris from my rental car, and true to form, he congratulated me but said he'd agree only on one condition: that Sony wire $8 million to our accounts on signing the deal, and that the deal had to be signed within forty-eight hours. I was slightly dejected when I called Jeff Berg, thinking no studio would pay 80 percent up front without even taking possession of the negative, but Jeff, also somewhat skeptical, said he'd do what he could. He called back very shortly later and told me we had a deal. Chris was happy—Calley must have thought we had other offers—and Larry Mestel, back in New York, breathed a sigh of relief. I took the picture to Telluride and Toronto, where it performed well for the festival audiences (in Toronto it was screened outside the festival, to long lines at the box office). I also did a deal for the soundtrack, put together largely by Power, with Steve Rifkind's Loud Records, a New York hip-hop label that would do a better job than we could in marketing and distributing it.

In Cannes, *The Cup* showed to an enthusiastic audience, and an even more enthusiastic press corps. Rachael Horovitz, then an executive at Fine Line Features, a division of New Line Cinema, had been following *Black and White* but knew her company wouldn't get into a bidding war or pay the kind of money it would cost to acquire, so I invited her to a screening of *The Cup* before Cannes. She loved it and said Fine Line would buy the distribution rights. In Cannes I met with her and Mark Ordesky, president of Fine Line, and we closed on a deal, quadrupling our investment in the film. By the fall of 1999, we were two for two in terms of profit on our films, but we still had no investors and Chris was impatient.

David Beal, meanwhile, was agitating for a bigger role at the company. He was working with Les Garland, an old friend and colleague who had been one of the first executives at MTV (and later at the interactive music video channel the Box, which Chris bought), on a venture called sputnik7.com, a digital music platform Garland and Chris started, and he was spending as much time with Chris as he could.

Chris had us down to Miami for meetings at his apartment at the Marlin Hotel, before heading to Jamaica for Thanksgiving that year. He told me he was unhappy with how the business was going, despite the profits, especially as he had come to realize that we couldn't sell the theatrical rights to any film without home video or DVD rights included—and certainly not for the kind of money we needed to make from each film. I felt that he was looking to cast blame for Palm not being the audiovisual company that he had imagined on anyone other than himself, and I was a convenient target. He said he had never wanted to be in the movie production business—he had done that before—but that he wanted to build a DVD-centric business, and with me selling distribution rights to our films, Palm couldn't be that. I reminded Chris that all rights to our films reverted to Palm after a certain number of years, depending on the deal (with *Black and White* spending the longest period, twenty-five years, at Sony, due to the until then unprecedented acquisition price), but Chris just wasn't satisfied. Exhausted, I didn't argue further, begged off going to Jamaica with him, and instead took a quiet break in New York.

Lockdown and *The Last Minute* were in post-production, and both would be sold for theatrical distribution in the United States and internationally. After the Thanksgiving holiday and Chris's return from Jamaica in December, he asked me to lunch at Michael's, a media-business restaurant that we had frequented since starting Palm. He was uncharacteristically uncomfortable with me, fiddling with his fork and not looking me in the eye. He said he was very unhappy with the way things were going at Palm, and he felt that I hadn't stuck to the original concept of creating content that could be distributed on DVD. I tried to defend my record, but I knew it was pointless. I knew Chris well enough by then, and when he decided to part with someone, or fall out with someone, that was that. Chris's character hadn't changed; my mistake had simply been believing that I would, because of the friendship—and especially the time with him and Mary when she was sick—be immune from his falling out with me. I was to leave Palm, he said, at the end of the year—a couple of weeks away—and stay on top of Norrington's film until it was complete, for which I would be paid. I walked away from lunch in shock. I had been working for Chris for more than a decade, and we had become like family. But family, I learned then and again later, didn't protect you from Chris's moods and his inability to accept blame for his own actions. Now I had no idea what could come next.

As I was leaving Palm and Chris, one former Island Records executive told me that they used to say at the label that I would be the last person standing, the last person to turn the lights out for Blackwell. His friends—Jeremy Thomas and Paul McGuinness, to name just two—were all supportive, knowing Chris's mercurial side. Because of all the work and flying around, I had been spending less time in person with him, and as Richard Bakalyan said to Gay Talese about his close friendship with Frank Sinatra after it had cooled, "I guess with Frank you have to be there every minute." I guess it was so with Chris, too. I didn't know it at the time, but if I had wanted to stay working with him, or even just to remain friends, I would have needed to join Chris on his plane to Kingston that Thanksgiving.

I had witnessed Chris's mercurial and capricious side myself. At Island Records, James Dowdall and Rose Noone, the husband-and-wife A&R team Chris had brought over from the London office to seek out alternative music acts in the States, were succeeding with their most recent signing, Tracy Bonham, and asked me for big raises. I was at Chris's that evening for dinner, and I told him that they told me Sony's Epic Records had approached them, intimating that unless I met their demand, they could go elsewhere to get what they believed they deserved. Though he liked them and had been supportive of their careers, he said to me, quite calmly, "Fire them. They should go to Epic." The fact that the team had been disloyal, as far as Chris was concerned, was enough to axe them from his work life, and I suspect that he believed—rightly, it turned out—that they weren't likely to have a second hit so soon after their first. When I called them into my office, they were smiling, confident. I watched their expressions change when I told them that we thought it better that they go to Sony. (I resisted using the phrase that the headmaster at Harrow had used when expelling the young Christopher.) They walked out of my office and were gone the next day, surfacing at Epic soon after. As far as I know, Chris never saw them again.

In the summer of 2001, Paul McGuinness invited me to his fiftieth birthday, a big affair at the Park, my friend Eric Goode's restaurant on Tenth Avenue in Chelsea. U2's present to Paul was a Hermès saddle (Paul was an avid horseman), but instead of gift-wrapping it, in a grand gesture and to everyone's surprise and delight, they arranged for it to come into the restaurant on the back of a horse. I was seated not too far from Chris and Mary, but neither of us spoke, or greeted one another. I left saddened, not sure how, when we had been so close, we could now be virtual strangers. Chris was an older brother to me, but more important, he had filled a vacuum in my life, not just providing me with a career that I was proud of, finally, but making me feel like his homes anywhere he had them were mine, too. It was silly of me, really, and naïve, after four decades of a suppressed longing.

Chapter 27

Another Chapter Begins

I wasn't sure what to do when I left Palm. Karri and I spent Christmas 1999 with Glenn and Gina at their house in Bridgehampton, and we were to have a big party—black tie—at the home of Abby Terkhule and his wife, Eva Faye, only a few doors down. Abby worked at MTV, responsible for animation, and his biggest show was the huge hit *Beavis and Butt-Head*. At the stroke of midnight we went out on the lawn, waiting for Y2K to hit, wondering if the power grid in New York or Long Island might go down. It was all rather anticlimactic—none of the doomsday predictions happened, of course, and the cold winter air forced us back inside where the lights were on and where our cell phones still worked. The new century had arrived, and I was forty-three years old and unemployed, just like twenty years prior. At least I wasn't an illegal alien this time, too, I thought.

When I was a child, I had always thought that I would be old in the year 2000, and couldn't really imagine what I would be like in the new millennium. But here I was, middle-aged with a useless degree and no readily definable skills about to go out into the world and look for work. As the weeks stretched on, I lived off the Polygram payout I had received in 1998, as the money Palm Pictures had agreed to pay me would be released only when all the elements of the picture *The Last Minute* were delivered, and that wouldn't be until a few months later. I soon discovered, though, that not unlike Chris's dilemma with investors seemingly shying away from him, I was not especially sought after, either. My reputation in the music business was tied up with Chris—I was his "guy"—and record companies didn't really have a use for Chris's guy if Chris wasn't there too.

Alain Levy had reluctantly tolerated me, Roger Ames had fired me, and I couldn't even go back to Davitt, who might recognize my value *sans* Chris, for when Universal Studios, owned by Seagram, bought Polygram in 1998—just as we were getting started at Palm—he was let go from Island (and Johnny Barbis was let go six months later). Levy and Ames were also let go, both ending up at different labels, but Davitt received a payout and didn't go back into the record business. Universal later separated the film and television businesses and the theme parks from the music division, naming it Universal Music and selling the other businesses to NBC, which became NBC Universal. As for the film business, I simply hadn't been doing it long enough, nor had enough credits under my belt, to seek out jobs in Hollywood. The only way I'd be making films would be if I started a production company like Dan Bigel (a former banker) and Michael Mailer (Norman's son), seeking investors for projects I might be able to find. I didn't have enough money to do that, nor did I know anyone with money who would want to partner.

Before the winter was over, though, Michael Zilkha told me about an investment that he and his father, Selim, had made in the cable TV (or satellite) business in Los Angeles. Selim Zilkha had been approached by a pair of French expats who had started a network called the Surf Channel, with an idea to broadcast surfing-related content—film, videos, interviews with the sport's stars, and associated material such as health and fitness videos—twenty-four hours a day. It sounded good—surfing was getting more popular in the United States and surfers (and anyone who admired surfers and surfing) would be a captive audience—but Michael was worried that the two Frenchmen weren't developing the channel into a viable network and were spending money without a proper plan. I knew Selim—I had met him with Michael in the eighties—and he agreed to hire me at the Surf Channel as COO, to see if there was a way to save the investment and perhaps build on it. It meant moving to Los Angeles, and I agreed, not only because I needed a job and the income it would provide. Karri was excited for a new adventure after living in New York for years. She was also happy that I would be gainfully employed after seeing me mope around for a while, hoping every day that I'd get that phone call asking if I'd be interested in a job.

In the spring of 2000, I put my apartment in Manhattan's London Terrace on the market and had my furnishings moved to Los Angeles, where they stayed in storage until I could settle in a new home. I rented a furnished apartment in West Los Angeles, not far from the 20th Century Fox Studios (about to be renamed 21st Century), and close to the Surf Channel offices in an office block housing satellite television stations and broadcast equipment on Olympic Boulevard. I was confident somehow that this next phase of my life would be a good one.

I worked on getting an understanding of the cable business as I found a house and settled, Karri joining me soon thereafter. I was flummoxed by what seemed to me the complete lack of any plan to market or promote the Surf Channel. Cyril Viguier, one of the original owners and president of the channel, who had been bought out by Selim, hired an editor to create video programming from stock footage, but he had no real ideas of what kind of other programming they needed to create or acquire that would make the channel viable. In the era before YouTube and social media, there was only one way to get your videos, shows, or films seen: cable or satellite television. Surf Channel had no cable outlet and didn't seem to have any plans to secure one. It had bought some time on a satellite channel that at other hours broadcast foreign-language programs for the immigrant community in Southern California and was on public-access cable in Malibu. Cyril seemed unconcerned that the network had essentially zero visibility.

I went to see Jeff Berg at ICM, hoping to get a sense from one of the top talent agents and savvy media investors in town what the viability of a surf network might be, and he was supportive but said he didn't know if the channel could be successful without diverse programming and a massive dollar investment. He suggested I call his friend Martin (Marty) Sugarman, a onetime professional surfer who published a magazine—or fanzine—called *H2O*, focused on everything surfing. I saw Marty a few times and found him both funny and intelligent. He was passionate about surfing and surf culture, and he loved the idea of a cable television network devoted to it. But when he saw what we were doing, he couldn't see how we were going to succeed—he told me that we had to both find a proper cable outlet and get much better programming. He was willing to partner with us, but when I showed his magazine to Cyril and explained how Marty was well known in the Palisades and Malibu surfing community, he couldn't be less interested.

I couldn't understand Cyril. I didn't know what it was he thought he and his staff were building, or whether they knew the whole thing would come crashing down sooner or later. They didn't seem interested in talking to cable operators, or to come up with a proper business plan, including where they were going to acquire content beyond the library of surf footage that they had already purchased. It wasn't enough to head to Zuma Beach with a cameraman; they needed professional films and videos, as well as original programming. They hired a friend of theirs to do marketing and publicity—another expat Frenchman—but he seemed befuddled, and I got the sense that he knew the whole thing was run on a wing and a prayer.

Selim's partner Mary Hayley's daughter, Emma, came to work in the summer to help with publicity and was as shocked as I was at the complete lack of any plan or real story to tell. I was talking to Michael about my concerns all along, and he understood, as his wariness about the enterprise was the reason he originally asked me to go to L.A. I also spoke with Craig VanDerMark and Joe Romano, executives at Selim and Michael's company Zilkha Renewable Energy in Houston, about the viability of the channel, which I felt was, at this point, not even a remote possibility.

I didn't want to disappoint Selim, and I didn't want to talk myself out of yet another job, but I couldn't let my friends continue funding a business when there was no "there" there. Cyril didn't want to give up control of the channel, but he was no television executive. His idea of a Hollywood bash was to throw a party for Pierre Cardin—yes, *Cardin*, the seventy-eight-year-old French fashion designer who had made millions by licensing his name to anyone who asked. I was flummoxed: how on earth was Pierre Cardin relevant to surfing? (Cyril should perhaps have persuaded him to license his name and logo to a surfboard company, years before Chanel stocked surfboards.)

Selim was quiet as I spoke, with Joe backing me up with a financial overview. I told Selim that even if he was willing to invest the millions necessary to build a *real* network, it wasn't guaranteed to be a successful and profitable enterprise. Selim listened carefully, and at the end simply said, "Okay." He turned to Joe and said, "Then let's sell it." The fledgling network did have a name and a content library that would have value to a media company, but beyond that, it was hard to say what it could be worth. Selim was fine with shutting it down while we looked for a buyer, and from the end of summer until the beginning of the new year, 2001, I tried to be helpful to the effort, but we had no success.

At the beginning of 2001, Karri, a yoga fanatic from her university days in Madison, Wisconsin, went to Mysore, India, with her college friend Ananda Sunshine Thorson to immerse themselves in two months of intense daily ashtanga practice in Mysore with Patthabi Jois, the world's preeminent practitioner. I was left alone in Los Angeles pondering my next move. The Zilkhas had generously paid me a good severance and Selim said he was hopeful we'd find something else to work on together, but I knew I felt more at home in New York than in California. One day while driving home, as I turned onto Elevado Avenue from Doheny Drive in West Hollywood. I saw Johnny Barbis walking with his wife, Edwina, very slowly up the street. I stopped the car and got out. I hadn't seen or spoken to them since Chris had fired him as president of Island Records, assuming these past few years that he hated me for being partly responsible for losing his job, even though I hadn't been. He looked very weak. "Johnny!" I said, and he looked at me and smiled, asking me what I was doing there. I said I lived on that street, and he told me he had just had open-heart surgery. I felt bad for him, seeing the once strong-as-an-ox Barbis in a very weak state. I hugged him and kissed Edwina (Eddi), and in that instant, we were back to being best friends. And have remained so ever since.

They had rented an apartment around the corner in a high-rise on Doheny, splitting their time between it and the apartment they owned in Manhattan. Johnny told me his older brother Dino, also in the music business in L.A., had died suddenly of a heart attack, and while in the hospital with Dino, Johnny had felt acute pain in his chest. "I was rushed into an operating room where doctors performed open-heart surgery after determining I was suffering a heart attack, Hoo," he said, calling me by the nickname he used to use. I told him how sorry I was to hear it, and that I was so very glad to be able to see him now. I explained that Chris had cut me loose from Palm, and that I had come to L.A. to work with the Zilkhas, but that I was thinking of returning to New York. We saw each other a few more times before I finally made the move back east in March, right around the beginning of spring and Norouz, the Persian New Year.

While Karri was in India, I moved into an apartment at the Carlyle Hotel that my friend the photographer Wayne Maser, whom I had met through Glenn O'Brien, had left with time remaining on the lease. My first night back in Manhattan, I had dinner with Glenn and Gina at the Mercer Hotel downtown. It was thrilling to be back in the city where I felt most at home on the crowded sidewalks, in the hustle and energy that simply didn't exist in Los Angeles. I was also happy to be in an expansive two-bedroom apartment at one of New York's storied hotels, where I was paying a fraction of what Wayne rented it for. He had redone the apartment in white: white carpeting, white fabric on the walls, and no art, but he had conveniently installed a professional espresso machine in the small kitchen. Karri joined me there upon her return to the States some fifteen pounds lighter, as always.

My brother, Saman, was now vice chairman of asset management at Deutsche Bank in London. He told me a close friend of his boss, Michael Philipp, was looking to get into the music business. Saman arranged a meeting for me in New York with Russell Kleinknecht, an electrical engineer and a music junkie, amateur songwriter, and guitar player. Russell had an idea for a new music company that would change the existing model: Artist Network would offer musicians and acts profit sharing rather than royalties, making them partners in business. Michael Philipp had committed Deutsche Bank to partly financing the venture; the Eurythmics' Dave Stewart, a client, was involved; and Russell asked if I would join his team in putting together a business plan. I, of course, agreed, and I started going to the offices he had taken at 500 Fifth Avenue on the corner of 42nd Street.

For our music business lawyer, I recommended Fred Davis, son of the legendary music man Clive Davis, whom I knew from when he was at EMI. Fred was enthusiastic, and he flew with Russell to London a few days later to meet Stewart and Philipp. Sometime later, Al Cafaro, formerly president of A&M Records, showed up and started working with Russell, but I didn't understand to what purpose. Dennis Lavinthal of *HITS* magazine called me, hearing rumors about a new label and about Cafaro, which I assumed had been leaked to him *by* Al. Russell had approached Chris Blackwell and asked me about him, and I said Chris would certainly be a huge asset to the company but couldn't be sure that he'd want to get involved given his focus was still on Palm and on his hotels. (I was still not speaking with Chris at this time.)

By the end of the summer, though, it appeared that Dave Stewart was frustrated with the pace of getting the business off the ground and took full control of the enterprise, with Russell becoming less involved in putting together a business plan. I asked him if I could get another advance against a future salary or earnings, but he told me there was no more money coming to him from Deutsche Bank, so I stopped going to the office. Stewart, with Michael Philipps's investment, went ahead with announcing the formation of the company in 2002, but it never attracted any new artists and does not exist today.

Chapter 28

September

In August 2001, Karri and I separated. She wanted a stronger commitment from me to get married and have a child together one day in the not-too-distant future, and I was unprepared, feeling unsettled about a career and my future for the umpteenth time in my life. I was saddened, but I also did not want to deceive her about a future I was uncertain of and wanted her to have the opportunities—a steadier life with kids as she entered her thirties—that she desired. So I was alone on September 11, having a cup of coffee and reading the newspaper, when my phone rang and a friend said to turn on the television. The North Tower of the World Trade Center—where not too long before I had visited my accountant—was on fire after a plane had hit it. The cause wasn't yet clear, but when the second plane crashed into the South Tower, the world knew we were under attack.

I walked out to Eighth Avenue and looked south, where I could see the smoke from the burning buildings. Karri, who had been teaching a yoga class just a couple of blocks away, managed to get through to me on her cell phone, crying and saying she was terrified. She later told me she witnessed people jumping to their deaths while paralyzed with shock and fear, unable to get on her bicycle and pedal away. My brother also managed to reach me from London; he had been having breakfast at the exact same time at Deutsche Bank's offices in the World Trade Center precisely one week earlier. Of course, he's not the only one for whom fate intervened, since the towers had thousands of employees coming and going and the adjacent area downtown was full of people on any given workday. My father and mother also got through to me on my cell phone sometime later, relieved that I hadn't been near the towers but anxious about what could come next. When the two towers collapsed, I (and almost everyone else) was in disbelief. How could hundred-story buildings simply collapse like that into a pile of rubble?

I was back to watching television when John Vlautin, former publicity head of Island, who was staying at the Tribeca Grand Hotel, called to ask me if we were still on for a lunch we had planned. We were all in shock, and I said yes as if nothing was amiss, and that he should come by my apartment, and we'd walk to a nearby bistro. He walked to Chelsea, where I'd moved earlier that summer—there were no cabs downtown—crossing Canal Street and reaching 22nd Street around midday. From there we walked together over to Tenth Avenue and headed downtown, watching trucks towing cars covered in layers of soot, dust, and crushed concrete inches thick; the detritus of the Twin Towers blowing away as the tow trucks headed uptown. I couldn't believe the sight of the vacant space from a mile or so away, still on fire, where once there were towers that were a landmark one could rely on to navigate in downtown Manhattan. At La Luncheonette on the corner of Eighteenth Street, the door was open and we were greeted by the owner/chef. He said no workers had shown up, but he'd be happy to cook a meal for us. It was surreal: thousands dead less than a mile away, cars enveloped in concrete dust being towed up Tenth Avenue, horrific footage on the television, and two guys having a steak frites lunch in a bistro within view of the disaster.

The days that followed are a blur, but Glenn said he was getting out of town and invited me to go with him, Gina, and their baby, Oscar, to Bridgehampton. Karri told me she was going to London to get away, and Davitt and his family were safely ensconced in their apartment on Riverside

Drive on the Upper West Side, miles from downtown—and from any tempting new target for Al Qaeda. (I was relieved and even happy to learn that in Tehran there were huge crowds at candlelight vigils, and that Iranians had forcefully denounced the act of terror, 60,000 of them at a soccer match a couple of days after 9/11 observing a moment of silence. I also knew Sunni Al Qaeda hated Shia Iran perhaps even more than it did America, and was a little anxious about Iran's possibility as their next target.) I took Glenn and Gina up on their invitation and went out to Bridgehampton for a few days but soon returned to Manhattan to find work of some kind, or at least come up with a plan of how I was going to live.

Life slowly returned to normal, but of course there was a pre-9/11 normal and the "normal" afterward. We went about our lives while always looking over our shoulders, worried that something else was going to happen. Then the anthrax scare and American Airlines 587 crashing into the Rockaways, killing everyone on board; an accident, but one we first thought might have been an act of terror. It was an uncomfortable time.

One night in the fall I was at dinner at the home of my friends Gad Cohen and his partner, François Vallée, with Glenn and Gina, who had introduced us. François had AIDS and was in perpetual pain despite the cocktail of pills he was taking. At one point during dinner, he disappeared into the bedroom. After he didn't return for a while, Gad went to check on him. We heard a scream and rushed to the bedroom, where François was lying on the bed, completely still, as Gad manically tried to revive him. Glenn joined in, pounding on his chest, tears streaming down his cheeks, but it was too late. He had taken all his pills at once—dozens—and had passed out and died. He left a note, saying he didn't want to suffer any more and didn't want to be a burden on Gad.

We were all in shock. François was fun to be around, and always had a positive attitude, despite his illness. He had brought his espresso machine to Karri's friend Ananda's wedding in the Catskills that summer, and plied anyone who wanted decent coffee with shots, beaming as he did so. He was simply a good person who cared about others—and especially about his partner, Gad, for whom he hated being a burden. I called Karri, who was also friends with both Gad and François, and she rushed over. We had been speaking, but were not yet a couple again. After the ambulance came and took François away, we comforted Gad as best we could, told him to go to bed and that we'd see him in the morning, and Karri and I walked home to my apartment, a block away. We have been back together ever since.

Chapter 29

Life in Slow Motion

In 2002, I still hadn't secured any source of income. Artist Network refused to pay my last invoice from the previous summer, and I stopped asking by the middle of the year. I still had money to live on, but the Polygram payout was getting depleted. I spent a lot of time with Glenn and with Davitt talking about ideas for work, or with Glenn and Gina about businesses that we might get investors for, but had no actual leads for a job. I decided to take my collection of short stories and turn it into a novel, which I thought might have a better chance of getting published.

When I was still at Island and soon after the sale to Polygram in 1989, an agent had called the offices looking for Blackwell. Leslie Gardner, an American expat literary agent in London, was inquiring to see if Chris would be interested in writing his autobiography. This was soon after the sale of the label had resulted in the sort of media attention that Chris had always tried to avoid. Chris laughed when I mentioned it, telling me he couldn't write (which he used to say all the time, asking me to write anything that needed to be written) and besides, didn't want to tell his story yet when he had so much more to accomplish. I called Leslie back and said that no, Chris wouldn't be writing anytime soon (he did, finally, write his memoir with Paul Morley, published in 2022, and proceeded to tell everyone in interviews that while it was all true, he hadn't written a word), but asked if she would be interested in a collection of stories that *I* had written. She replied that she would, so I mailed her a copy to London. (The xeroxed copy that Michael had originally sent Chris still sat in the sauna at his house in the Bahamas years later, up until the last time I visited in the late nineties. He told me often that one day he'd get around to reading all the stories, but I knew that he wouldn't.)

Leslie liked the stories very much, she said, and while she didn't sell them as a collection, she was able to sell one to Serpent's Tail, an independent publishing house in England, to be included in a 1991 collection with other short stories about exile. Now in 2002, I told Leslie that I was going to turn the stories into a novel. She said she'd be happy to see if she could find a publisher for it. I began to think that if I couldn't get a job in the entertainment industry, *I* would have to provide the entertainment.

In the meantime, Karri was telling me that I needed to go to Iran. She knew that my entire life I had been longing for a homeland that I still felt was mine. "You need to go there," she said, "and see if it still is your home." She made the point that my writing was about Iran and Iranians, and I needed to see the country as it was now. I didn't disagree, and the idea was planted in my head.

By the time 2003 rolled around, I was getting nervous. Nothing seemed to go my way, and the Polygram payout was dwindling rapidly. Glenn had introduced me to Michael Hainey at *GQ* magazine, telling him that I should be writing for him. Michael was keen, but unable to place any of my submissions. When I finished my novel, Leslie began submitting it to publishers, but we received one rejection after another. Then she told me that Sonny Mehta, the legendary editor in chief of Knopf, loved it and wanted to meet me. I could not imagine a better place, or better editor, for my novel. I thought it a delicious irony that my career in the music business had begun with a set of short stories that Davitt sent to Michael, who then

01.

01.
With Glenn O'Brien and his son Oscar (right) and Eric Goode (left) at Glenn's house in Bridgehampton, early 2000s

told Chris he should meet me, whereupon I entered the entertainment business; and now those stories, turned into a novel, might be leading me to yet *another* new career, one to which I suppose I had always aspired.

But as time went on and we never heard back from Sonny, I was both confused and dejected. Why would he show enthusiasm but not follow up? Leslie was infuriated—she knew him from London—and tried reaching out a few times before we gave up. I realized much later, when Sonny was chief of the Random House publishing group, which encompassed Doubleday, future publisher of my books, that the enthusiasm he had expressed to Leslie was more for *me* than for the novel, although as a fan of crime novels—and mine had plenty of Iranian gangster crime—he may have enjoyed reading it but wasn't necessarily keen on *publishing* it. He was interested in my nonfiction, though, and I met him several times, including at his house in the Diplomatic Enclave in New Delhi, where we both, along with his wife, Gita, chain-smoked cigarettes as servants served us drinks and appetizers. He told me he thought I should continue writing fiction—a proper crime novel, he said. I could see that he found me an interesting character, as I did him, and I was saddened when I heard that he died in 2019. I wrote to my editor at Doubleday, Kristine Puopolo—who had first taken me to drinks with Sonny across from the publishing offices on Broadway—as well as to Gita Mehta, expressing my sadness and condolences.

وزارت کشور

اداره کل آمار و ثبت احوال

ماه

۹۵۸۲۵۲

آقای

شناسنامه ۹۵۵

خانم

شناسنامه ۱۱۵

۱۳۳۴

در شهر

دهستان

کوی

متولد شده است

صادره از حوزه

ثبت احوال

Chapter 30

Encounters with Officialdom

It was in 2003, with little else on the horizon, that I finally followed Karri's advice to try to get an Iranian passport. (Iran, even under the Shah, did not recognize dual citizenship, and neither his regime nor the Islamic Republic would ever issue a visa to me on a foreign passport.) I had long before lost my Shah-era passport, but surprisingly, given the number of moves and the overnights on friend's couches, I still had a photocopy of the main page. Nor could I find my birth certificate—only the English translation document certified by the embassy in London back in the sixties, but that showed my certificate number, which in Iran is assigned as a sort of social security and identification number. Mine was 434, issued in 1957, and was still presumably in the paper records of the interior ministry in Tehran. (I found my Shah-era birth certificate a few years later buried among some papers in a folder.)

My father connected me with Ali Khatami, the president's brother, a successful businessman who'd joined Khatami's administration as chief of staff when he was reelected in 2001. Ali was happy to hear from me after so many years had passed, and he told me to call the Iranian Interests Section in Washington, D.C., and make an appointment with the head of the section, Ali Jazini, who would be expecting my call. After President Jimmy Carter broke off diplomatic relations with Iran in 1980, the Iranian government arranged with its Pakistani counterpart (which represented Iranian interests in the United States) to have an office physically separate from the Pakistan embassy, staffed by Iranians resident in the States, and it was to that office that I needed to make any consular requests. Despite the years of uncertainty—for me and my parents—about money, career, and life in exile, somehow my father's and family connections on both sides of the revolution brought me the good fortune of being able to make calls like this.

Mr. Jazini was very accommodating on the phone, and I went to Washington on the train, taking a taxi to Georgetown. Jazini was extremely helpful, filling out forms for me in Farsi (there were none in English). His office made a photocopy of my U.S. passport and my old passport, keeping the latter. Jazini hesitated when I told him I wouldn't sign a power of attorney granting the Interests Section the authority to see my U.S. immigration file, as I had already admitted that I received political asylum in the eighties and there was no reason to complicate things. Then he shrugged it off. Again, family connections paying off dividends.

Jazini told me it would take a couple of hours, if I wanted to go and have lunch. I walked around my old haunts in Georgetown, amazed at how much it had changed since my college days, with more stores and chain stores. When I returned two hours later, Jazini greeted me and handed me my new passport. "Say hello to Mr. Khatami," he said, and then, "You Ardakanis stay close to each other, don't you?" with a smile. I thanked him profusely, with as much *ta'arouf* as I could, and went back to New York *officially* Iranian.

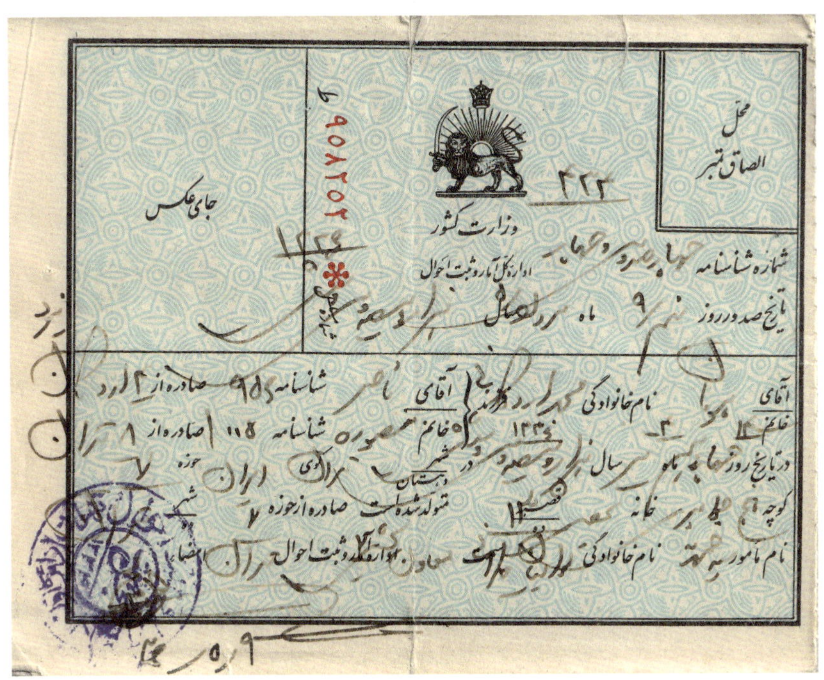

محل
الصاق تمبر

وزارت کشور
اداره کل آمار و ثبت احوال

جای عکس

شماره شناسنامه
تاریخ صدور روز ماه سال

آقای نام خانوادگی شناسنامه صادره از
خانم شناسنامه صادره از
در تاریخ روز ماه سال در شهر دهستان کوی حوزه
کوچه خانه متولد شده است صادره از حوزه شهر
نام مامور نام خانوادگی اداره کل آمار و ثبت احوال امضاء

01.

01.
My original Imperial-era
Iranian birth certificate, 1957

Chapter 31

Back in Los Angeles

I had my Iranian passport but no plans yet to go to Iran, still hoping something would come of my attempts at journalism. In late 2003, I reconnected with James Truman, editorial director of Condé Nast, whom I knew from when I was at Island Records and we'd have lunch from time to time and talk about music. James was launching a men's version of *Lucky*, the successful women's fashion and shopping magazine he'd started, to be called *Cargo*. He put me in touch with Ariel Foxman, whom he'd hired from *InStyle*. Perhaps because he'd heard Glenn praise my stylishness, Ariel suggested I write a monthly column on "ageless style" to be called "Classic" in the front of the fashion pages, focusing on one product or clothing item that would always be fashionable, no matter the era. My first short column in early 2004 was on the mackintosh raincoat—I borrowed one to shoot from Andy Spade, a friend of Glenn's and mine who had a store in Soho.

Still, I was despairing about my future, as payment for the *Cargo* pieces would only pay a fraction of my rent. Then Selim Zilkha called me about a film company he'd invested in, Arenas, which specialized in marketing mainstream films to the U.S. Hispanic community, traditionally underserved by Hollywood but growing beyond traditional enclaves in California, Arizona, and Texas to the east and north. The founder, Santiago Pozo, had secured an investment from a major Spanish media company, Marco Polo. Selim, despite his reluctance to enter the film business, was willing to invest in Arenas, he told Santiago, as long as I was brought on board as COO to Santiago's CEO, and that the financials made sense. It was decided that I should move to Los Angeles and help put together the business plan.

Emma Hayley, Selim's partner's daughter, who was now buying houses in Los Angeles and remodeling them, suggested I stay with her at a mid-century house she had finished—very stylishly—in Brentwood while I looked for an apartment to rent. Off to California I went again, my furniture and my Vespa (which I had bought to replace the car I'd sold in pursuit of cash) following me in a truck. I thought, and hoped, that this might be the last move across the country that I'd have to make. For the first couple of months, I lived in Brentwood and drove a newly leased Mini every day to the Arenas offices in Beverly Hills, before finding an apartment in West Hollywood just above Sunset Plaza. Karri was excited to go back to L.A. and joined me there. Discussions with Selim and Santiago continued while I read scripts that were coming into the offices as news filtered out in the industry that a new player was in the film production business. The scripts, and the films, were to be in English, but the subject matter had to be Latino- and Latina-related in some way, or culturally appealing to a Hispanic audience.

I had been in Los Angeles for about three weeks when Selim changed his mind and decided he didn't want to be a partner in the company, nor a silent investor. The back-and-forth with ownership percentages and Santiago's somewhat antagonizing positions and demands had soured Selim, and I couldn't blame him. The film business is inherently risky, and even with a great script, a film can turn out poorly or underperform at the box office. The old joke about the airline business—that the way to make $100 million is to invest *$200 million*—applies equally to film. Santiago asked me to stay on at Arenas to see if we could find other investors. There were a few promising leads—and we pursued each one as diligently as possible—but in the end no new investor came on board. In the fall, Santiago told me that he couldn't justify keeping me on salary, even as he would like me to stay and continue to advise and assist him. I told him it was hard for me to work and not get paid at all and wished him the best for the future.

I wasn't sure what my next move would be, although I doubted I would be staying in Los Angeles permanently. And then, in November 2004, I received a call from Cathy Snipper, who'd worked at Island Records in London with Suzette Newman when I first met her at St. Peter's Square. Cathy now worked for Chris Blackwell in Jamaica and Miami. (I still call her "Moneypenny," after M's secretary in the James Bond movies with whom Sean Connery flirted, as she was as loyal a Blackwell employee as could be.) She told me that Mary Vinson had died, and that Chris wanted me at the funeral, which was going to be held at Pantrepant, the hideaway where Mary had been able to relax without the hubbub and streams of visitors at Goldeneye, and where she had wanted to be buried.

I had run into Chris at a music event in New York in 2003, and unlike at Paul McGuinness's birthday two years earlier, we approached and said hello to each other. It felt like old times, and we never mentioned the falling-out. He told me he had had cancer himself during our time apart, but was well and cancer-free, and that Mary was doing well, too. I had known her disease was one that came and went—I had seen it myself back in the nineties, visiting her at Sloan Kettering and thinking she would die in the hospital, then going to Jamaica or the Bahamas later with her in fine fettle. I realized how much I missed her presence in the years Chris and I didn't speak—I had written to her after my dismissal from Palm, saying I hoped that we could still see each other, but didn't hear back. I didn't expect to, really, as I knew her to be fiercely loyal to Chris, who would have been annoyed if she had. Nonetheless, I wished I had at least reached out to her after Chris and I had spoken at the music event.

Farhad Azima chartered an airplane—a Boeing 757—to ferry the funeral attendees to and from Jamaica and New York, so I got on a flight to JFK right away. Chris had rooms booked at the Half Moon Hotel on

01.

02.

01.
Mary's funeral: Chris next to Diane Jobson and his sister Eileen, who is next to me; Carl Bradshaw, Jamaican actor, on my left next to Suzette Newman; Glenn O'Brien in foreground next to Jeremy Thomas

02.
Mary's funeral: the author and Jo Menell, South African filmmaker and close friend of Chris, photo by Michael Zilkha

the beach for everyone, and vans to take us up the mountain to the farm on the day of the funeral. It was a somber day, but with beautiful weather, as Mary would have liked. She undoubtedly would've also liked Chris's arrangements: a Jamaican preacher beautifully dressed in a black suit and wearing a black fedora presiding. I was doubly sad that after being so close to her for years, I had missed the last few years of her life. Walking around the farm with old friends who had Mary, Chris, and Jamaica in common, I reflected on the value of friendships. The day after the funeral, Chris had a Jamaican feast at Pantrepant, and afterward we left Mary in a grave in her favorite spot on earth, to visit her whenever we could return to Jamaica. (I went with Suzette in 2018.)

Chapter 32

Going Home

When I returned to Los Angeles, I decided that the time was finally right for me to go to Iran. Karri and I had planned to go to London for Christmas to spend it with my parents and sister and her family, and I had no work to return to. Perhaps Iran would spark something, and perhaps I would finally put to rest my longing for a home I could call my own.

I spoke with my childhood friend Kaveh Bazargan, with whom I'd stayed in touch over the years and who had been going back and forth from London to Mashhad, where his father still lived, to see if he'd be interested in going with me, and he was enthusiastic. He booked us into his favorite Tehran hotel, the Simorgh, which used to be the Miami Hotel in the Shah's time, in the center of town on Vali-e Asr Street, formerly Pahlavi Street after the Shah's dynasty. Iranian citizens paid their bill in rials, while foreign tourists paid in dollars, and for us the hotel was something like forty dollars a night. I was excited but also a little anxious, especially after nightmares

I'd had about not being able to leave Iran. I would be going to my home country after a *thirty-two*-year absence, and to a country that had radically changed since I had last been there as a teenager on Christmas holidays. Would Iran be the homeland I thought it was, or would it be so alien as to make me feel even more unmoored?

I left my parents' apartment for Heathrow Airport with exhilaration and a queasy stomach. I had a last shot of vodka with a smoked salmon sandwich in the terminal, not knowing when my next drink would be in what was technically a strictly Islamic, and therefore dry, country. In 1979, I mused on the plane, I had assumed that I would return to Iran only when its radically new form of government changed, which didn't seem so far-fetched then. The revolutionary government had been fragile in its early days, and we Iranians in exile thought its incompetence in governing a country without the indispensable technocrats and experts that had maintained stability would be its downfall. Of course, the graveyards of the world are littered with "indispensable" people; whether in government or in business.

Like the Russians in the Paris of the twenties, a generation of older Iranians who left Iran—or those already abroad who merely refused to return—sat in cafés, bars, and in one another's homes, drinking to the day (*soon*, they reassured themselves) when they surely would return home and resume their rightful lives. What most didn't comprehend in those early days was that Persia, *L'Empire de L'Iran* as it was identified on our passports despite the passing of empire centuries ago, had not just changed with Khomeini's revolution; it had been fully reborn. The national emblem—the lion and sun, sometimes with a crown, sometimes without—that had greeted us for generations, from the center of our flag to the surface of our stamps and currency, was gone, and a stylized *Allah*, the symbol of devotion to Islam, had replaced it. I realized now how wrong we had all been about Iran; about its fragility, about its longevity, and about the cunning of the clergy who had changed a nation for what now seemed forever. I was just one of the many Iranian exiles, like the Iranians on the full-capacity flight I was on, or like my friends Maryam Malakpour and Moji Sangi before me who had left at a very young age, who had come (or been forced) to accept Iran for what it was, as the saying goes, and not what we *wanted* it to be.

The surprise election of the wildly popular Mohammad Khatami and a staunchly reformist government in 1997 had changed the political stance of the Islamic Republic from one of revolutionary, even rude, defiance, to one of accommodation with the outside world. In the late nineties, many Iranians in the diaspora began to feel that perhaps Iran could become a country a bit *closer* to what we wanted it to be. For us in the West who had not endured revolutionary Iran, Khatami was a revelation: in an interview with Christiane Amanpour soon after he was elected, he proclaimed "Dialogue Among Civilizations" as his initiative to create an opening with the west. He "regretted" the taking of hostages (but couldn't apologize for it, for doing so would have doomed him in Iranian politics). It was to this Iran that I was returning, one in which my family now held positions of power. It was also an Iran that now fortuitously turned a blind eye to dual citizenship, a sort of "don't ask, don't tell" policy, not unlike at the Clinton administration's Pentagon.

I'll confess to a certain hesitation when I arrived at Tehran's Mehrabad Airport at dawn, a certain dread at what might await me once I stepped out of the safe cocoon of a European airplane. Would I be interrogated for not having returned to Iran to fight in the Iran-Iraq War? Would authorities be disdainful of me, someone who had lived—in their minds—in the lap of luxury and security of America? The last time I had walked the corridors of Mehrabad International, the Shah of Iran, self-proclaimed Kings of Kings and Light of the Aryans, was ensconced in his palace in the hills above Tehran. If you had told me then that he would flee his "empire" only a few years later, defeated by an ascetic ayatollah he had exiled to Iraq fifteen years earlier, I would have laughed at what was, surely, a joke. But then I would have also begged you to hush, for SAVAK, his secret police, was probably somehow listening.

In the immigration line, I was surprised that two of the officers, staring at old green-and-white screens on their computer terminals and stamping passports loudly and with a great flourish, were female, young, and of course completely covered in the black hijab compulsory for government officials. When my turn came, I handed over my Iranian passport with a forced smile. The woman looked at me sternly and then carefully flipped through the blank pages of the document. She frowned, and I began to worry—just a little. "Do you have an American passport?" she asked, slightly accusatorily to my ears. "*Baleh*," I replied, reaching in my pocket to retrieve it, thinking perhaps that it might be the last I'd see of it and I'd have to go to the Swiss embassy to get a temporary replacement.

"No," she said quickly, raising her palm. "I don't need it." She looked through the empty pages of my Iranian passport again. "When was the last time you were in Iran?" she asked, more out of curiosity, it now seemed. "Uh, 1972," I replied. "Maybe thirty-plus years?" I added, not knowing how to convert the Gregorian calendar to the Jalali (Iranian).

"Yes," she said, looking at a small, printed notation on the last page of the passport that I hadn't paid attention to, a mark indicating the date of my last exit from the country. "You have a lot of patience," she continued, a smile barely perceptible on her lips. "What took you so long?"

"I'm not sure . . ." I said hesitatingly, wondering if it was a trick question designed to identify enemies of the government, or if she was merely scolding me for being unpatriotic. "*Befarmaied*," she said—welcome (to the homeland)—cutting me off in a genial tone and handing me back my passport. She gave a curt nod and turned away. It was an odd feeling, stepping past immigration control into Iran. It occurred to me that I was in a place—for the first time in my life, really—where if a stranger asked me where I was from, it wouldn't mean what country, but from what *town*. I breezed through customs, no questions asked, and into the welcoming embrace of numerous cousins who had come to the airport to escort me into the city—a Persian tradition that thankfully hadn't fallen by the wayside in the age of universal transportation.

The city, though, like some of my cousins, was unrecognizable to me, as I sat in a car stuck in snarled traffic on the highway into town. It was now a city of twelve million, four times as many as when I had last been there, every last one of them, it seemed, behind the wheels of automobiles going somewhere or nowhere. "Going for a drive" was a custom Iranians seem to have fully mastered since the dawn of the automobile age, and with gas prices firmly controlled at 1960s levels and cars available to the masses in the twenty-first century, they had expanded it. What occurred to me on my first day in Tehran, and what I later learned also struck my American journalist friends, was the ordinariness of Iran—a place often portrayed as "the other," an enemy of the West, a defiant and revolutionary country filled with angry, unfriendly people. I knew, of course, that Iranians are far from unfriendly, but I wasn't sure what thirty-plus years under a revolutionary government might have done to the national character, especially those secular-minded Iranians who had remained in their homeland. Nothing, I soon discovered.

I found that Persian customs—everything from the extreme politesse to social etiquette and generous hospitality—remained intact inside Iran, whether practiced by die-hard revolutionary Islamic fundamentalists or by rabidly anti-regime dissidents (and those customs have survived among the diaspora for decades, far from home). For centuries, Iranians had learned to not reveal their true selves or their real opinions, and in general they are still wary of doing so, particularly to outsiders. But within Iranian society, I found that Iranians were as they had been not just for centuries, but for millennia. Formed by pre-Islamic Zoroastrianism and molded by martyrdom-obsessed and recusant Shia Islam, Iran was still proud of its past and dismissive of what it believed were lesser cultures of the region. Yes; at least culturally, it felt very much like home, and I was happy.

I spent the two weeks or so in Iran catching up with family I hadn't seen in years—decades, in some cases—such as my cousins Nahid and Fatemeh, both religious and headscarf-wearing, or Mohammad, who I last saw in college in Washington, all first cousins of the president—and family I had never met; children of cousins already in adulthood. I visited my father's hometown in the desert where he was born, the village of Ardakan, now a city, which he had called a "shithole" way before Donald Trump used that term to describe African countries. My father, without shame, would slip back into the accent he'd abandoned with fellow Yazdis. I loved Ardakan (where the new president was also from) and Yazd for the architecture, the ancient wind catchers invented centuries ago to provide natural air-conditioning, the weather, and the history of my family, but I could understand why my father left. There was nothing there for an ambitious, irreligious young man who was fascinated by modernity. Not even in 2005.

Before I left for Iran, I had spoken to Michael Hainey at *GQ* to see if the magazine would be interested in an interview with the Iranian president. Khatami had not, since the one interview with Amanpour for CNN, given another to the U.S. media. Hainey had said absolutely, and Ali Khatami made an appointment for me to see the president at his office in Sa'adabad

01.

02.

01.
With Mohammad Ziaie, my aunt's husband, father of my cousins, uncle of President Khatami, in Yazd, 2005

02.
Posing with Khatami before the interview for *GQ* magazine, 2005

03.
GQ magazine interview (page 1 of 2), 2005

The Other President Speaks

by Hooman Majd

*In his first interview with an American journalist in eight years, Iranian president Mohammad Khatami tells GQ about his country's alleged nuclear program, mocks George W. Bush's "axis of evil," and offers some surprising words on the 1979 hostage crisis

When the moderate and staunchly reformist Mohammad Khatami was elected president of Iran eight years ago, many observers hoped that the days of a rabidly anti-American, anti-Western, anti-Zionist Iran would soon come to an end. After his election, some Western journalists were quick to declare a new era in Iranian politics. But those who hoped for an eventual reestablishment of ties with the United States and a significant relaxation of Islam's social strictures were in for a disappointment, for although Iran has changed considerably since the early days of the revolution, it is still very much a theocracy and often a bastion of anti-Americanism in an increasingly American-dominated world.

The president of Iran does not readily grant interviews or audiences to foreign journalists. As such, I was told that my Q&A was to be "informal." The interview was held at Sa'adabad Palace on one of the two days a week that the president uses it as his office. Although not opulent by any stretch of the imagination, the palace has a sparse, midcentury-chic air about it, and the setting, in a park of mature trees comfortably set off from the smog-choked city, says much about why the president is keen to spend some of his working hours here. In the spirit of informality, he left his translucent black *aba* (cloak) hanging on the coatrack and joined me at the coffee table for tea and what proved to be an unusually candid conversation.

President Bush has included Iran in his "axis of evil" and is pushing for Iran's nuclear program to be referred to the U.N. Security Council, which could result in sanctions. Is there any reason why America should be alarmed by Iran?
Terrorists and warmongers and those who seek to negatively influence world public opinion: This is what constitutes an "axis of evil," and Iran has actually been the victim of both terrorists and warmongers. If humanity is respected everywhere and justice prevails everywhere, this kind of wickedness will disappear. There is nothing that proves or indicates that Iran is intending or trying to acquire nuclear weapons. And this is not just what we declare, for every international-agency report confirms it. No matter what we do, it is America's habit to lob accusations at us. This is not at all a question of our ability to acquire nuclear capability. The U.S. is simply opposed to Iran becoming an independent force in the region.

In a unipolar world, with America the lone superpower, what does Iran intend to achieve by retaining its anti-U.S. stance?
America has done us great harm, and the past few decades of Iranian history prove this. Many examples could be mentioned. Our policy of avoiding conflict and tension naturally applies to all countries, and we have no desire to be in conflict or to have tense relations with any country. The severing of relations between America and Iran was initiated by the United States, and I believe that for the reestablishment of ties or relations, it is America that needs to take the practical steps necessary in accepting Iranian principles for rapprochement. But regrettably, it appears that it is in their interests to maintain the status quo.

But what can America do so that it will no longer be "the Great Satan" in the eyes of the Islamic Republic? Under President Clinton, Secretary of State Albright made an official apology for America's role in the 1953 coup against Prime Minister Mossadeq. Was that a missed opportunity for Iran to make a friendly overture to the United States?
With the many factions in American politics, there is no single policy toward Iran. I believe that the president of the United States, by including Iran in his "axis of evil," reversed the previous administration's positions with respect to Iran, and whatever progress could have been made was brought to a complete stop or, even worse, moved in the opposite direction. In spite of this, in the instances of Afghanistan and Iraq, we have shown our goodwill and made positive moves in the interest of peace and tranquillity.

Since your election to the presidency of Iran, you have repeated your desire for a "dialogue amongst civilizations" as a way to better understanding and world peace, and it became an initiative that the U.N. took up based upon your suggestion. Do you think your campaign has been successful?
The entire world welcomed the "dialogue amongst civilizations" initiative when it was introduced at the U.N., and this demonstrates that there is a powerful underlying message within: that establishing peaceful coexistence in the world can be achieved through such an initiative. The wave of protests and strong public opinion against the American warmongers during the Iraq war is itself a sign that this initiative is affecting world public opinion. Of course, those whose interests lie in war and strife do not welcome this initiative or any spreading of the idea. I think that the criminal events of September 11 and the subsequent wars, terrorism, and upheaval were a direct response from those who oppose or don't find to their advantage the "dialogue amongst civilizations" initiative.

Americans' views on Iran are still somewhat influenced by the hostage crisis of 1979. The vast majority of Americans of a certain age vividly remember the images of blindfolded American hostages on their TV screens. How can Iranians and Americans put this episode behind them once and for all?
In this connection, it has been said many times that we understand the feelings of the great American nation, and we regret that those feelings have been hurt. But it is the American nation, more than us, that should be unhappy with their leaders and should question why their leaders treat nations that wish to be independent in such a way as to provoke such harsh reactions—in the same way that American public opinion put the blame on their government during the Vietnam War. And in the case of Iraq, almost 50 percent of the American people showed their opposition to the war by voting for the opposing candidate.

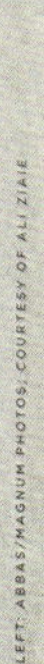

03.

Palace, formerly one of the Shah's, in Shemiran, the hills above central Tehran. There Khatami entertained foreign dignitaries and, two days a week, worked away from the presidential compound in downtown Tehran, where the air was drastically more polluted. My cousin Ali Ziaie (also a first cousin of the president), an insurance executive with whom I hadn't spent any time since he left George Washington University before the revolution, picked me up at the Simorgh Hotel (which, incongruously for a hotel affiliated with the Iranian armed forces, boasted a Christmas tree in the lobby), and we drove north on Valiasr Street all the way to Tajrish and the palace entrance.

Ali Khatami met us and showed us into a room where the president stood waiting for me. Khatami greeted me warmly, asking after my father, whom he had known, and also my mother, my brother, and my sister, whom he either barely knew or had never met. We Ardakanis did indeed stay close. While Khatami didn't reveal any secrets of the early stages of the nuclear crisis with the West, the fact that he—representing one member of what President Bush termed the "Axis of Evil"— spoke to an American magazine was news enough. It received attention in the media, including Fox News, which asked to interview me when I returned to the States and questioned whether Khatami was "evil." It was hard to not laugh on camera.

When I left Tehran, as the plane took off and I saw the lights of the city disappear into the darkness preceding dawn, I already missed being there. I felt I needed more time to get to know the country I had left as an infant, even as I admitted to myself that Tehran, while giving me a vague sense of familiarity, wasn't really "home" in any meaningful way. But I promised myself: I would be back.

Arriving in the United States from Iran, the immigration officer asked no questions but simply said, "Welcome home," as he stamped and handed me back my American passport. I remembered the first time I had traveled with a U.S. passport, in 1994, when those same words had been the most comforting I'd heard since 1979. I knew that "welcome home" was part of what America was—welcoming to immigrants and people with strange names who could indeed be home in a land not necessarily of their birth—but this time, after returning from Iran, it felt different again; I felt I might have *two* homes, both of which embraced me as their own, even as I hesitated to think of myself truly at home in either place.

Chapter 33

Another Career

When I returned to Los Angeles, I began working on when to head back to New York and how to get rid of the Mini Cooper I had leased for three years. Selim Zilkha often invited me and Karri to his house for meals; at one dinner Kirk Douglas was present and I said hello, although I didn't bring up that we had met years ago, as I wasn't sure he'd remember, especially since suffering a severe stroke almost a decade earlier. At one luncheon, I met Arianna Huffington. She was about to launch the *Huffington Post*, and over lunch, after Selim understood what blogs were, he suggested to both of us that I write for her. She liked the idea of an Iranian on the site, and I started to think that perhaps blogging might be the path to a career in freelance journalism.

Selim's daughter, Nadia, also introduced me to her friend Allison Silver, a style editor at *The New York Times*, who asked me to come up with an idea for the Style section. I suggested a profile of Dan Tana's, a restaurant on Santa Monica Boulevard just east of Beverly Hills in West Hollywood that had been an industry hangout for decades since the former Yugoslavian soccer player had opened it, famous for its steak with spaghetti, where any given night you were bound to see celebrities or studio executives. Allison was keen on the idea, and it became a big spread with a photograph of the restaurant's interior, a framed copy of which still hangs on its wall. I was excited that I might have some credibility as a journalist, if the Gray Lady would publish me.

Not long afterward, Karri and I drove in the Mini out of Los Angeles with a promise of a check for the security deposit from our landlord. We stopped in Las Vegas for the night, and the next morning headed toward rural Wisconsin, where Karri is from, through Utah, Colorado, Nebraska, and Iowa. Karri, mostly vegetarian, had brought along various snacks in a cooler, along with a large tin of Iranian caviar that I had been given by Ali Khatami in Iran. One evening, at a gas station in Utah, Karri said that we should just pull over, watch the sunset, and eat caviar for dinner. (My father would often send caviar back with me from London, having received it as a gift from Khatami himself, and we had extra tins.) Once opened, the tin would have to be finished, which we found not to be a problem, carelessly spreading heavy layers of the world's finest beluga on small crackers, adding a drop or two from a squeezed lemon, and devouring every last pearl. Two unemployed adults—Karri a yoga instructor now between studios—in a car they couldn't afford to keep, driving across the country and eating a dinner that would embarrass even a millionaire, but we enjoyed it thoroughly, sitting in that gas station's parking area in remote Utah, that I can still remember every bite.

It reminded me of the time in the nineties when I accompanied Chris Blackwell to Martha Stewart's office opening at the Starrett-Lehigh Building in far west Chelsea, a newly hip location for creative businesses after an extensive remodel. Among the appetizers was a bowl of caviar and some tiny mother-of-pearl spoons that one was supposed to use to gather a few eggs onto blinis or toast points. Chris tried to navigate the delicate task but quickly gave up. I took out two of my business cards and, handing one to Chris, used mine to scoop up a rather large mound of the caviar and then just scraped all of it into my mouth. Chris followed my lead, and we both laughed at the absurdity of our greedy improvisation. The caviar, while decent, was not Iranian due to U.S. sanctions on Iranian goods, and therefore of inferior quality, as any Iranian (or even Frenchman) will tell you. Sturgeon, you see, from which "real" caviar is harvested, while roaming the entire Caspian and therefore fished by all the littoral states including Russia, prefer the warmer waters in the south, on the coast of Iran. At least that's what Iranians tell themselves.

After a week in Dodgeville, Montfort (where Karri grew up), and Livingston, Wisconsin, we continued our drive and stayed at my brother's house in Connecticut. I wrote my blog for the *Huffington Post* every second or third day, joining a handful of Arianna's friends in opining on everything and anything that I felt needed to be discussed. Having recently returned from Iran, I naturally focused on the Middle East and Muslim issues and gained some attention. Another *Huffington Post* blogger was Jann Wenner, founder and owner of *Rolling Stone*, and I decided to pitch the magazine an Iran story. I met with Will Dana, the managing editor, who loved the idea of me going to Iran to write a long piece—10,000 words at a dollar a word—on what Iran was like and what we should know about it.

I was getting ready to leave for Tehran when Glenn and Gina suggested we rent their friends' loft, two floors above theirs on Bond Street, for the rest of the summer, as the owners, both artists, were going on their annual trip to France. The only caveat was that we had to take care of the two cats. We moved our suitcases there, and I left for Iran. In addition to the wage, I hoped the piece would raise my profile and my credibility. Print journalism (and its presence online) was still, in the age just before social media took over, commissioning long, thoughtful, and interesting stories that weren't "breaking news" or on the subject du jour. *The New Yorker*, *The Atlantic*, and *Harper's* were of course the granddaddies, but *Rolling Stone*—the wilder grandchild (Hunter S. Thompson, anyone?)—also covered politics and social issues. It's a shame that fewer and fewer magazines can afford to commission the kinds of pieces they once did, and even if they do, can't afford to pay the kind of compensation that a 10,000- to 20,000-word piece deserves.

I had asked my cousin Ali Ziaie to book a room for me at the Homa Hotel, formerly the Intercontinental, in Vanak, a busy shopping district in the northern central part of town, which with my Iranian rial rate was affordable on the expenses I could submit. I planned to stay two to three weeks and also travel outside Tehran. The Homa is a high-rise with a beautiful outdoor pool (unavailable for swimming due to Islamic clothing restrictions), and a marble lobby with décor stuck in the 1960s and '70s, the last time I had been there. I had a room on a high floor with a balcony—and a special, even more deeply discounted nightly rate that my cousin had arranged—but my friend Khosro Etemadi from California, with whom I had reunited over a cup of coffee at the Simorgh after more than twenty years when I had been to Iran at Christmas, told me I shouldn't waste my money and should move to his house on Safi Alishah Street in downtown Tehran, where I could have my own bedroom and full privacy. I'd not only enjoy the company, but I was sure to learn more living in a home than staying in a hotel.

I visited Khatami again in the president's office, and attended his farewell event to celebrate his eight years in office. Iran, like the United States, limits its presidents to two four-year terms, and in that summer's presidential election, the hard-line populist Tehran mayor Mahmoud Ahmadinejad had prevailed over the frontrunner, Ali Akbar Hashemi Rafsanjani, president in the 1990s. Rafsanjani was a pragmatist with a foot in both camps: conservative but not a hard-liner, reformist but not radical, although he couldn't overcome his reputation as the face of politics as usual, thought of by many to be corrupt.

I also visited Qom, the center of Shia Islam in Iran, where seminary students are visible on the streets in clerical garb in numbers not seen anywhere else (other than the Twelve Imams' shrines). There, I had hoped to see Ayatollah Lankarani, and I sat in a waiting room with dozens of other men. The protocol, apparently, was to just say hello and leave. Lankarani was a noted hard-liner—extreme, even—but his son was courteous and insisted I go with him to the ayatollah's library, where all his works and his edicts were stored along with other religious texts. The library (and his office) was equipped with fiber-optic internet cable—rare if not entirely unavailable to the public—and seminarians sat at computer terminals working, maintaining his website and taking down questions to be answered later by the ayatollah.

I left Iran after three weeks, in mid-August, armed with copious notes and not a few photographs. In New York, I worked on my piece for a few

01.

01.
Waiting for the Ayatollah,
Qom, summer 2005

weeks and handed it in to Dana in September. I gave a copy to Davitt to see what he thought; he loved it and said I should send it to Jann Wenner as well. Yet after a couple of edits, Dana called me and said that Jann had decided not to publish the piece. Will loved it, he assured me, but he had no choice in the matter as Jann had to make room for his own extensive interview with Bono in the same issue. Will promised me, however, that they would pay my full contract and not a "kill fee," and I would own the article, freeing me to take it elsewhere. There weren't a lot of outlets that would want a piece like mine, and certainly not at the length it was, so I decided that I'd save it for a nonfiction book that I had started to think about writing soon after my first visit to Iran with Kaveh, imagining the wealth of stories that could be told. Jann never responded to me directly.

After I had returned to New York from Los Angeles earlier in the year, Ali Khatami had introduced me, via phone, to Hossein Fereidoun, Iran's ambassador for cultural affairs at the Iranian Mission to the U.N.—the only outpost for Iranian diplomats on U.S. soil. The host agreement that the United States signed with the United Nations for it to be based in New York meant that the USA was impelled to allow diplomats of member countries such as Iran, North Korea, and Cuba, with which it had no diplomatic relations, to work and live in New York. For diplomats from those countries, the USA restricted their movements to a twenty-five-mile radius of Columbus Circle, which includes JFK Airport. I had also met Mohammad Javad Zarif, the ambassador and permanent representative, as ambassadors to the U.N. are called (the country being "permanent" and not the ambassador), who would travel back and forth to Tehran every couple of months. He jokingly once said to me, after the *GQ* interview with Khatami was published, that he told Khatami he was impressed that he had given an interview to a "sexy" magazine. I don't know if anyone in Iran remembered that Ayatollah Khomeini, founder of the republic, had once given an interview to *Playboy*—although, to be fair, perhaps without knowing which media outlet he was talking to.

Ahmadinejad's victory over Rafsanjani in 2005 had come as a surprise to reformists and moderates who made up most of the intelligentsia and the urban middle class, as Rafsanjani had come in first against multiple candidates but had fallen short of 50 percent of the vote, forcing a runoff. Fereidoun had been incredulous. He told me he believed that the reformists—meaning Khatami—had made a big mistake in not asking his brother, Hassan Rouhani, the secretary of the Supreme National Security Council (SNSC) and chief nuclear negotiator with the West at the time, to run for the presidency and back his candidacy. There was no way, he insisted, that Ahmadinejad would have defeated Rouhani. Rafsanjani had been president before, and only Rouhani could match Ahmadinejad's militant nationalism and pair it with a pragmatic approach to the West, he argued. Later, I thought about what he had said when in 2013 his brother, with Hossein as his senior advisor, ran and handily defeated all comers in the first round of the presidential election that year. That time, Khatami *had* backed Rouhani publicly and all the way, with campaign posters picturing the two men side by side. (Rouhani's last name was also Fereidoun—a purely Persian one that predated Islam—before he changed it when becoming cleric to Rouhani, meaning "cleric" or "religious.")

Hossein Fereidoun put me on a list of journalists to be invited to any events with the new president when Ahmadinejad decided to attend the U.N. General Assembly in person a little over a month after he was elected. In the past (and even under the Shah), Iran's heads of state usually gave their country's address during "U.N. week" only once or at most twice during their time in office, and rarely in their first year, leaving it to the foreign minister. (Rafsanjani never bothered at all.) Ahmadinejad was about to break the mold in more ways than one. When he arrived in New York in September 2005, I was among a handful of journalists and editors invited to a meeting with him at his hotel. It was eye-opening less for what he said than the way he treated Zarif, Iran's ambassador, who sat next to him in the conference room while a simultaneous translator sat in a makeshift booth in the corner. When the interpreter got something wrong and Zarif corrected the mistake, Ahmadinejad said to him, "*Toh tarjomeh kon!*" or "*You translate!*" And using *toh*, like the French *tu*, instead of *shoma*, like the French *vous*. Zarif, red in the face, told him it wasn't the place of an ambassador to be an interpreter, and let the interpreter continue while Ahmadinejad scowled. It was clear to me that Zarif—a reformist with close ties to Khatami and Rouhani, with whom he'd worked during nuclear negotiations from 2003 until 2005 before Ahmadinejad and the new negotiator Ali Larijani shut them down—would not survive for much longer in New York. Afterward, I shared an elevator with Mike Wallace of *60 Minutes*, who asked me what I thought of Ahmadinejad. I said the Q&A was interesting, but not very revealing. He agreed. "I want to interview him, but not here," he said. "I want to go to Iran." He never did.

I had started freelancing for the *New York Observer*, a weekly newspaper that many media executives picked up every Wednesday. It was known widely for Candace Bushnell's "Sex and the City" column, made famous later by the television series, although nothing I wrote for Suzy Hansen, an editor to whom I was introduced by Michael Hainey, would garner nearly as much attention. One story I wrote for the *Observer* was on a new tradition Ahmadinejad started: yearly catered dinners in a hotel ballroom for some five hundred or so Iranian Americans (or Iranian residents in the States), to forge better ties between Iran and the diaspora and, of course, to garner support. That year it was at the Hilton on Sixth Avenue, and the crowd was lively. In a vivid display of his populist credentials, after dinner and obligatory speeches, Ahmadinejad stood in a corner and shook hands with every single attendee (or bowed, in the case of women guests) who wished to see him and say hello. It was easy to see why he attracted admirers, even in New York. But the line was long, and I took my leave instead.

Karri and I were living in another loft by then, on Great Jones Street, renting from friends who had moved to Los Angeles. Before we finally found an apartment to lease on Park Row, Ahmadinejad made his infamous statement that Israel must be "wiped off the map," causing outrage and concern the world over. (The translation, many have since argued, was technically incorrect: Ahmadinejad was slightly misquoting Ayatollah Khomeini, who had said, "*Een rezhim-e eshghalgar-e Quds bayad az sahneh-ye rouzegar mahv shavad*," or "This Jerusalem-occupying regime must vanish from the sphere of time.") Regardless of what was meant by the statement—and Iranian politicians from the supreme leader down were at pains to insist that the country by the name of Israel vanishing doesn't mean its *citizens* should be vanished, too—the reputation of Ahmadinejad and indeed the Iranian regime itself as anti-Semitic was cemented. And my work as a journalist working on Iran stories was now potentially in demand.

Chapter 34

The Voice of Iran

In the late spring of 2006, struggling to pay most of my bills and running up some credit-card debt, I received a call from Mehdi Faridzadeh, formerly a diplomat at the Iranian Mission to the U.N., who had remained in America after his assignment was over, heading an institute that aimed to cultivate cultural ties between the United States and Iran. President Khatami was accepting invitations to speak in the States—at universities, institutions, organizations, and at the Washington Cathedral—and he wanted to know if I would be willing to join the tour, which would take Khatami to Chicago, Boston, Virginia, Washington, and New York, as an informal advisor. I said of course I would, and then spoke to Suzy Hansen about an essay I could write at the end. I was excited to get to know Khatami and his team of advisors better and to gain entrée to the diplomatic world that had been my family's but had been denied me by the revolution—the very revolutionaries I was going to spend time with.

There was a brief dispute in Tehran, I later learned, when the foreign ministry under Manouchehr Mottaki, a conservative former MP I had interviewed for the *New York Observer* who had said that Iran's new international stance under Ahmadinejad was "no more nice guy," had refused a diplomatic passport for Khatami, who as a former head of state refused to leave the country without one. After much back-and-forth—I presume it was taken up with the supreme leader—Khatami arrived in New York and was whisked by the State Department's Diplomatic Security Service (DSS) to the U.N. ambassador's residence on Fifth Avenue, a town house nestled between two co-ops and facing Central Park, a block from the Metropolitan Museum. I met him and Ali Khatami there, and was introduced to the rest of his party, Sadegh Kharrazi and Gholamali Khoshroo, both former ambassadors under Khatami and now working for his Dialogue Among Civilizations organization, and Iman Mirabzadeh, a distant relative from Ardakan who worked in his office and was serving as a general aide and photographer on the trip. Zarif, the ambassador, not only hosted him at the residence (which drew criticism from Ahmadinejad's people), but arranged a few dinners, too. Karri came with me to one dinner for select Iranians in New York, and I went alone to the others, including with think-tank fellows and other executives. I was impressed with and a little surprised by how much Americans, especially, liked Khatami and what he stood for. The dinners were a hot ticket, with not a few journalists calling me to ask if they could receive an invitation. It gave me hope that Iran and the United States might not remain mortal enemies forever, after all, despite a new Iranian administration that seemed to revel in its revolutionary stance.

We flew to Chicago first, where Khatami was scheduled to deliver a speech to CAIR, the Council on American-Islamic Relations. Mehdi gave me a copy of the English-language version of the speech, translated in Tehran, to which I made numerous language and grammatical corrections, but I knew Khatami was going to speak in Farsi. Sitting with Ali Khatami and Faridzadeh in the lobby of the hotel in the afternoon, I asked them who the interpreter was going to be. They looked at each other and then to me. "Can *you* do it?" they asked. I replied that I wasn't a simultaneous interpreter, which was a very specific skill, or indeed a translator at all, to which Mehdi said that I could just sit near the former president, and as he said a sentence or two, he could pause, and I would read off my translated document—essentially be a consecutive interpreter. I reluctantly agreed, and that was established as the format for all the speeches, everywhere.

I was surprised (as was Khatami and the rest of the party) with the level of security that the State Department provided the former president. Armed agents were with us twenty-four hours a day, taking rooms on the same floor in hotels, traveling with us on planes, and sending armored cars from Washington to Boston and Chicago ahead of us. The Diplomatic Security Service—ordinarily tasked with protecting the secretary of state, State Department officials, and foreign ministers or other dignitaries visiting the USA—coordinated with police departments in cities to give us escorts: in Washington, while driving near the White House, we were cheered by some, thinking that in our limo was George Bush, Dick Cheney, or some other high official; and jeered by others thinking exactly the same. Condoleeza Rice, then the secretary of state, had instructed the service to pull out all the stops for Khatami, who had called for diplomacy and dialog in contrast with Iran's new president (and perhaps she remembered that under Khatami, Iranians held public vigils for the victims of 9/11).

On the drive to the University of Virginia, I sat in a black custom Chevrolet Tahoe in a jump seat facing Khatami; I was told by the agent sitting up front, with two of his men pointing machine guns out the rear window, that it was *Condi's* usual vehicle. The only kink in the plans was when Mitt Romney, then governor of Massachusetts, forbade the Boston police or the state police to offer us any courtesy or protection while Khatami was in town to deliver a speech at Harvard, calling him a "terrorist." The State Department agents were unconcerned, but when we got on a JetBlue plane at Logan Airport heading back to New York, two people, seeing armed men escort a man in robes and a turban onto the plane, asked to be let off. I was amused, but to be fair, it was only five years after 9/11. While in Boston, Khatami received a letter from Jimmy Carter, inviting him to meet with him at the Carter Center in Georgia. It was left to me to respond, politely and diplomatically, that unfortunately Khatami was unable to add Georgia to his itinerary on this trip due to previous commitments. Had he met with Carter, it is safe to say that he might have been hanged, drawn, and quartered on his return to Iran—or worse.

01.

02.

03.

01.
Khatami exiting a State Department car with DSS security in Manhattan, Kharrazi exiting driver's side at top; photo by the author

02.
Khatami speech at Washington Cathedral, with the author on the left, translating

03.
With Khatami on a JetBlue flight, 2006

When we returned to JFK, a good number of cars awaited us on the tarmac, and we were led off the plane before everyone else descended another aircraft stairway. We set off with an NYPD police escort—motorcycles in front—and were on Fifth Avenue at the Met in fifteen minutes flat. I watched in amazement as police motorcyclists went ahead, stopped all traffic on an expressway to let us enter from a ramp, held the cars for a minute or so, and then gave us a clear highway ahead. As anyone who has spent as much time riding on the Long Island Expressway from JFK to Manhattan as I have will understand: it was one of the most thrilling car rides of my life.

The Khatami visit made me feel very Iranian, and close to the reformists in the regime who I felt, lacking any other alternative, might be the best hope for the future of my fellow Iranians. My father, no fan of the Islamic system, had begged me to wear a necktie to distinguish myself from the rest of the party; I instead promised to stay clean shaven. The Iranian regime, an autocracy camouflaged by a democratic façade, has former revolutionaries challenging, if not always publicly, the autocratic element, which I appreciated but my father was suspicious of as he thought it was all a mirage, and one set of clerics wasn't going to be radically different from another. I understood his rationale. Khoshroo, a diplomat with a strong sense of humor and understanding of the ridiculous, started calling me "Ayatollah Hooman" whenever I questioned the Islamic aspect of something, and I came to see him and Kharrazi as staunch reformists stymied by the system and by the election of Ahmadinejad, who ironically would more openly defy the supreme leader and even question his authority over the government than anyone ever had.

Kharrazi, whose sister was married to one of Ayatollah Khamenei's sons, became a friend, inviting me to his house in Tehran and calling me every time he visited New York in later years for cancer treatment. It was hard to reconcile his relationship—and even friendship—with the supreme leader while he was fiercely loyal to Khatami (and served as his ambassador to France), but he managed to be one of the very few Iranians—if indeed there were any others—who comfortably straddled the extreme hard-line and radical reformist factions in the leadership and in government. Kharrazi also had impeccable taste—from his bespoke suits to his house, fitted out with Persian antiques and tiles—and in Paris he renovated and refurbished the Iranian Embassy, which had been left decrepit after years of neglect. He reopened and revitalized the Foreign Ministry Club in Tehran during a stint as deputy foreign minister under his uncle Kamal Kharazzi's ministerial term; it had fallen into disrepair after the revolution, the notion of a private "club" anathema to the revolutionaries.

In 2007, Reza Noorsalehi, a diplomat who had served under my father in London and who my father took with him as his deputy to Japan, invited me there for lunch one weekend. He, in a suit and tie that he had clearly bought in the seventies, stood out among the shabbily dressed diplomats and their wives in full chador, but he didn't seem to care. A cultured man of great intellect, who in London had taken me and my brother to the Roundhouse arts and music theater in Chalk Farm before we knew it existed, was a lifelong bachelor living out his retirement in a small apartment in Vanak rather than in London or Paris. It depressed me that the revolution had eliminated some of its best human resources, either by forced retirement in his case, or by exile in so many others'. I was deeply saddened to hear of his death a few years later.

01.

01.
Reza Noorsalehi leaving the Foreign Ministry Club, Tehran; photo by the author

Chapter 35

The Persians

After Khatami and his party departed New York, President Ahmadinejad was shortly due to arrive for the U.N. General Assembly in September. As the date grew closer, Ambassador Javad Zarif asked me if I would do the interpreting at the U.N. for Ahmadinejad's speech—people in the president's office in Tehran had seen videos of Khatami's visit to the States. I reiterated what he already knew: I was not a simultaneous translator. He was unconcerned and suggested that I simply do what I had done for Khatami, read the English translation as I listened to his Farsi through headphones while watching him from the interpreters' booths above the assembly room. I thought it sounded like an opportunity for an article, so I agreed, as long as I could write about the experience and nothing would be off the record. Zarif was fine with my demand. I wasn't especially flattered by the request: there were countless other Iranians then, many of them born and raised in America, who could read a speech in accentless English, but I suppose fewer in Tehran, and especially not in the circles of power. For some, a strong command of English was more a badge of shame than pride.

Zarif received the president's address to the U.N., in Farsi and in Tehran-translated English, a few days before Ahmadinejad arrived in New York and asked me to look it over at the mission residence. There were many mistakes, and I told him that if the interpreter was to sound halfway competent and intelligent, which presumably was what the Iranians wanted, we'd need to fix the translation and grammatical errors in the text. Zarif shook his head reading the Farsi, knowing in advance what a bad reaction the speech would elicit among not just the Western diplomats and media, but even some of Iran's allies. I could tell that he was embarrassed to have Ahmadinejad as his president, an embarrassment I presume many American foreign service officers experienced later during the Trump administration. (When he was elected, Trump was referred to as America's Ahmadinejad by many Iranians.) But as a loyal soldier of the revolution, Zarif continued in his job, knowing that while Ahmadinejad wanted to replace him, the supreme leader would block any change, insisting that Zarif stay in New York. (The supreme leader has traditionally only really cared about and insisted on approval over four ambassadorships: Beirut, Baghdad, Damascus, and New York.)

On the day of Ahmadinejad's speech, the Iranian Mission arranged for a U.N. pass for me, and I was in the booth a good forty minutes before Ahmadinejad took to the podium. I read his address to the General Assembly over and over, hoping I wouldn't be confused and go too fast or too slow, trying to catch up. It was the usual bombastic speech, and when it finally ended, I was relieved and headed home. I wrote an article for the *New York Observer* that night, and it was published on the front page, titled "Mahmoud and Me" with, admittedly, a rather unflattering caricature of Ahmadinejad and me with sweat pouring from my forehead, which was not entirely inaccurate.

I spoke to Ahmadinejad later at an event for Iranians and found him oddly charming, one of those politicians who, when they speak to you, make you feel as though you are the most important person to them at that moment, that what you're saying is of great interest and at the top of his or her mind, and I understood his appeal inside Iran among many nationalist

THE NEW YORK OBSERVER

OCTOBER 2, 2006 · NEW YORK'S WEEKLY NEWSPAPER · DOLLAR

Gore Awakens Sleeping Booty Of '00 Donors

Convenient Truth: Silent Al Warms Up Old Money; Ex-Veep Squeezes Branson, Boogies in Chelsea: Brazile, Chafing-at-Bit Backers Vow Support

BY JASON HOROWITZ

In suit pants too short and black boots too polished, Al Gore stepped haltingly to the podium of the Sheraton New York on Thursday afternoon and took credit for helping to solicit an enormous donation to fight global warming. Mr. Clinton patted him on the back and joked, "Al's the enforcer." Mr. Gore ignored the whiff of condescension as his puffy, aquiline face beamed in the direction of the adulation.

AL GORE

To the Democratic-leaning audience, he was their favorite political martyr. But for a series of major donors and operatives across the country, he's still very much their candidate for 2008.

"I might host a reception here for Mark Warner, I might attend some event for John Edwards, but I think certainly because of my background with Gore, they wouldn't expect me to be committed to them if Gore were to come in at the last minute," said Charles W. Bone, one of Mr. Gore's major fund-raisers in 2000, who is hosting a reception this weekend for Mr. Warner in Nashville. "I think a lot of folks are just going to stand on the sidelines to see who strikes the hearts of the Democrats, and if nobody does that, it just makes the case stronger for Al Gore."

These quiet, influential members of Al

CONTINUED ON 9

Steve Kornacki on Bill Clinton's Big Weekend, Page 9.

@$#&*% KEN BURNS! PBS SCRUBBING G.I. MOUTHS WITH SOAP

WWII Memory Film May Get Bleeped for F.C.C., Bush's Indecency Fines

EVEN *FRONTLINE* QUIVERS

Oath Can Cost $325,000; Lowell Bergman Explodes

BY REBECCA DANA

NYTV

War can be hell on public television. It just can't contain any "fucks" or "shits" before 10 p.m.

Scenes of war on PBS in which soldiers use profanity have been cut or elaborately avoided in two upcoming *Frontline* documentaries. According to the journalists and PBS executives responsible,

CONTINUED ON 17

INDEX

Serene Dean Baquet Has a Birthday Cake In *L.A. Times* Newsroom

'I Made a Wish,' He Says; Baltimore, Hartford Staffs Back Editor vs. Tribune

BY TOM SCOCCA

OFF THE RECORD

On Sept. 21, *Los Angeles Times* editor Dean Baquet turned 50 years old. When he stepped out into the newsroom that afternoon, following the daily page-one meeting, he was greeted with a birthday cake and a prolonged, loud ovation.

The crowd numbered more than a hundred. Two hundred? It sprawled uncountably out of view, around an angle of the newsroom: columnists and top editors and copy editors all mingling, upbeat and merry. The *L.A. Times* celebrates birthdays, but not like this; at the edges, it was impossible to hear Mr. Baquet's remarks, let alone hope for a piece of cake.

"It was sort of a cream-filled cake with my picture on it, which was very nice," Mr. Baquet said.

The crowd sang "Happy Birthday" with gusto. "It was a very moving scene," Mr. Baquet said. "I felt very close

"I Began to Sweat": Hooman Majd with Iranian President Ahmadinejad: "A few extra words here and ... headlines."

Mahmoud and Me

Ahmadinejad's Wild Week, by His Translator: 'I Heard You Sounded Great!'; Meet the Wife; Asks for Michael Moore; Big Dinner at Hilton

BY HOOMAN MAJD

On Tuesday, Sept. 19, the day of his now-famous speech, Iranian President Mahmoud Ahmadinejad entered the General Assembly at the United Nations and sat down with his foreign minister and the Iranian U.N. ambassador. He waved in my direction, and I waved back. *Me and Mahmoud*, I thought to myself.

I had seen the text of Mr. Ahmadinejad's speech before he'd even arrived in Manhattan on Monday, Sept. 18: I was his interpreter, or at least his English voice, at the U.N.

My father was an ambassador under the Shah, and I've spent most of my life in the U.S. After a career in the entertainment industry, I had written about President Khatami for U.S. publications and made contacts within his government. That experience, along with my credentials as an apparently trustworthy Iranian, led to my invitation to be Mr. Ahmadinejad's translator, and to attend some of his public pit stops, as well as an Iranian-only (and media-free) celebration at the Hilton. There, I thought, I'd glimpse the real Ahmadinejad.

His speech used the simple "man of the people," anti-intellectual language that Mr. Ahmadinejad is known for, and was translated expertly. Any nuance would be in Mr. Ahmadinejad's tone or body language, neither of which I would be able to reproduce from my booth overlooking the General Assembly.

Nuance in Persian is in any event difficult to translate, but it can be most misleading—sometimes comically so—during interviews with the American press. When Brian Williams of NBC asked about Mr. Ahmadinejad's attire—a suit rather than his trademark windbreaker—the

Cancer Vixen Tells All

Marisa Marchetto, Mme. Da Silvano, Publishes Graphic Memoir

BY TONI SCHLESINGER

On the evening of Thursday, Sept. 21, the Champagne and rosé were flowing yet again at Da Silvano on Sixth Avenue, this time in celebration of owner Silvano Marchetto's wife, Marisa Acocella Marchetto, and her graphic memoir, *Cancer Vixen*

01.

01.
NY Observer cover story on Ahmadinejad

02.
With President Ahmadinejad and Hossein Fereidoun (foreground) in New York, September 2006

02.

and underprivileged Iranians, despite the embarrassment he appeared to be outside the country.

When the paper hit the newsstands, Masoud Modarres, a New York–based publisher of Farsi newspapers and someone who had been in the Khatami party, called me and said he liked the article, but was worried about what he called the "terrible" drawing of Ahmadinejad. I wasn't especially concerned and doubted the *Observer* was even on the radar of Iranians in government. Jed Alpert, however, a Democratic political operative I knew who was in public relations, saw me in the Village the next day and said, "*This* will get you a book deal." I hoped, for the first time, that he might be right.

I'd had lunch with the writer Simon Van Booy sometime before, telling him about the novel I had written but that my agent couldn't seem to get published. He generously offered to put me in touch with a former girlfriend of his, Lindsay Edgecombe, who worked as an agent at the Levine Greenberg literary agency. She had liked my novel and gave helpful editorial suggestions when I sent it to her, but after Jed's optimistic comment, I asked her if we should instead present a nonfiction book on Iran and Iranians, with Luigi Barzini's bestselling *The Italians* as a comparable title. She thought it was a great idea, and we set about writing a proposal.

We met with several editors who expressed interest, all of whom thought the proposal good, but only one, Kristine Puopolo of Doubleday, was willing to make an offer on the spot. I thought her very perceptive and smart, but more important, truly interested in my writing *and* in Iran. Kristine gave me a copy of Edward Luce's *In Spite of the Gods*, his book on modern India, thinking that it would be comparable to my book, too. My idea was that I would go to Iran for two months, and the experiences I would have there—political and cultural—would form the narrative, along with my own opinions and an examination of Iran's modern history. And so, in January 2007, I left for Iran, this time having arranged to stay with Khosro at the house on Safi Alishah in Tehran and to travel the country. Finally, some of the stories from the *Rolling Stone* piece that was never published would see the light of day.

Chapter 36

Again in Iran

As much a revelation as Iran had been to me in 2005 when I had gone there for *Rolling Stone*, it was far more so in 2007. Emotionally, I still felt both close to and alienated from the country. It simply seemed to have passed me by, because of my own prejudices, politics, and desires. My thoroughly Anglo-American upbringing, more in sync with the Iran of my youthful vacations, now clashed violently with Islamic Iran, even as I wanted to respect the beliefs of millions of my fellow Iranians. For my secular countrymen—and there were many, especially in the urban areas—Iran in 2007 was not as severe an environment as Saudi Arabia, for example: liquor was widely available at the same price as in the West, unless you wanted to be *absolutely* certain it was the genuine thing (in which case you had to pay a premium); Jews, Christians, and Zoroastrians existed along with churches, synagogues, and fire temples; and unlike in some other Islamic countries, life didn't grind to a halt at the first sound of *azan*, the call to prayer, which was not heard publicly in most parts of Tehran to begin with.

On my trip in 2005, I had met one of my father's best friends, Iraj Aliabadi, a poet who had worked in insurance with my father before his sitting for the foreign service exam. Over the years he had become close to my oldest cousin, Ali Ziaie. I met Aliabadi's daughter Shirin, who invited me to a party at the apartment she shared with her husband, Farhad Moshiri, a painter and sculptor, one of the best-known artists working in Iran. Shirin herself was an admired photographer, and at the party in their art-filled apartment I had come face-to-face with Karan Vafadari—the youngest son of Ardeshir Vafadari, my father's childhood schoolmate from Yazd—whom I hadn't seen since childhood in Tehran. I called Karan and his wife, Afarin Neyssari, in 2007, and they insisted on inviting me to their house for dinner.

I took Khosro with me, and Shirin and Farhad were there, too. The house, in the foothills, had once been Karan's father's summer escape from the oppressive heat of downtown Tehran. Karan had returned to Iran from America to reclaim his family's properties and put their various businesses in order. The Vafadaris are Zoroastrian—an officially state-sanctioned pre-Islamic religion (and the oldest monotheistic religion)—considered apolitical by the revolutionary government and therefore generally left alone, their businesses and property not routinely confiscated by the regime. The house sat on more than an acre, with a pool and a tennis court and lushly manicured grounds, all surrounded by twelve-foot walls in the Persian manner. Outside of the presidential compound and the Shah's palaces, there was probably no other house comparable to it in all of Tehran—those that hadn't been requisitioned from owners in exile and subdivided into lots or torn down were used for a government or school building. Khosro was shocked at the sight of a private home like this: he told me on the drive back downtown that he worried they wouldn't be able to keep it, given that high-rises built after the revolution with the northward spread of the city had views directly onto the property that the walls couldn't hide. But parties at their house became regular events for me every time I visited Iran. It helped the mood of any party that as a Zoroastrian, Karan was allowed to have liquor in his home.

Much later, in 2011 when I was in Iran with Karri and our newborn son, Khashayar, we were at their house almost every week, with Khashayar sleeping in their bedroom as the loud parties extended into the early morning hours. I would see the British acting and deputy ambassador Jane Marriott, who would drive herself from the embassy compound in an SUV, speeding down the hill late at night; I assumed that the intelligence ministry and the Revolutionary Guards knew full well the comings and goings at the Vafadari residence but chose not to intervene. Not, that is, until 2016, when Karan and Afarin were both arrested and sent to Evin Prison, their house ransacked, and their gallery closed. They were finally released in 2018 and I saw them in New York a couple of years later, after they had been cleared of charges (but their art was not returned to them).

Shirin Aliabadi sadly died too young in 2018 from cancer, leaving Farhad, who himself passed away six years later at the age of sixty-one, devastated. Karan, Afarin, Shirin, Farhad, Khosro, and so many others, including my family, often made me feel Iranian to the core, and proud of my countrymen and -women who persevered in an Iran that they loved, but which didn't love them. And often, especially in later years, something would happen that would make me feel like an alien in my own country. I felt at home in religious circles and was not judgmental—my own grandfather had worn the Shia clerical garb and my mother had made pilgrimage to Mecca, after all—but the disdain that some of the die-hard revolutionaries-turned-fascists had for any Iranian not like them made me feel that I couldn't *possibly* be their compatriot.

I had experienced the full brunt of Shia Islam in the winter of 2007 when I went to Yazd and Taft, a village in the province known for its theatrical displays in the town square. Ali Khatami introduced me to his brother-in-law, Hojatoleslam (Shia clerical title one grade below ayatollah) Mohammad Sadoughi, and he took me to Shia mourning ceremonies. These occur every year on Tasua and Ashura—the ninth and the tenth day of the Arabic month of Moharram, when the third Imam, Hossein ibn Ali, the prophet Mohammad's grandson, was massacred in the fields of Karbala by the armies of the ruling Imayyad Caliph Yazid. The ceremonies can be thrilling to watch: grown men weeping for the prophet's grandson lost

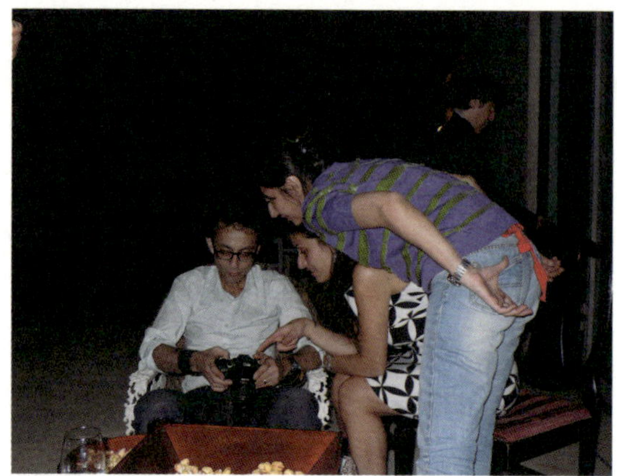

01.

02.

01.
With Farhad Moshiri, Shirin Aliabadi, and Afarin Neyssari at Karan and Afarin's house, Tehran, 2008

02.
With Mohammad Sadoughi (in turban) and guards at the square in Taft, Yazd Province, 2007

thirteen hundred years ago, men—and boys—self-flagellating with chains and whips with varying degrees of enthusiasm, drawing blood in some cases and welts in many others.

In Tehran I had rushed to find a black shirt to wear for Ashura and could only find a polyester one made in China that itched like mad, so I wore a T-shirt underneath, which I realized later was jarring in its whiteness, but then again, not unlike a cleric's shirts worn under a black robe.

I witnessed not only religious fanaticism but religious nationalism too, on the anniversary of the revolution, February 11, when Ali Khatami picked me up from Khosro's house and we drove as close as we could to the marches and rallies celebrating the victory of the revolution. We joined former President Khatami's contingent—he was mobbed as soon as he exited a car, and guards tried to keep supporters (and enemies) from getting too close—but soon the crush of a surging crowd made the situation dangerous and he was whisked away while I, pressed on all sides and starting to feel the pressure too great, pushed my way to a side street with Ali following. While government employees had the day off and were encouraged to attend (the government being the single largest employer in Iran), it was undeniable that there was a sizable contingent of supporters of the Islamic regime in attendance. This was, of course, only a year and a half after Khatami's term and before the Green Movement and subsequent other protest movements, but after Ahmadinejad had proclaimed the Holocaust a myth that needed further research (and wasn't taught in Iran). Ahmadinejad had yet to proclaim that "there are no homosexuals in Iran" during a Q&A after a speech at Columbia University during that year's U.N. General Assembly, which would have come as a surprise to not only homosexuals who were undoubtedly among the crowd of millions, but to those mullahs who have, from time to time, been accused of enjoying same-sex relations, too.

On my trip in 2007, I visited Qom again, the ski resorts in the mountains above Tehran, and Isfahan, and paid a visit to the former president Khatami, who had been given offices in Jamaran, Khomeini's old headquarters in a villa once owned by one of the Shah's ministers. Khatami was guarded by the IRGC (Revolutionary Guards), who had a car parked outside twenty-four hours a day.

I would take taxis and *agence* cars, as car services were known in Iran, around town and to appointments, but a man who worked for Khosro, Ali Akrami—whom we called Ali *Amreekaee* because of his love of all things American—would take me for long rides anywhere I wanted to go on the back of his motorcycle, a ubiquitous 125cc Chinese model assembled domestically. (Iran banned the import or manufacture of anything bigger than a 250cc on the theory that assassins, terrorists, and even ordinary thieves would have an easier escape on larger motorcycles.) It was a good, though terrifying, way to capture life in the capital, amid the gridlocked traffic and reckless driving of many of Tehran's residents.

I also visited Sadegh Kharrazi at his house, along with former reformists who reminisced about the better days before Ahmadinejad sidelined them all, career diplomat or not. I returned to New York with a beard, plenty of material, I thought, and an outline for my book, which I had already titled *The Ayatollah Begs to Differ*, as it just rang true to me, after seeing all the different clerics with different, and often contradictory, opinions.

After my trip to Iran, Chris Blackwell invited Karri and me to Goldeneye for a few days of rest. It was a radical departure from Iran: the beach, endless (and legal) cocktails, Jet Skis, and seeing Chris in good form and wanting, I felt, to make up for the time we had lost. It was now as if we never had a falling-out—not that he would ever admit to being in the wrong. Since I was no longer working with him, I felt oddly more on an equal footing, and I sensed that he felt the same. Friendship with Chris, I realized, could never be complete unless you didn't *need* him. He knew that, consciously or otherwise.

I had rented a car at the Kingston airport and driven across the mountains to Oracabessa on the north coast—this was before the Chinese, expanding their influence in the hemisphere, built a toll highway that cut through mountains—a three-hour-plus drive that I nonetheless enjoyed because of the views and the lush greenery of the rainforest we traversed, and the shacks and roadside food stalls that more often than not had delicious snacks and fresh coconut water for thirsty travelers. One Friday night we drove into town to a bar in a rickety shack where we danced with the locals, some in their sixties and some dancing alone and nursing a beer, relishing the moment. I had always thought Jamaicans were not unlike Iranians—

01.

01.
With Ali "Amreekaee," on the back of his motorcycle, Tehran, 2007

religious, sharp-witted, smart, and willing to break the rules—and this night I felt, after being in Iran and not even once witnessing a public expression of happiness or joy there, a sadness for my compatriots who had only reveled in grief during Moharram, and warm-heartedness for Jamaicans, rich or poor, who tried to make the best of whatever life they were fated to live.

I spent most of the rest of the year writing my book, interrupted only by saying farewell to both Javad Zarif, who was finally forced to resign his post in July, and to Hossein Fereidoun, who was recalled back to Tehran and sidelined from the foreign ministry. I delivered the manuscript in the fall, and Kris Puopolo and I spent a few months massaging it into shape to give readers what we hoped would be a truer image of Iran than what was portrayed in the Western media. Once it was considered a "delivered" manuscript by Kris and Doubleday, I was paid the balance of my advance, without which I worried I would soon not be able to afford to pay the rent on our apartment. *The Ayatollah Begs to Differ*, a collection of stories and observations of my time and travels in Iran, was scheduled for a fall 2008 release.

In the winter of 2007, my aunt Shusha Guppy (née Shamsi Assar), my mother's younger (and only) sister, called me to say she would be in New York in December. I always made time for Shusha, in London or in America. She was a writer, singer-songwriter, and all-around intellectual who had gone to Paris to study as a teenager, then married Nicholas Guppy, art dealer and explorer, and moved to London. As a child, we would visit Shusha and her family whenever we were in London—she had two boys, Darius and Constantine—either at their house in Chelsea or their cottage in Cambridge, and she was a constant in my life from infancy. She had been inspired by my experiences in Iran to finally go back herself after a decades-long absence. She had a wonderful time and loved the Simorgh Hotel, which I'd recommended to her. I could just imagine her making friends with the staff, telling them stories and being the ball of energy that she always was.

We met at a Pain Quotidien on Hudson Street in Greenwich Village near where she was staying—she seemed to have friends everywhere in the world who were happy to host her, except in Iran. She was a little less energetic than usual and coughing a lot, which she put down to a mild cold. A few weeks after she returned to London, my mother called me to say Shusha had lung cancer—although she had never smoked. She deteriorated very quickly, and in the early months of 2008, my mother went to her house every day. At the onset of Norouz, the Persian New Year and the first day of spring, a holiday she and my mother had loved from childhood, she died at home.

Shusha had collected many friends from her decades in artistic and intellectual circles—many after her divorce from Nicholas in the late seventies—including Prince Charles (now king), an admirer of hers (and of Sufi Islam) who twice visited her in her final months in Chelsea. My mother, ordinarily starstruck by the British royals, even having attended the Queen's Garden Party in her younger days, was too heartbroken to even acknowledge she met the future king of England. They'd had a contentious relationship at times—Shusha couldn't understand why or how my mother could stand "just" being a housewife, and not use her talents otherwise—but they loved each other, and it was especially difficult for my mother to have her younger sister die literally in her arms.

My brother and I went to London for the funeral, attending it with my mother (my father left for Tehran that day, for a preplanned trip) and my sister, and our cousins Darius and Constantine. Darius lived in South Africa then, after a sojourn in Ireland, where he had gone after being released from prison. (Darius was convicted of staging a jewelry heist in New York—he was a gem dealer at the time—to collect insurance from the London insurer Lloyds, an episode that caused great distress for Shusha, who was passionate about her children and believed they could do no wrong.)

Darius had been a classmate of Boris Johnson at Eton, and they remained friends long afterward, a fact the British tabloids liked to point out when Johnson became prime minister. From his schooldays Darius was also very close to Charles (Earl) Spencer, Princess Diana's brother, which made him a target of the paparazzi, and the media in general, after his trial. Earl Spencer had suggested he go to Ireland after his release from prison to avoid the media glare, and he then followed Spencer to South Africa. It was good to catch up with Darius, whom I had seen only once in California after he graduated from Oxford and was touring America in the early eighties, and to see his brother, too. I stayed in touch with Darius after Shusha's death, and one year he sent me photographs he had taken of our grandfather's grave, at a shrine south of Tehran, on one of his frequent trips there.

After my aunt's funeral, my brother and I stayed for a few days in London with my mother, who was inconsolable. One morning, she said she couldn't breathe properly, and that her chest hurt. We called an ambulance and our sister, Marjan, who lived nearby and was a doctor herself, and went to the hospital with my mother semiconscious. Doctors said that she'd had a heart attack—she was, quite literally, *heartbroken*. She thankfully survived and came home later, and we returned to the States.

Later that year in the summer and quite out of the blue, an editor at *GQ* magazine, Dan Fierman, asked me if I would be interested in profiling the Jewish community in Iran, having discovered their existence—a surprising fact to the editors at the magazine. I said yes, of course, and prepared to fly to Tehran on the magazine's dime. I called Ali Khatami, now a civilian businessman again but managing former president Khatami's office and still very connected to the various centers of power. He arranged for me to meet Morris Motamed, the former Jewish MP in the Iranian parliament and someone with tight connections to the Tehran Jewish Committee. Motamed and I chatted for about an hour, after which he invited me to Shabbat services at the Yousefabad Synagogue the following Friday and told me to go and visit.

Motamed also told me to say a fond hello to Khatami, whom he praised as a great president. (Motamed had, incidentally, publicly denounced Ahmadinejad's Holocaust denial when he served in parliament.) I went to synagogue for Orthodox services, visited the hospital, and met with members at the offices of the Tehran Jewish Committee. I saw several other prominent Iranian Jews, some of whom had homes in Los Angeles but still liked to spend time in Iran. The one common thread I found was that Iranian Jews, some of whose families had not just decades or centuries but millennia of history in the land, loved the country despite the Shia theocracy and its anti-Israel stance. At synagogue, I sat next to an older man who somehow knew I didn't belong but also welcomed me. He gestured to his prayer book. "See, we pray in a language we don't understand, and have to read the Farsi translation. You do the same with your prayers." He was, of course, correct, and I wondered if my mother, who performed *namaz*, or ritual prayer, all her life, knew what it was she was reciting in Arabic three times a day.

01.

02.

01.
My mother (left) and Shusha (right), in their youth in Tehran, 1940s

02.
Detail from outside wall of Yousefabad Synagogue, Tehran, 2008

The relatively short visit to Tehran over, I returned to New York to write my piece for *GQ*. The contract had asked for 5,000 words, but I eventually handed in 13,000. While Dan said he loved it, I also knew it would never be published at that length in the magazine. We spent the fall of 2008 editing it down to more reasonable length, while I was engaged in promoting the release of *The Ayatollah Begs to Differ*. Nicole Dewey, the publicist at Doubleday, booked me on *The Daily Show* with Jon Stewart, by then an important promoter of books. Guests on the show were told to not try to be funny—that was Jon's job—and I wasn't, I'm sure. But I enjoyed being interviewed by him and found him to be genuinely interested. He came into the greenroom before the show and chatted for quite a while, which I appreciated. He did the same a few years later when I was on the show again for my third book, and he remembered who I was. My appearance on Jon Stewart spiked sales of the book to such a degree that it shot up the Amazon rankings—all the way to number eight on the overall sales—and landed it on the *New York Times* bestseller list, a sort of holy grail for writers, who from then on would be referred to in any publicity materials as "*New York Times* bestselling author . . ."

By the end of the year the *GQ* edit was done, but I still hadn't been given a publication date. In the meantime, I was busy with the release of my book, being interviewed by radio and television, and accepting engagements through a speaker's bureau, the Lavin Agency. After much back-and-forth and editing, and after Dan and Michael Hainey were very happy with the *GQ* piece, Dan emailed me at the end of January and said Jim Nelson, editor in chief of *GQ* at the time, had decided to not publish it, though they'd paid me in full. His reasons weren't entirely clear to me, but Dan had the sense that Jim had been looking for something wilder, more controversial, which the Jews of Iran simply weren't and, more important, didn't *want* to be. And so, like my *Rolling Stone* piece, I kept it and later included another version as a chapter in my second book, *The Ayatollahs' Democracy*, written in the aftermath of the Green Movement, the disputed presidential election of 2009, and the associated protests.

In 2008, Peter Brant, the owner of *Interview* magazine, hired Glenn O'Brien (his second term there, after being at the earlier *Andy Warhol's Interview*) and his old friend and colleague Fabien Baron as co–editorialdirectors of the magazine. Glenn put me and Davitt on the masthead as "contributing editors." I was fortunate to be able write three pieces and interviews for the magazine, interviewing Gwen Ifill, then the PBS *NewsHour* anchor and author of a new book; James Toback, who always has interesting stories to tell; and Chris Blackwell, who, as an extremely private person, nonetheless agreed to be interviewed by me and, I'm happy to say, loved the story. Sadly, by the summer of 2009, Fabien and Glenn had a major falling-out over editorial content, and Glenn left the magazine. Davitt and I both asked that our names then be removed from the masthead, and I missed the opportunity to bring Iran to *Interview*, or *Interview* to Iran.

DOWN WITH
THE U.S. A

Chapter 37

NBC News

In 2009, Nisid Hajari, the foreign editor at *Newsweek*, asked me if I would be interested in a cover story on Iran, in a special issue in anticipation of the presidential election that June as Ahmadinejad vied for a second term. I jumped at the chance. Just before I left for Tehran, an NBC News reporter, Robert Windrem, introduced me to a producer colleague, Richard Greenberg, who had read my book and wanted to go to Iran. I knew Bob Windrem from 2006, when I had consulted for NBC regarding an interview it had secured for Brian Williams with President Ahmadinejad during the U.N. General Assembly. Rich Greenberg and I met at a steakhouse in midtown Manhattan.

Greenberg was looking to produce an Iran special for NBC to be aired on *Dateline*, anchored by Ann Curry. (*Dateline* was then still a general-interest program, like *60 Minutes*, but not nearly as popular among foreign policy or politics junkies.) He wanted Ann and a crew to spend two or three weeks in Iran and come back with a program that would show Americans

01.

01.
Brian Williams, NBC News anchor, interviews Ahmadinejad in New York. Standing with the author is then Iranian ambassador to the U.N. Mohammad Javad Zarif

what Iran was really like, behind its president's outrageous comments and belligerent speeches at the U.N. Iran's nuclear issue, too, was no closer to being resolved than when Khatami had left office four years prior.

Rich wanted to know if I'd be willing to go with the network to Iran as a guide and consultant, and I naturally said yes. I suggested that the first step should be for Ann Curry and him to meet with Iran's ambassador to the U.N., Mohammad Khazaee, who had replaced Zarif and was a compromise choice for Ahmadinejad and Ayatollah Khamenei. Khazaee had been Iran's representative at the World Bank in Washington, was familiar with the United States and American culture, and could smooth the way for NBC to secure visas and press credentials for the trip. The press officer at Iran's mission, Mohammad Mohammadi, was sure to be supportive, too. I set up a meeting with the ambassador and Mohammadi, and Ann charmed them both. Before long, we had approvals from Tehran, and plans were made for a trip to begin in mid-May for the presidential campaign season, limited by law to thirty days.

Meanwhile, I left for Tehran in the third week of April and traveled to Isfahan, Yazd, and Qom for *Newsweek*. Fareed Zakaria, who had recommended me to Nisid Hajari at the magazine, was going to write an article for the issue, and Maziar Bahari, *Newsweek*'s correspondent in Iran, was assigned to interview former president Khatami. (He told me later that at the Ministry of Culture and Islamic Guidance, where press credentials are issued, he was asked why *Newsweek* was sending *me* to write the cover story while he was the Tehran bureau chief. He told them they should ask *me* why.) Upon return to New York, I hurriedly wrote my piece and submitted it; Nisid and I worked on edits, and I left with the NBC team for Tehran in mid-May, before the June 1 issue of *Newsweek* hit the stands.

While in Iran for NBC at the end of May, I was emailed the image of the cover and was horrified. The editors could not have picked a less complimentary photo of Ahmadinejad, and with me inside Iran, I worried that I'd be called into the culture ministry soon enough. In fact, the entire issue, including Fareed's piece, was much kinder overall to Iran than most Western media coverage. I assume the officials at the ministry were too busy with the upcoming election to notice or to care, and I never was called. My story was called "Tehran or Bust," and I was quite proud of how it turned out, showing a side of Iran most Americans would not ordinarily see, sort

01.

POLITICS | SOCIETY | TRAVEL

BY HOOMAN MAJD
PHOTOGRAPHS BY KARIM BEN KHELIFA

TEHRAN OR BUST

A journey through the heart of Iran.

ON A WARM FRIDAY IN LATE APRIL, AS I RODE back from prayers at the Molla Esmail Mosque in the dusty central Iranian town of Yazd, my companion was a loaded Kalashnikov rifle. The weapon belonged to the man who had just led the Friday prayers, as he does every week: Hojjatoleslam Mohammad Sadoughi, a kindly 60-year-old cleric who normally uses a cane but leans on the rifle when he delivers sermons. Sadoughi is the official representative of the Supreme Leader of the Islamic Revolution for Yazd province. This means that, in addition to leading Friday prayers, he plays host to Ayatollah Ali Khamenei whenever the Iranian leader visits Yazd, where his mother's family is from. This afternoon I too would be a guest at Sadoughi's sumptuously restored historic home in the ancient city center. While I have spent most of my life in the West, Yazd is my hometown as well, and whenever I visit Iran I return there to see relatives, one of whom (through marriage) is Sadoughi's wife, Maryam. Mrs. Sadoughi is a highly educated and erudite woman who, notwithstanding her black chador and obvious Islamic piety, holds reformist—even liberal—political views and is a strong supporter of her brother, the former president of Iran, Mohammad Khatami. So too is her husband, owner of the Kalashnikov that lay next to me.

The layers of contradiction that make up the modern Islamic Republic of Iran are both pervasive and confounding, and not any less so in Yazd. Set amid the blistering deserts of central Iran, the city is home to the kind of fierce religiosity bred in Islam's starker landscapes, and many of its sons were sacrificed to the bloody war with Iraq. Yet it is also a capital of pre-Islamic Persia, and is well known for its Zoroastrian temples and grave sites. (At one fire temple, priests continue to tend a flame that they claim has burned for more than 500 years.) It is the only city in the world that can boast two native sons, Khatami and Moshe Katsav, who simultaneously served as presidents of Iran and Israel. Even the mosque where Sadoughi leads prayers is named after a Jewish convert.

The sermon that Sadoughi had delivered that morning had been equally impossible to categorize. He defended the inflammatory speech that President Mahmoud Ahmadinejad had delivered earlier that week at a United Nations conference on racism, chiding Western nations who "allegedly are ... defenders of free speech" for walking out. But he also criticized the government, in this case for failing to ensure that Iranian pilgrims traveling to Iraq were adequately protected, a large number of them having been killed the day before in a suicide bombing near Baghdad. And he conceded that the United States had elected a new president who had promised to change its relationship with Iran. He declared that Iranians were waiting to witness real deeds from Washington, not mere rhetoric. But at the end of his 30-minute sermon, unlike past Friday prayers and prayers that same day in Tehran, there were no chants of "Death to America" or "Death to Israel," not even halfhearted ones. Later that night in his office he repeated, wistfully, the same sentiment—that words alone were not enough from the United States, not for Iranians, who are master rhetoricians, and who well understand the many uses to which they can be put.

Anyone reading a translation of Sadoughi's sermon would quite likely miss the sincerity of his appeal, the doors it carefully left open. After 30 years of enmity, the United States and Iran have almost entirely lost the capacity to interpret such subtle signals. Very few serving U.S. officials have met their Iranian counterparts, and almost none have ever visited Iran. Yet such expertise is more critical than ever, as the administration of President Barack Obama prepares to embark on what could be months of difficult negotiations aimed at halting Iran's nuclear-enrichment program.

After Obama videotaped a Persian New Year's message for the Iranian people, reiterating his offer of unconditional talks, most Western commentators interpreted Khamenei's lengthy and defiant response as a slap in the face. But what would have been most significant to any Iranian listening was a passage at the very end of the speech, when Khamenei said, "If you change, our behavior will also change." Iran's supreme authority had never before

4000 B.C.
Tribes settle in isolated villages protected by mountains or desert, in territory that is now modern Iran.

IRAN AND AMERICA: AN INTERSECTING HISTORY

NEWSWEEK.COM N 29

02.

01.
Newsweek cover story

02.
Newsweek cover article

of a companion to my book, and complementary to what I thought NBC wanted to accomplish.

Adding the piece to others I had written for major media outlets (*Newsweek* wasn't then the shell of itself it is today), I felt my journalism career was well on its way. Later in the summer I wrote for *The New Republic* about the 2009 election that gave Ahmadinejad another four years in office, which to me seemed if not outright fraudulent, at least extremely suspicious. I had a good time in Iran with Ann and the NBC crew, and I found television work—both being on camera and coming up with stories—to be fascinating and enjoyable. We had plenty of time to witness and document not just the political environment, but the excitement of the youth yearning for what appeared to be change on the horizon. I hoped that television news might be another component in my career as a journalist and author.

It was a fortuitous time for NBC to be in Iran, as the campaigns for the presidential elections were in full swing when Ann Curry arrived for her first-ever trip to the country. The mood, especially among the young, was festive. Mir Hossein Mousavi, the main challenger to Ahmadinejad, was a reformist who, unusually and in a first for Iran, campaigned with his wife. More important, he sought the support of Khatami, who not only endorsed him but joined him at rallies, one of which, in an overpacked Tehran stadium, we attended with the NBC camera crew. Campaign posters even had Mousavi and Khatami pictured side by side, in an unsubtle hint to voters that a vote for Mousavi was a vote for a return to the Khatami era—one of relative openness, more liberal social attitudes, and better relations with the West. The youth, and especially in the urban areas, were excited.

We traveled to Isfahan and shot footage there, to the mountains north of Tehran, and all around the city. Ann interviewed Khatami, and though Mousavi was too busy, Mousavi's wife, Zahra Rahnavard, was willing to sit down with Ann at their campaign offices. It remains the only interview she has ever given to Western media, and as of writing, she has remained under strict house arrest with her husband since 2011. The through line in all the interviews at the time was "hope"; whether by politicians, activists, or young people on the streets and at rallies. The excitement Iranians felt for

01.

02.

01.
Ann Curry interviewing the author in the gardens of the Abassi Hotel in Isfahan, May 2009

02.
With Richard Greenberg of NBC News, Tehran, 2009

the future, at least in the urban areas, especially impressed not just Ann, for whom Iran was new, but me as well. That that hope was soon dashed, rather violently, was distressing to me and countless of my fellow Iranians, inside and outside Iran.

Chapter 38

The Aftermath

The Iranian presidential election of 2009 was held on June 12, but NBC and I were long gone. The aftermath, with massive, millions-strong demonstrations not seen since the revolution thirty years prior, was chaotic, with Mousavi claiming he was robbed and insisting on a new election. In less than twenty-four hours, Ahmadinejad, having received more than 60 percent of the ballots cast, was announced the winner, though many doubted the veracity of the result. Millions, mostly in Tehran, took to the streets demanding, *Where is my vote?* It was a dubious result at best, in a country with such a huge percentage of the population under twenty-five. I was soon busy with requests for interviews and writing a second book focused on what had happened in 2009 in Iran. The rest of the year was a whirlwind. I was suddenly seen as an Iran "expert," and though I pointed out that no "expert" had predicted the outcome of the 2009 election, and certainly not its aftermath, I did feel a sense of duty in trying to explain Iran to a curious

American audience. I appeared on *Real Time with Bill Maher* on HBO, wearing a pair of green Persian shoes in support of the Green Movement, which apparently caused some inside Iran to decide I was a troublemaker.

In the fall that year, I was ecstatic and terrified when Karri told me she was pregnant, and that I would become a father in 2010 at the geriatric age of fifty-three. Karri had always wanted a child, and in our getting back together after a brief separation nine years earlier, I had accepted that a child would be in our future. Karri had gone along with all my upheavals in life and work, and now with some stability she and I both felt responsible enough to become parents. My happiness outweighed any terror soon enough, although I had a nagging doubt about how I was going to support my child if my career(s) didn't work out—doubt being a constant, it seems, in my life post-revolution. Karri was happy—perhaps happier than she had been in a long time—and that gave me some comfort. But now, with the frenzy surrounding the election fading, I wasn't sure I could continue to successfully pitch as many stories or be invited to give talks and paid speeches with the same regularity. I tried to remain optimistic, and reflected on the fact that somehow I had managed to survive (and even occasionally thrive) over the years, and would do so again.

At this time, one of my mother's dearest relatives, Shamsi Davis, née Ashraf Naini (it was not uncommon for women, especially, to use a different name from their legal one—my mother was born Mansoureh but inexplicably was called Badri from birth), had been diagnosed with pancreatic cancer, and was undergoing treatment. We children had always called her "Cousin Shamsi," ever since she was sent to London from Tehran to study and baby-sat for me and my brother. After we left London for San Francisco, Shamsi stayed and became an au pair at the English conductor Colin Davis's house; they fell in love and married in 1964. With their five children, they lived and loved together for more than four decades, but I had little contact with them in the years before I left the music business. Karri and I, however, saw them with my parents soon after my sister's wedding, and we then would get together every time we'd go to London, or when Colin came to New York as a guest conductor of the Metropolitan Opera or the Philharmonic, and we sat in the conductor's box with Shamsi.

She would tell Karri tales of my childhood, laughing at what she said was my impertinence. When she died in 2010, I was doubly sad that she didn't live to see my only child. My mother was again heartbroken, losing another close relative, and I think the only thing that gave her solace later in the summer was the birth of my son.

In the spring of 2010, before our son was born and when Green Movement protests had died down in Iran, the government planned a "nuclear energy summit." *Foreign Policy* magazine was interested in me going to Tehran to cover what the mood was like, and what, if any, changes had occurred since the uprising in 2009. Blake Hounsell, the editor, was keen on a story from "on the ground" rather than analysis from afar, as most coverage of Iran had been in the aftermath of journalists being expelled. I asked the Iranian Mission to the U.N. if I could have a press pass ready in Tehran when I arrived in May. My father, however, was dead set against me going. He said that with all my appearances on television in support of the Green Movement (including the appearance with Bill Maher) I would be in danger of being arrested. I tried to assuage his concerns by saying that if the Iranians granted me a press pass, it would be okay. "You can't trust them!" he cried. "Your book alone is a mark against you and is something they've probably read and translated."

The Iranian ambassador to the U.N., however, assured me that I would be fine, and I decided to ignore my father's advice, spending ten days in the capital before returning to New York to finish my piece. I wasn't questioned or stopped, despite my press pass not being ready when I arrived and having to jump through bureaucratic hurdles to secure one. Then I focused my attention on the last days of Karri's pregnancy and getting married (so our child would have married parents, crucial for Karri and him to receive Iranian citizenship), both in the States and in Iran, which simply meant having a Shia mullah marry us in a mosque in New York and have the certificate sent to the interior ministry in Iran, which would then issue Karri an identification number. When the mullah asked Karri if she accepted Islam, she wanted to say she accepted *all* faiths, she told me, but held her tongue. Born a Protestant Christian in rural Wisconsin, she nonetheless always had curiosity and respect for all religions, and Islam was simply an addition to her earlier interests in Buddhism and Hinduism. She was fine with it if Shia Islam wanted to consider her a Muslim.

Our son was due to be born on my birthday, July 5, but was late and emerged into the world on July 17. We had already decided to name him Khashayar—Persian for Xerxes—but give him two other English names, Keith and Jinkins, from Karri's family. For the rest of the summer, I was preoccupied with him, with family and friends, and with Skype calls with my parents in London. With him in my arms, I didn't feel fifty-three years old, and it actually reminded me of how I felt with my sister, Marjan, when she was a baby and I was already a teenager. But I realized happily that Khash, as we call him, was going to play a prominent role—physically present with me or not—for the rest of my life, and I couldn't imagine ever loving or having loved anything or anyone more.

My second book, *The Ayatollahs' Democracy*, was due for publication in September, but having received only a small advance for it, I was already thinking of my next book and how I was going to support my family. By this time, I had switched agents and was with Andrew Wylie at the Wylie Agency. He had already sold my first book in the U.K. and Poland, and with the second book had secured Swedish, Polish, Dutch, and U.K. deals. I was with Helen Conford at Penguin UK for both books (and later a third) but didn't know the European publishers. The Swedish and Dutch publishers wanted me to visit Stockholm and Amsterdam to promote their editions, and in the fall of 2010, I went on a short trip to London, Stockholm, and Amsterdam, where they had arranged interviews and appearances, and happily, took me to their favorite restaurants, too.

I had an idea to do a third (and I promised myself *last*) book on Iran, now that I had a child: What if I proposed to move my family to Tehran for a year, chronicling what it was really like to live there? Still finding myself both attracted to and alienated from Iran, I thought I might finally be free of my decades-long obsession, and Karri, who had first told me to go to Iran before I even had a passport, would experience Iran and Iranians and understand my culture even better than she already did. Andrew was keen on the idea, and we put together a proposal that Kris Puopolo, my editor at Doubleday for my first book, loved and agreed to sign up. Sonny Mehta, she said, was keen too, and that sealed the deal for me.

Before heading to Iran, though, NBC News asked if I would accompany Richard Engel, the chief foreign correspondent, on a trip to Tehran, where he would report on the nuclear issue and visit the Tehran Research Reactor, supplied by the United States in 1967 to produce medical isotopes. So, in January 2011, I flew to Tehran with Richard and was almost immediately summoned to the culture ministry to be "interviewed." The deputy minister for foreign media gave his office over to intelligence agents who proceeded to grill me on virtually everything I had written, asking me if I still believed that Ahmadinejad had lost the election of 2009. They had stacks of documents—mostly my articles and books translated into Farsi—but had really wanted to scare me more than anything else, I thought. I told them at the end of the interrogation that I intended to return to Iran in a few weeks with my family to live there for a while, and I hoped we would be okay. Their response was yes, but only as long as I didn't write anything for the foreign media. I didn't tell them I'd be writing a book. I left Iran with Richard after only a few days, and once back in New York I started to make the arrangements for our lengthy stay.

We were living in a loft in Greenpoint, Brooklyn, having moved there in 2009 after some twenty years in Manhattan, and we were lucky to find a neighbor to sublet it while we were gone. I asked Khosro if we could stay at his house while we looked for a place of our own, and asked my cousin Ali if he could ask around about furnished apartments for us to rent for a few months to a year.

During the ten months or so we spent in Iran, I felt, much as I did before, both at home *and* alienated from my homeland. I sensed that I had very little in common with most of the people, and certainly nothing in common with the uncompromisingly religious ones. Even for secular Iranians, after decades under a strict Islamic regime their outlook on life was simply different. It is of course a folly to ignore the Shia religious culture of Iran—the Pahlavis learned that lesson the hard way—and as the religion fully encompassed political life, I knew it could never be a true home for me. I couldn't be sure what life was like for ordinary Iranians—the millions who fought traffic every day to get to their jobs and struggled to make ends meet with low wages and high inflation. It seemed to me that unless you were independently wealthy, were in trade (such as in the bazaar or in import/export), or had connections to the government, just getting by was increasingly difficult. My son, of course, was oblivious to all that, but Karri, despite being fascinated and impressed by many things in and about Iran, was equally aware of these issues. She liked the way people shopped locally for food, and the way family was of such importance, but couldn't relate to the dress and behavior codes that overwhelmingly targeted and punished women.

My father's extended family—all first cousins of the previous president—were a source of comfort to me. In typical Yazdi fashion, they were always inviting us to lunches and dinners at their homes, and often on weekends there would be big family gatherings at the country villas of cousins who had getaways (from the smog and traffic of Tehran) in the mountains. I wondered what emotional compromises they had to make to live in Iran—even the onetime revolutionaries among them—and whether I would have been happy to make similar compromises in order to work and live. I knew my father had made those compromises and had lived with them. But despite feeling alienated from what should have been home to me—the hospital I was born in still stood—I also felt some comfort in waking up in Iran every day, going to the bakery to buy freshly made flatbreads, *sangak* and *barbari*, baked as I waited in line, and taking Khash in his stroller to the market for fruits and vegetables while Karri did her yoga practice at home. Chatting with my favored produce seller, he would steer me to the freshest and best, and when I caught him hiding a lit cigarette once during Ramadan, he looked at me and said, "*Een yeki ra nemeetoonam tark konam!*"; or, "*This one I can't quit!*" I also mused about walking the streets that my parents and their parents once did as if it were the most ordinary thing in the world to do, while for me it was both novel and somewhat exotic.

In the time we spent in Iran we had, perhaps unwisely, attended embassy parties with many Westerners in attendance, even becoming friends with the Polish ambassador, Juliusz Gojlo, and his wife, and met the Canadian chargé Dennis Horak and his wife, Sally, with whom Karri started spending some time. We had attended multiple parties at Karan and Afarin's house where the guest list on any given night included Western diplomats, dancing, and free-flowing alcohol; the parties contributed to their being incarcerated at Evin Prison a few years later. Given the tension with the West over the nuclear program, and my previous run-ins with the intelligence services, I felt that staying in Iran the full year might not be wise. Having planned to go home to the States for Christmas anyway, we decided not to return to Iran in January and instead I would focus on writing my book.

In October 2012, before the publication date of my third book, *The Ministry of Guidance Invites You to Not Stay*, on our life in Iran, my father passed away at the age of eighty-four from lung cancer, after some sixty years of smoking and only a few years after he quit the habit. He spent his last days in Charing Cross Hospital with his sons visiting from America and his wife and daughter by his side every day. He was very weak and didn't speak much but would ask me every day that I visited him how Khash was, and what kind of mischief he was up to. "*Khash ra kay meyaree*," he'd say, "When will you bring Khash?" (My father also loved Khash's nickname—in the Yazd and Ardakan dialect it meant "happy" and "good.") After returning to New York from a visit a week earlier, my brother and I had booked flights to London with our families, knowing that it might be the last time my father would see his grandchildren, and I had promised I would bring Khashayar to see him the next time. But sitting at home, packed and ready to leave for the airport, my sister called and said our father had passed away peacefully, holding my mother's hand, his wife of almost sixty years. We flew that night to London.

Chapter 39

The Ann Curry Unit

The Iranian presidential election of 2013 was held in the late spring, and this time Hassan Rouhani won in what appeared to be an entirely legitimate victory over his conservative rivals, with no interference from any quarter. I was flown by Al Jazeera to Doha, Qatar, to cover the election from their headquarters.

Although Rouhani was not known to be a strict reformist, his alliances were on the reform and left side of the political spectrum, and he was considered a pragmatist in the Rafsanjani mold. Khatami endorsed him, a crucial factor in getting the liberals to come out and vote, which they did in large numbers after essentially boycotting parliamentary elections earlier. I was reminded of Hossein Fereidoun, his brother, telling me how Khatami should have promoted him in 2005, and thought how happy he must now be.

Tom Bettag at NBC News was a veteran television producer working with Ann Curry, who had been given her own "unit" after being unceremoniously taken off *The Today Show*, mainly because Matt Lauer simply didn't want her as a co-anchor. Tom, an extremely smart, highly experienced, and savvy journalist, asked me if I thought NBC could interview Rouhani in Tehran *before* he attended the U.N. General Assembly, which was a great idea that somehow no other journalist had thought of. Rouhani had promised in his campaign that he would resolve the nuclear crisis, appointing U.S.-educated Javad Zarif as foreign minister and authorizing him to have direct talks with his U.S. counterpart. An interview with a new president who was radically different from his predecessor would be a real scoop, Tom argued.

I spoke about it to Ambassador Khazaee, and then emailed Zarif, prodding them for an answer as to whether we could go to Iran. I also called Hossein Fereidoun in Tehran, Rouhani's closest advisor. My pitch was that with a new approach to foreign relations, why not telegraph to the international community—before going to New York and having the opportunity to meet other world leaders—what Iran's foreign policy would look like under his administration? Although he had been the chief nuclear negotiator under President Khatami, Rouhani wasn't well known in the West and had up till then never given an interview to the Western media. But I knew from working with her and from our deepening friendship since our first time in Iran together, that Ann would do a great job, and that he would like her. Her style of interviewing is intentionally unconfrontational and polite, yet she manages to elicit responses to her questions, sometimes pressing, that are revealing. (Rouhani liked Ann and the interview so much that he requested her again the following year.)

My pitch worked, and we prepared to fly to Tehran. David Verdi, senior vice president of worldwide news gathering and therefore responsible for NBC's Tehran bureau, came on the trip, and we flew on Emirates Airlines, through Dubai, to Tehran's Imam Khomeini International Airport, arriving late in the evening. The U.S. passport holders were shown to a room to have their fingerprints taken (at that time, because Iranians were fingerprinted entering the United States, Iran reciprocated with Americans), and I, having passed immigration with my Iranian papers, waited for them. After a few minutes, I thought I heard my name over the loudspeaker, barely audible at immigration, but clear downstairs in the baggage claim area. A harried man in a gray suit and white shirt ran up to me and said, "Are you Mr. Majd? We've been calling you; follow me." He led me to an office next to the room where the NBC team was being fingerprinted and asked for my passport. He scribbled something on a receipt and handed it to me. "You will go to that office in two weeks," he said. "But we're here to interview the president and leave the next day," I replied. "I have to have my passport back so I can leave the country." In the meantime, I was told on the phone by an NBC employee in Tehran that the hotel we were to stay in wouldn't give me a room, as the culture ministry, responsible for press credentials, wouldn't authorize it.

Ann Curry and David Verdi emerged from the fingerprinting room, and I told them that we had a serious problem. The door to the office where I had been taken was open, and so Verdi went in and asked if the man, presumably an intelligence agent, would return my passport so that we could do what we came to do, namely interview the president *at his request*. The agent replied that it was out of his hands and that that was not possible. David suggested that in that case, he should at least let me get back on the Emirates flight that was due to return to Dubai in a few hours with my U.S. passport, to which the man responded that I was not allowed to leave the country until I went to the office whose address he had written down on the receipt. David told him we—the NBC team—were therefore not going to leave the airport until my issue was sorted out.

I called Ali Khatami and told him what was happening, and he told me to immediately call Majid Takht-Ravanchi, who had been appointed deputy foreign minister and was in Tehran while Zarif had already left for New York. I knew him, a former high-level diplomat in the Khatami administration and a colleague of Sadegh Kharrazi. Ravanchi told me to leave the airport and the new administration would fix everything the next morning, as it was getting to be late at night. I told him NBC didn't want to leave the airport unless it was resolved, and he begged me to make sure they didn't cause an international incident just as a new president had been sworn into office. So I called Khosro, who said he'd be happy for me to spend the night, but he sounded worried. David Verdi, on the other hand, didn't want me separated from the NBC team and wanted to send one of their crew members with me so that I wouldn't be alone. I told him I couldn't ask my friend to put up *two* people for the night, so he finally relented, and the NBC contingent picked up their equipment, which by now was piled up high on the side of the silent baggage carousel, and left in hired vans.

I took a taxi to Khosro's house and told him I was quite confident that things would be worked out in the morning. He remained skeptical and said that someone must really want to get me—Rouhani and Khatami be damned. He reminded me that the last time I was in Tehran with Ann and NBC, just two months prior for Rouhani's inauguration, NBC had pulled me out of the country when I started receiving anonymous threatening phone calls, asking me what I was doing in Iran, and telling me that I wasn't welcome there.

We went to bed, and when I was having coffee in the morning, Hossein Fereidoun called me on my Iranian cell and told me someone would contact me shortly. True to his word, my phone rang from an unknown number, which in Iran was possible only for top government officials or the intelligence apparatus. "Mr. Majd?" "*Baleh*," I replied. "Do you know the Esteghlal Hotel?" I replied that I did—it was the old Hilton. "Go there to the lobby at nine a.m. the day after tomorrow, and I will meet you there with your passport." I asked how I should know him, and he replied, "I will find you." A few minutes later, I received a call from the head of the foreign correspondents' division at the culture ministry, a Mr. Shiravi, asking me what the problem was. "The problem is that the hotel won't give me a room because you won't authorize it," I replied. Ironically, the hotel the ministry had assigned us was named Evin because that is the district where it *and* the notorious prison are located. While it occurred to me that no one would ever complain about being *refused* entry into a place called Evin, I told Shiravi that I needed to be there to do my job and that the ministry needed to fax over an approval for me to get a room. He replied that he would make sure that would happen—undoubtedly after receiving a stern message from the president's office—and that I was free to go there right away. I thanked Khosro and said goodbye, taking my suitcase in a car service uptown to the hotel.

Ahead of the appointed time, I took a cab to the Esteghlal and sat on a sofa in the lobby facing the entrance. A few minutes later a young man in a gray suit, white shirt, and closely cropped beard approached me. "Mr.

Majd," he said matter-of-factly. He took out an envelope from his jacket pocket and handed it to me. "Please open it," he said, "and look at every page." I took my passport out of the envelope and started flipping through its blank pages. "Are there any marks?" he asked. "No," I replied, "but after we interview the president, we're leaving Tehran. There won't be any issues at the airport, will there?" "No," he said, and turned around and left. Before everything was fully computerized in Iran, a small mark, a code, in the back of one's passport would signal extra scrutiny or even an exit refusal. I imagine that the agent thought I still believed that might be a way for them to stop me, or at least alert the airport immigration officers.

I returned to the hotel and informed the team, with Ann, Tom, and David *very* happy to hear that I had my passport and was cleared to leave with them, and we could proceed stress-free to the presidential palace for the interview that afternoon. It went well, Rouhani seemed happy, and NBC was ecstatic. It received much attention in the States, the White House even asking for a copy of the entire interview. The Rouhani administration was seen as potentially being the key, after more than three decades of mutual animosity, to a breakthrough in relations with the USA. The interview garnered much praise, too, mainly for Ann; it also got nominated for an Emmy (losing, not surprisingly, to a *60 Minutes* segment), which ended up being my one television award credit as producer. I now had all three entertainment industries on my resumé: music, film, and television. But no real, stable career.

Chapter 40

Nuclear Talks Begin

In his interview with Ann Curry, President Rouhani had prognosticated a new day in nuclear negotiations. Zarif and his team were authorized to talk directly with their counterparts, and during the U.N. meetings, Zarif met with John Kerry, agreeing on a timetable to have P5+1 meetings (the five permanent members of the U.N. Security Council plus Germany) at the ministerial level to negotiate an agreement that could result in a triumph of diplomacy over conflict—what both the Obama and Rouhani administrations desired. The first meeting would be in Geneva on October 15. NBC wasn't the only network interested in the talks: most Western and indeed Eastern media wanted to be present to witness Kerry and Zarif huddled together to avoid a crisis—or even war—over Iran's nuclear program.

Ann Curry and Tom Bettag wanted not only to cover the talks but to produce a documentary on what they believed was a turning point in U.S.-Iranian relations. They received approvals from the network brass and in

October we flew to Geneva to stay at the Intercontinental Hotel, where the negotiations would be held. Once there, I contacted Susan Morrison at *The New Yorker*, for whom I had written for Talk of the Town, asking if the magazine would be interested in dispatches from the front, so to speak, as it was the first time that an Iranian minister would negotiate a sensitive issue directly with his American counterpart. Over the next few rounds of talks I wrote a couple of dispatches about the mood at the talks, while the content of the negotiations was reported extensively by the international media. We received access to Zarif and his team, including being allowed to film them in his suite while they strategized, but while Ann tried to get Wendy Sherman, John Kerry's deputy in the talks, to give her an interview, at first she was unsuccessful. She told me she thought we were being ignored by the Americans, ironically, because of the evident closeness we had with the Iranians.

The issue was more complicated than that, although I didn't doubt that there were people in the U.S. negotiating team who might have been annoyed at our noticeable and easy access to the Iranians. Ann was eventually able to talk to Sherman in later rounds of talks, and the mood was still quite optimistic. When we got back to New York, NBC News offered me a one-year contract as a paid contributor, and I was happy to have a steady monthly income, officially on the Ann Curry Unit budget.

I had become quite close with Ann, who I admired and respected after seeing her work. I thought her journalistic integrity was second to none, and besides, she was fun to hang out with. On my first trip to Iran with her and Rich Greenberg, we stayed in an all-suite hotel, and one night, through contacts, I arranged for a bottle of whiskey to be delivered to the three-bedroom suite I shared with the cameramen. I offered a drink to everyone, and Rich, nervous as the representative of a major U.S. network and not wanting to break the law, refused. Ann joined me and David Lom for a few shots, thoroughly enjoying the moment. As time went on, we became closer still, and as a family spent time with her and her husband, Brian Ross. She remains a great friend today.

For the November talks I asked Zarif if, for the purposes of the NBC documentary, I could fly with the Iranians, with a camera, from Rome—where Zarif was making a stop—to Geneva. (For political reasons he couldn't allow any of the NBC *Americans* on an Iranian government jet.) He said that would be fine with him, but NBC had to get clearance from its legal department due to issues with a U.S. citizen (as far as the United States was concerned) aboard an Iranian government aircraft. I was cleared, though, and Mike Simon supplied me with a high-definition video camera. I was shown a seat in the front of the aircraft, where the officials sat; the Iranian journalists accompanying the negotiating team were seated behind a curtain in the rear. It was a short flight, but I was able to get some footage of Zarif and his team.

When we arrived at the Geneva airport, we descended stairs onto the tarmac, where there were vans, cars, and a police escort waiting. One Iranian official had all the passports in his hand and asked me for mine. I told him I was on my U.S. passport, and he shrugged, motioning me to get into one of the first minivans. I thought, foolishly, that we would go to the terminal and clear immigration and customs, but instead the convoy went through open gates and onto the road into the city. When we arrived at the Intercontinental, I was worried. There was no record of my arriving in Switzerland, not in my passport, and not in any Swiss immigration computer file.

As it happened, I was leaving Geneva on that trip separately from the rest of the NBC team, on Air France from Geneva to Paris to connect to a New York flight. When I went to the airport, I was a little nervous about not having an entry stamp in my passport. I saw a sign for "France" departures, though, and one for "Swiss" and followed the France sign, remembering that the airport was on the border, and I was in fact leaving from French territory, not Swiss. I also realized that years before, I had driven from the Geneva airport to and from my brother's house in Chamonix, France, and had never had to show a passport crossing the border. The French immigration officers barely looked at my passport, and I was off to Paris.

There was one final round of talks in Geneva before the end of 2013, and we attended again, although NBC was getting concerned with the expense of flying Ann, Tom, me, and a crew for the purposes of a documentary that they weren't even sure would conclude with a breakthrough agreement. Due to end before the Christmas and New Year holidays, we anxiously awaited an announcement from the negotiating parties, which came on the final day

01.

02.

03.

01.
Mike Simon, NBC cameraman, shooting the Iranian negotiating team in Geneva, October 2013. Zarif (far right), photo by the author

02.
Ann Curry, Foreign Minister M. Javad Zarif, and the author, Geneva, 2013

03.
On the Iranian government plane from Rome to Geneva. Clockwise from top, Zarif, Ravanchi, and Araghchi; photo by the author

in appearances at the press center by both John Kerry and Javad Zarif, when they explained that the P5+1 and Iran had reached an agreement, called the Joint Plan of Action, or JPOA, a pact that temporarily froze some aspects of Iran's nuclear program while the United States eased some economic sanctions in anticipation of negotiating a final and permanent agreement. It was a celebration of sorts, and another positive sign of a thaw in the deeply antagonistic relations between Iran and the West, exacerbated during the presidency (and obstinacy) of the Ahmadinejad administration until earlier that year. In January 2014, I went with Ann to the State Department in Washington to interview Secretary of State John Kerry, and to Vienna in February to interview Javad Zarif and cover the continuing talks between Iran and the P5+1.

Chapter 41

Iran Talks, Part Two

The next series of negotiations were to take place in Vienna, at the exclusive Palais Coburg, where no rooms were made available for journalists and where access to even the small lobby was restricted. Fortuitously there was the Marriott across the street and a press tent set up in the plaza, and it was only steps to the Palais, where NBC needed to gain access to shoot footage for the documentary, now called "Twitter Diplomacy" after Zarif's active use of the platform to disseminate his views of the talks and of foreign policy in general.

It appeared that things were moving in the right direction, but there was little actual "news" to report, and NBC executives in New York were getting frustrated by the cost of the documentary and of our expenses. Not every senior correspondent from the three U.S. networks was attending *every* session, and while the wire services and correspondents from various media flew to Geneva or other locales to file reports, Ann was by far the most senior to be present at every occasion.

At around this time I was invited to participate in two public speaking events: one was to be on a panel at the *India Today* Conclave in New Delhi in March, and the other, a few days earlier, to debate the motion "This House Believes Iran Is Just a Wolf in Sheep's Clothing" opposite Rabbi Shmuley Boteach—the outspoken author of *Kosher Sex*, fierce critic of Iran, and self-described "America's Rabbi"—at the Oxford Union. Karri and I flew to England, where I won the debate handily despite Boteach presenting an impassioned case against Iran (no surprise, really, amid media coverage that presented a "reasonable" Iran, that the students voted with their feet—a tradition at Oxford University's debating union—walking through the "nay" (to the proposition) door in much greater numbers than the "yea"). I left for India alone the next day, and upon arrival I was excited to see a text on my phone from Sonny Mehta, who had seen my name in the conference program and insisted I visit him at his home in Delhi during my stay.

Returning to New York, the next steps at NBC News were editing and finishing "Twitter Diplomacy," with on-air appearances by Ann and me to promote it. In July, while another round of talks in Vienna was scheduled, David Gregory, the host of *Meet the Press*, indicated he was interested in an interview with Zarif, and I told Zarif that I would fly to Vienna with Gregory for the interview at the Palais Coburg if he would agree. It went quite well, with Gregory seemingly inclined to give Zarif and the Iranians the benefit of the doubt. But when the show aired, he invited onto the show Jeff Goldberg, who proceeded to pour cold water on the notion that Iran would negotiate in good faith. I don't think Zarif saw the show, but I was disappointed that David felt the need to not just balance it, but to end on a negative view of the talks.

After I had left Vienna for New York, Jason Rezaian, a *Washington Post* reporter in Tehran whom I knew from when he first started freelancing as a journalist and traveling to his father's homeland, had arrived to cover the last couple of days of that set of talks and attend a press conference. A few days after his return to Iran, he and his wife, Yeganeh, a reporter for the Emirati paper *The National* and before that at Iran's English-language media Press TV, were arrested and jailed in Evin Prison, making me wonder if his trip to Vienna had had anything to do with his arrest. When I was back in the States, his brother Ali contacted me through a mutual friend to solicit my help in convincing Zarif that Jason was innocent of the spying charge leveled against him. Zarif told me that while he had no actual power in getting anyone released, he was clear that he didn't believe arresting dual citizens and journalists benefited Iran in the least, especially at a sensitive time when he was trying to convince the world of Iran's benevolent intentions in not just its nuclear program, but its ballistic missile program too. The fact that many of the accused were arrested by the IRGC intelligence division and not the intelligence ministry under the president meant that he had even less influence. He didn't think Jason or anyone else was necessarily guilty, but he also wouldn't discount that there *could* be spies among dual citizens and other journalists.

Ali Rezaian became a regular from then on at the nuclear talks, always arriving at the hotels and trying to talk to anyone he could, and to confer with me as well. I began a conversation with their mother, Mary Rezaian, who was living in Istanbul. I urged her to go to Iran, thinking that it could help get her son released or at least make the Iranians have some sympathy and treat him better, but Ali was worried that I could be wrong. My argument was that while the Iranian authorities might think they had a case against Jason, they'd never argue one against his American mother. I checked with Zarif, who agreed with me, and who said he didn't see any reason for problems. We left it at that, until Mary could decide whether to go later in the year.

At the end of summer, Tom and Ann asked if I thought we could interview Rouhani again in Tehran ahead of the U.N. General Assembly. Zarif, Gholamali Khoshroo—now the new Iranian ambassador to the U.N.—and Hossein Fereidoun were all positive, and at the last minute, Rouhani gave his approval. It was too late to pick up visas at the Iranian Interests Section for the Americans on the team, so we were told that they would be ready at the Iranian consulate in Dubai. When we were on the way to the airport to catch the Emirates flight, though, I received an urgent message from Zarif, who was on his way to New York, to not go to Iran. I called Ali Khatami, who said I should take Zarif's advice and not go to Tehran with NBC, as he would know if there was a danger. I agreed that it would be best to avoid travel to Iran for now. In frantic discussions with Rich Greenberg at the office, we decided I would go as far as Dubai, help the team with their visas at the consulate, and monitor the interview from there. I met the team at the Dubai airport on their way back from Tehran, and we had a celebratory meal in the duty-free zone. I didn't know at the time, especially with my contacts and friends in high places in Tehran, that 2013 would be my last time visiting Iran.

It is ironic, I now think, that after twenty-five years of longing for a homeland, having nightmares of going there and not being allowed to leave, and then finally setting foot in Iran, it is now more than a decade since I've been able to go back. I'm told, courtesy of one specific individual in the IRGC, that I would end up prison should I risk it. The occasional nightmare has returned, of going and not being allowed to return to my family in America. The Islamic Republic of Iran, it seems, is determined to deprive me of my homeland, just as it has for anyone it deems a potential critic, or worse, an enemy.

Chapter 42

NBC, Continued

At the end of September, I joined Ann and the NBC team nominated for an Emmy at the awards, held in New York. Although we didn't win, we had a good time there and at the after-party. Tom Bettag had asked me that summer if I'd be interested in coming aboard NBC News as an employee, as he was being asked to contemplate running the Ann Curry Unit out of New York (he was still based in Washington, D.C.). At the Emmy after-party, he stepped away to take a phone call from his attorney in Los Angeles. He came back a few minutes later and said that NBC was not going to renew his contract, which came as a shock to me and Ann both. It did not bode well for Ann's unit. We had never been quite sure of NBC News president Deborah Turness's support for Ann. She had heartily congratulated Ann on her first exclusive interview with Hassan Rouhani—it was during Turness's first year as president, after she had come to New York from ITV in London—and was gracious otherwise, and to me as well. I took her to a breakfast meeting with Rouhani in September 2014, after Ann's second interview with him in Tehran, and she said she was happy to be in the "Iran business." But she was, we sensed, displeased with what we were spending to cover the nuclear talks, and it wasn't clear if she thought the documentary, "Twitter Diplomacy," was worth the expense. Nonetheless, we persevered, albeit sadly without Tom.

In mid-November, Farhad Azima, who had been a constant at the nuclear talks, invited me to dinner in midtown Manhattan. Accompanying us was Jay Solomon, the *Wall Street Journal* correspondent who was covering the talks in Europe (and who later got fired for allegedly partnering with Farhad on arms deals in the Emirates, adding to the intrigue that surrounded Farhad wherever he went). A week or so later, Ann and I left for Vienna for the final round of talks before Christmas, with Ann still being asked to do live shots from outside the Palais Coburg, and the talks ending with plans, we were informed, to resume in early 2015 with a goal of coming to a successful conclusion by July.

Farhad asked what could be done about Jason, and I told him I was doing whatever I could—lobbying Zarif and Fereidoun as well as contacts in Tehran—to see if his case could be resolved quickly. In fact, I asked Zarif at the end of November if Mary could visit her son in prison over Christmas, and Zarif replied that he thought it might be possible. Mary was at first hesitant but finally agreed to travel to Tehran, and I, remotely, helped her set up a secure *hushmail* email account for communication from Tehran that couldn't be monitored by the authorities, giving her my and Ali's addresses to use for all emails. She flew to Tehran, stayed at Yeganeh's parents', and had no issues other than the stress of dealing with government and judiciary personnel. But Zarif was able to arrange her visits with Jason, and she returned home happy to have at least seen him.

At the end of February 2015, Ann and I were on our way back to Switzerland—this time to Montreux—for a couple of days to interview Javad Zarif and to get a sense of where the talks were heading. The press contingent covering this round was much smaller, and the talks appeared to be a starting point for the final deal, which all sides were expecting, or at least hoping, would be concluded before the end of the year. We met Hossein Fereidoun in Montreux, too, as he had started joining the Iranian team, helping communications with his brother, the president, in Tehran.

We broadcast live to New York from the promenade near our hotel, including Ann and I live to the *Morning Joe* show on MSNBC, and returned to New York with more footage for "Twitter Diplomacy, Part Two." But we were beginning to wonder if it would ever see the light of day. I wanted to visit Ardeshir Zahedi, who lived nearby, but in the end, there was no convenient time. When he died a few years later, I regretted not having seen him.

In mid-March we were back to the talks, now being held in Lausanne at the grand Beau-Rivage Palace Hotel and coincidentally where the Treaty of Lausanne, ending conflict with the Ottoman Empire, was signed in 1923. Zarif, who we wanted to interview again, invited me on a walk to discuss possibilities and to hear about what the media was saying. I again pleaded with him about Jason, and he said he was doing all that he could, including speaking with the IRGC intelligence people, but so far they were not convinced of the journalist's innocence. It was also becoming clear that the Americans in prison were being held hostage for some future demand from America, as well as to hinder the nuclear talks, which hard-liners were against from the beginning. A CNN camera crew followed us on the walk, resulting in footage of me with the Iranian negotiating team being seen in Tehran, causing me even more trouble with the hard-line conservatives who despised Zarif and the reformists. They had always accused Zarif of having too-close relationships with Americans (even calling him part of the "New York Gang") and believed that the footage (and later photographs) might indicate that to be the case.

But a few days into the talks, on March 20, President Rouhani's (and Hossein Fereidoun's) mother died in Tehran, so the Iranian delegation took a break and returned for both the Norouz holiday and for consultations with the leadership, as well as for her funeral. Ann went to Paris for a few days, and I went to London to see my mother and sister, deciding that it was more cost-efficient to stay in Europe than to fly back and forth from New York. We returned to Lausanne on the 24th, but to our surprise were, like all the journalists, not only barred from staying at the Beau-Rivage, but we weren't even allowed in its halls or in the bar, where we—the press corps—previously had spent huge amounts on food and drink while passing the time. We understood that the request had been made by the American team, feeling

01.

02.

01.
With Ann Curry and Hossein Fereidoun in Montreux, 2015

02.
With Zarif and Al'Habib, his chief of staff, left; Araghchi and Ravanchi to right of the author

crowded by the large contingent of reporters following them or hanging out in the bar, depriving them of any privacy. We checked in at the Beau-Rivage's sister hotel, a small boutique hotel, the Angleterre & Residence next door, and hoped to be able to follow the talks and still get more footage. That hotel could accommodate us only for a few days, and we had to move to another one, farther away, for the rest of the trip. It was at that hotel that I got sick, at first thinking that I had a cold, then the flu, and I stayed in my room while Ann brought me soup and juices and vitamin C tablets.

After a day or so, I couldn't get out of bed, and Ann said she was worried. "I'm taking you to a doctor," she insisted. She asked the front desk for a medical office nearby and put me in a taxi and took me to a clinic, where a doctor saw me after a while and proclaimed that I had the flu. He suggested rest and we returned to the hotel, but by the next day, I had slept the entire time and Ann was getting scared. "This is not okay," she said, "we're going to a hospital." She took me to one where I couldn't even stay awake in the waiting room, and when doctors saw me, they hospitalized me right away, saying that I was suffering from pneumonia. Ann contacted Adrienne Mong, a vice president of news gathering in London, who immediately sent a producer to check on me, pay the hospital bill, and ensure that all was clear for me to travel back home.

Ann took me to the airport after I was discharged, and flew back to New York with me, insisting that she deliver me to Karri at our apartment in Brooklyn first before heading to her home in Connecticut. She had, I told Karri, saved my life, for I didn't realize at the time that I had been delirious, sleeping all day and night and interrupting my semi-comatose state only to get up and vomit in the bathroom—dry vomit—probably from my nicotine withdrawal. I don't think I was worried especially during the illness, other than feeling absolutely wretched, but was certainly grateful for Ann and her considerate concern and friendship. I had lost some twenty pounds when I went to my doctor in Brooklyn, and she advised me to not start smoking again, as I had presumably by now been cured of my physical addiction if not the mental one. Almost ten years later, I still miss it, and have kept the duty-free Camels I bought on the way *to* Lausanne but never finished smoking. I've kept them sealed in a drawer for when I'm in my seventies, as my father suggested.

While I was incapacitated, the talks in Lausanne ended on April 2, with Federica Mogherini (who had replaced Catherine Ashton as high representative of the EU) and Mohammad Javad Zarif holding a press conference announcing that an agreement had been reached on a "framework deal" for a Joint Comprehensive Plan of Action, or JCPOA, and which they said was to be completed by June 30. By this time Deborah Turness had removed Brian Williams from his role as anchor of *Nightly News* because of a scandal surrounding his exaggerating the details of an experience he'd had when covering the Iraq War, further creating uncertainty for Ann, who had at times substituted for Brian when he was unable to anchor the program. She had lost her unit with NBC but was to continue with a production deal providing content to the network, and to continue to cover Iran—or at least that was what was promised.

Our next trip, at the end of June, was meant to be the last, to wrap up the talks with an agreement between the P5+1 and Iran. This was to be "the big one," a historic agreement and an end to the nuclear crisis, and it felt like the entire world's media descended on Vienna, with the Austrian government once again hosting the negotiations (and paying the tens of thousands of dollars a day the Palais Coburg was charging the delegations). There were satellite television trucks lined up along the Parkring road in front of the Marriott, but I was unable to get a room there as it had been fully booked by journalists from around the world as well as some of the Iranian journalists and foreign ministry officials. NBC put me at the Ritz Carlton down the road—I couldn't complain—with Abigail Williams, Andrea Mitchell's producer at NBC, as Andrea was taking over coverage of the talks. It was unclear what Ann's role would be with the talks, with the Iran coverage, or indeed at NBC.

The talks proceeded slowly, and while the U.S. delegation (and some of the American reporters) were hoping to be finished in time to get home for the July 4 holiday, the day came and went, and John Kerry hosted an Independence Day barbeque at the U.S. Embassy instead. The following day happened to be my birthday and, I found out, *The New York Times*'s David Sanger's as well, so some of the other reporters planned a big dinner at an outdoor Italian restaurant within walking distance, and we were back to waiting, and waiting, the next day.

It became a routine of sorts; no one had any real news to report, so often one would see reporters at a café, for breakfast or a late-night drink at Café Schwarzenberg on the corner of Parkring and Kärntner Ring, or just hanging out in the lobby of the Marriott, where often there was no place to sit. (The number of Wiener schnitzels consumed during July 2015 at the Marriott in Vienna must have set a record for the hotel chain.) On more than one occasion, the Wi-Fi in the hotel lobby couldn't handle the traffic and would stall, leaving reporters frustrated and unable to file stories. One such time I was sitting with Anshel Pfeffer, then a senior correspondent for *Haaretz*, and he offered me his password for a portable Wi-Fi router his paper had given him before leaving Israel. I accepted, thinking Mossad undoubtedly by now had the entire contents of my laptop, and Anshel and I were, for a short while, the only ones with a connection to the internet from our computers.

During almost two years of talks, I had become friendly with reporters from the English-language media covering the talks, often spending hours with them over lunch, dinner, or drinks. The Russians kept to themselves, as did the Iranians whose budgets didn't allow stays at the Marriott or other upscale hotels, and for whom halal food was organized daily by the Iranian embassy. (I was friendly with a few of the Iranian reporters.) I had no illusions that any of our conversations, or communications, were private.

I continued to see the Iranian delegation, taking notes and photos for the second documentary (its airing, however, now a distant possibility). I also wanted to set up an exclusive interview for Ann with Zarif, and I went one day to discuss that possibility with him. Zarif's suite had a terrace facing the plaza and the media tent, and normally there were cameras set up and trained on the hotel, where foreign ministers would come and speak on the street. The Iranian negotiating team would often step out onto Zarif's terrace for fresh air (and I presume to whisper, away from what were certainly bugged rooms), and that day I stepped out with Zarif after talking to him about NBC, interviews, and documentaries (he hadn't seen "Twitter Diplomacy" yet). The Iranian journalists fired away with their cameras and long lenses. A photo of me arguing a point with Zarif landed on *Fars News*, a hard-line Iranian website affiliated with the IRGC. Perhaps more than any other issue, that photograph has become responsible for hard-line elements

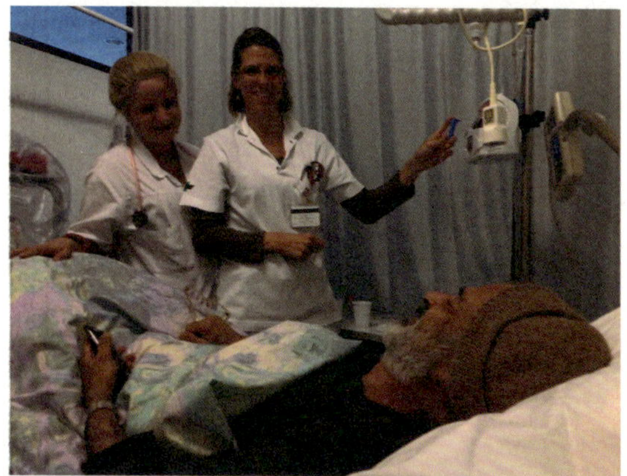

01.

02.

01.
In the hospital in Lausanne before discharge, 2015

02.
My shared birthday dinner with *The New York Times*'s David Sanger, Vienna, July 5, 2015. Matt Lee, AP's diplomatic editor who closely followed the talks as State Department reporter, at top, and Indira Lakshmanan of Bloomberg holding phone camera, with Laura Rozen of Al Monitor in the background

in the regime assuming nefarious intent on my part, and a reason I cannot safely visit my homeland.

After the photo was published, along with a video of me walking with President Rouhani when NBC interviewed him in Tehran in 2013 posted on hard-line Telegram channels, I was referred to by some in Iran as the "puppet master"—an American spy infiltrating the upper echelons of the Iranian leadership and dictating the surrender, as the hard-liners deemed it, to the Americans in the form of a nuclear deal that limited Iran's program. The truth was that yes, as an author with connections to the Iranian leadership I had indeed been approached by intelligence agencies, sometimes in roundabout ways, and I had always said to them exactly what I told anyone who asked: that my views and sentiments were no secret and were published in books and my opinion pieces. I was a journalist who, yes, had sympathy for a progressive Iran that would have no conflict with the West or the outside world, that would respect freedom of speech and democratic rule, respect minority and women's rights, and would be a place Iranians in the diaspora would want to visit, invest in, or even live in. But as Ann Curry had taught me, I had to be objective if I wanted to be respected as a journalist, which is always a struggle when one's passions are involved.

Iran, in some ways not unlike the United States, has factional politics, but with far more dangerous consequences for the weaker faction. The hard-liners could toy with the Zarifs and the Rouhanis and the Khatamis of the world, while they had no recourse except to cry foul every now and then. That Zarif would be called to Parliament for a dressing down every now and then; that Khatami—two-time popularly elected president who in the early days of the new regime resigned from his position as minister of culture rather than censor books and the arts as was demanded of him—couldn't leave his house without permission was indicative of how power politics played out in Iran. I was unimportant, as the various intelligence agencies knew well, but they also knew I might, like some others before me, be a useful pawn.

By July 10, journalists camped out in Vienna (some with smaller budgets moving from Airbnbs to cheap hotels) had run out of steam. Ali Rezaian again came, but I had no new information to share with him. I had argued many times with whoever would listen that any trip Jason took to the

U.S. consulate in Dubai (which the Iranians claimed was a hotbed of CIA activity directed at Iran) was merely for his wife's green card application, and besides, what possible information could Jason have been gathering in Iran that wasn't already public? I suspected at this point that the foreign ministry types knew all that, and the judiciary probably did, too, but there were elements of the regime that believed he, and any other Americans they held, were pawns in negotiations over sanctions, frozen Iranian funds, and the nuclear deal.

Gholamali Khoshroo, now the Iranian ambassador at the U.N., would call me every now and then from New York to see if I had any specific news or a read on what was happening. I knew that the Iranian team couldn't communicate from the hotel—their mobile phones barely worked, presumably due to twenty-four-hour interference from the remote listening equipment of every major intelligence agency—and we were advised to not log on to the Palais Coburg's Wi-Fi network at any time. John Kerry, we were told, had a secure communication system always accompanying him, and he stayed at a different hotel anyway. The Iranians had their embassy, where they could send secure messages back to Tehran. It was also reported that Hossein Fereidoun would talk to his brother the president in a dialect, Sorkhei, that few could understand—in Iran or outside—but in general, communication was limited outside of a very few people. I thought it ironic that Khoshroo, who once told me how funny it was that had we met at the time of the revolution, he would have considered me his mortal enemy, was now a friend who called me every day to be updated on his revolutionary government's negotiations with the Great Satan.

Ann Curry, whose relationship with NBC as an employee had been severed at the end of 2014, still had authority from the network to cover the nuclear talks, and she finally arrived in Vienna—with some encouragement from me—on the last days of negotiations. On July 15, a breakthrough was announced, and the JCPOA was signed. Zarif did a round-robin set of interviews with the U.S. media, arranged by his press officer, Alireza Miryusefi, and it was Andrea, not Ann, who conducted it for NBC. An implementation date for the accord was set for January 2016, to be announced officially, again in Vienna, once all the *planned actions* by the parties were taken, and I was relieved to return to New York in time to be with my son for his fifth birthday on July 17. The media had been in Vienna for almost three weeks—the longest continuous set of negotiations in the last two years.

In August, only a month after the talks ended successfully, I asked Zarif if NBC could interview President Rouhani again, for the third time, in Tehran. Rouhani had been happy with the previous interviews, I argued, so why shouldn't he stick to what worked? NBC, however, with Lester Holt as the new *Nightly News* anchor, wanted *him* to conduct the interview, not Ann. After much back-and-forth, Ann agreed to conduct the interview *with* Lester, although she continued to harbor doubts that it would turn out well. It was in the end a moot point, as Rouhani decided he couldn't do three interviews in a row with the same network, and the Iranians granted a long-standing request by *60 Minutes* for an interview in Tehran in September. Steve Kroft, the correspondent, upset the Iranians when he couldn't pronounce the name of Supreme Leader Ali Khamenei, and referred to him as "your boss" to Rouhani, further upsetting him, and in 2016 I was successful in getting Rouhani to commit to NBC again when he would be in New York for the U.N. General Assembly. This time, however, Lester Holt was moderating the upcoming first presidential debate between Donald Trump and Hillary Clinton, and at the last minute we had to substitute Chuck Todd, moderator of *Meet the Press*, in a successful but not especially newsworthy interview. Lester was finally able to interview Rouhani in both 2017 and 2018 during his visits to New York—the latter after Trump had withdrawn the United States from the JCPOA, angering the Iranians to no end.

In October 2015 I was invited to the Conrad Literary Festival in Kraków, Poland, and I was thrilled to have the opportunity to meet with my Polish publisher, Karakter, which had faithfully translated and published all my books. That year, the festival—named after Joseph Conrad—received greater attention than usual when, right before its start, another invitee, the Belarussian writer Svetlana Alexievich, was awarded the Nobel Prize for Literature. While media attention was naturally on her, my event was also sold out and there was a lively discussion with the Poles in attendance. The writer who perhaps has had the greatest influence on my nonfiction was a Pole, Ryszard Kapusciński, the celebrated journalist who wrote, in my opinion, the definitive account of the Islamic revolution, *Shah of Shahs*. A witness to the revolution while reporting for the Polish state news agency, he brought to life for me what it was like to be there as an observer, not a participant, and all his other books of reportage, whether in Africa or Central America, have impressed me.

I enjoyed visiting Poland—Kraków especially—and my only disappointment was that while we were staying in the same somewhat faded but once grand hotel in the city, I never got to meet Alexievich.

After the JCPOA was signed, I continued to work with NBC on Iran issues and starting in 2017 went each year to the Munich Security Conference to help with interviewing Zarif. I also arranged with Zarif and Majid Ravanchi, who had replaced Khoshroo as U.N. ambassador in 2019, for Lester Holt to go to Iran in August of that year for the first time to interview Zarif and several top officials, including the Speaker of Parliament, Ali Larijani. That year, Chuck Todd also interviewed Zarif in New York for *Meet the Press* while Ravanchi was at Sloan Kettering Hospital being treated for cancer. Zarif was not allowed to visit him, as according to Mike Pompeo's State Department directive, Iranian diplomats at the U.N. and any other Iranian officials in New York for U.N. business were now *further* restricted to a few blocks of the U.N. and Kennedy Airport. Sloan Kettering was outside the permitted zone, as was Central Park, directly across the street from the ambassador's residence, where Zarif would hold meetings, and he was not granted an exemption to visit his sick friend and colleague. In late February 2020, Richard Engel interviewed Zarif in his suite at the Bayerischer Hof hotel, the venue for the conference, only days before the Covid-19 pandemic interrupted, and then changed, our lives. It was Zarif's last visit to Munich.

I continued to see Ravanchi after his cancer treatment in New York, even breaking State Department rules and going for a walk in Central Park with him where we could be without masks and presumably out of range of long-range microphones. Ravanchi, like Zarif, had been educated in the States—at the University of Kansas, in the state where, ironically, Mike Pompeo was from, and at Fordham University in New York—and as a student had gone to the Iranian Embassy in Washington in 1979 to vote in the referendum that created the Islamic Republic. We talked about the coincidence of being friends now, when we likely met each other on the

01.

02.

01.
From left: Araghchi, Ravanchi, Zarif, and the author on the balcony of Zarif's suite at the Palais Coburg, Vienna, 2015, published by the IRGC-affiliated Iranian news agency Fars News

02.
At the Conrad Literary Festival, 2015

day of the vote at the embassy without knowing it, with him casting "yes" on his ballot, and me casting "no" on mine. In 2021, he helped arrange an interview at his residence for Andrea Mitchell with the new Iranian foreign minister, Hossein Amir-Abdollahian, appointed by the new hard-line Iranian president, Ebrahim Raisi, in New York for the first time for the U.N. General Assembly. Because of the pandemic, that year Raisi gave his inaugural address remotely from Tehran.

Back in New York, I continued consulting with NBC News. In January 2017, Glenn O'Brien, who had been diagnosed with cancer, was beginning to decline in health. Over the next few weeks, I tried to visit him every day at his and Gina's loft, and he weakened drastically as time went on. On many days, after I dropped Khashayar off at school in the East Village, Glenn would call me and ask if I could go see him. I would spend much of the rest of the day with him. Friends would visit; the artists Tom Sachs, Nan Goldin, and Richard Prince; the portrait photographers Kate Simon and Lynn Goldsmith; and many others in the fields of art and entertainment—or Art and Commerce, as the agency that represented him was called. Michael Zilkha would come to New York and see Glenn every day he was in town, and Eric Goode, an old friend who lived around the corner, was there almost every day, too. We all celebrated Glenn's seventieth birthday on March 2, but sadly he continued to weaken and died in hospital on April 7, after a day when many of his friends stood around his bed for hours, keeping him company and playing him the songs that he loved while he was unconscious, but which we imagined he might somehow be hearing. The first three months of 2017 were difficult ones, and when Glenn died, I felt a deep loss. A close friend for more than twenty years, he was unfailingly loyal and loving. At his fiftieth birthday bash in an event space on 58th Street, Madonna sang "Happy Birthday" to him in the same manner as Marilyn Monroe famously did to John F. Kennedy, a reminder of the love and respect his many friends who gathered to celebrate his half-century in this world had for him. I miss him today, and I always will.

Chapter 43

Back to Jamaica

In the spring of 2016, Suzette Newman called me from London and said she was going to Jamaica with Nathalie Delon in August and was hoping that I and my family could join them at Goldeneye for a week or so. I knew Nathalie from my earliest days working with Chris Blackwell—the ex-wife of Alain Delon, she had been Chris's girlfriend and they remained close years later, even after Chris married Mary Vinson. I often saw her in Los Angeles at Chris's house in the Hollywood Hills above the Chateau Marmont, where her son Anthony Delon would sometimes stay with his dog. We flew to Jamaica *en famille* for my son Khashayar's introduction to my third "home." We stayed in one of the villas near the main house, which was now blocked off and kept private for paying guests, and it was great fun to see Nathalie after almost twenty years. I had seen her in 1999 at her house in Sundance, Utah, after returning from California with Chris on his plane and making the stop there to spend the night. She hadn't changed

01.

02.

01.
Nathalie Delon (right) with Karri and Khash, Jamaica, 2016

02.
Khash and Nathalie at Hotel Costes, 2019

03.
Khash, Liv, and Lou Delon at lunch at the outdoor table overlooking the sea at Goldeneye's main house

03.

much, except for no longer smoking the Gitanes International cigarettes she once loved and was never without.

Khash took to Jamaica (and especially to Goldeneye) right away, proclaiming it his favorite place in the world, and was thrilled when Suzette announced we'd all be back the next summer. It was Chris's world again—old Island Records friends and artists, such as Grace Jones, who had an apartment in Ocho Rios, were regulars.

In the summer of 2017 we returned to Jamaica, this time staying in the new village of huts that Chris had built on one end of the property, by what used to be called James Bond Beach in the days before Goldeneye was a resort, and which was now Button Beach, James Bond now being the name of a public beach across the bay. Unfortunately, on the day we arrived Chris and Suzette flew to London when they received news of the death of Chris's mother, Blanche, and so we busied ourselves with Nathalie until they returned to Jamaica. We saw them for only a few days before heading back to New York.

Again, in 2018, we were back at Goldeneye and in a hut right off the beach, while Suzette and Nathalie were staying at a villa on the lagoon. On that visit, Suzette and I took a car up to Pantrepant to visit Mary Vinson's grave. We had a memorable roast chicken meal and swam by a waterfall on the property before returning to Goldeneye on the bone-rattling ride down the mountain. We didn't go to Jamaica in 2019, instead going to France to expose Khash to that country, and had dinner with Nathalie at Hotel Costes, which would be the last time we saw her.

With the pandemic, summer in 2020 in Jamaica was out of the question, and sadly Nathalie had by then been diagnosed with cancer, so it would have been impossible for her to travel anyway. Chris was stuck in New York during the early days of the pandemic, and I would go for walks with him in Central Park, where on occasion we'd take a bottle of wine and a few sandwiches and have a picnic. He longed to get back to Jamaica, and left New York as soon as it was possible for him to do so without having to quarantine in a hotel in Kingston. Nathalie died in Paris in January, and in the summer of 2021, we went to Goldeneye with Suzette, Anthony Delon, and his two daughters, Liv and Lou, who Nathalie adored, to spread her ashes in the sea. It was her final wish to be at one with the sea at Goldeneye, one of her favorite spots on earth, a place that held memories for her of the love she had had for Chris.

The week before heading to Jamaica, we had attended a party that Chris threw on Shelter Island for Blackwell Rum, a premium rum he had started producing in Jamaica. It was outdoors on the grounds of the Ram's Head Inn, but Chris was mobbed by friends and acquaintances the entire time. When we arrived in Jamaica, having had our PCR Covid tests done in time, Chris called from New York to say that he had tested positive and couldn't come as planned. It was no surprise, really, given that he wasn't wearing a mask and hundreds of people had gathered very close to him at the party. He was going to test every day in the hope that he could join us soon, but in the end he never was clear, and we returned to New York without performing the ceremonial scattering of ashes.

Anthony left his mother's ashes in Chris's office for safekeeping until we could all return another time, and he left with his daughters for Paris. That year, Chris and Cathy Snipper had arranged for us to stay at the main house (and its two separate villas), with its private beach and swimming pool, which was a delight for Khash, who had never been in the restricted area of the resort, as well as for Nathalie's granddaughters, who had never been to Jamaica and were thrilled. Khash was especially delighted with the private chef who made him whatever he wanted to eat for breakfast every day—usually *mounds* of bacon with eggs from the chickens on the property.

In May 2022 Chris finally went with Anthony and his family to Jamaica and they were able to perform Nathalie's ceremony at Goldeneye. We were unfortunately unable to join them, as my mother was unwell in London, and I was about to make a few trips there to be with her.

Chapter 44

Losing Childhood

My mother, who after leaving the flat in Chiswick had spent a few years in a nicely furnished "granny flat" above my sister's garage in Walton, a suburb of London, had in 2020 moved to a nursing home when she could no longer take care of herself, even as Marjan carefully juggled monitoring her along with her busy life with her children still in school. The nursing home was only a few minutes away, and my mother had a private room overlooking the gardens and was very happy. Due to the Covid pandemic, my brother and I couldn't visit for a while, and when I finally did, in 2021, I had to get tested every day to be allowed into the facility. In the spring of 2022, Marjan called to say that our mother had been admitted to hospital with stomach pains. Within a few days, her health declined, and my brother and I flew to England to see her. After a week, when she seemed stable but still very ill, we returned to New York, planning to go back as soon as Marjan asked us to. Within a week, we were back in England, and my mother was being moved to a different section of the hospital for hospice care. She had a private room this time, and we could spend as much time with her as we wanted, but I was not sure she always knew we were there. She was barely conscious, on heavy doses of painkillers fed intravenously. We thought, and the doctors assured us, that she was at least comfortable and not in pain as she had been.

She died on June 9, at ninety-five years old, with her three children at her bedside, holding her hands. She was the last of her siblings to die, having witnessed her brothers Nassir's and Nasser's deaths, and her sister Shamsi's. Throughout her life and in my adulthood, she would tell me to kiss and hug her properly, as I would always be her child—her little boy. I was finally no longer a child to anyone, but I certainly hadn't wished to no longer be hers.

Back to New York, two weeks before my sixty-fifth birthday, Chris had a party for his eighty-fifth. Many old friends were there, including Farhad Azima, a constant presence in Chris's life for more than twenty-five years. Some people believed that I was the last person to turn out the lights at Island Records in the days that we ran it, but Suzette, who had started working for Chris when she was seventeen and had been at his side for more than fifty years, was *really* the last person at any of Chris's enterprises. She wasn't at the party, however, as Chris had finally had a falling-out with her, too, and pulled me aside to tell me quietly that he had felt betrayed by her. Neither I, nor indeed any of Chris's other friends, took sides in the divorce, though, and we all remain friends of both, recognizing all the while that if there was a fault to be assigned in the break, it had to be to Chris. He had, too many times in his personal and professional life, fallen out with people (exactly as Davitt had warned me all those years ago, when Chris first offered me a job), and had tended to lay blame on others for whatever he was unhappy about at any given time.

Then, in September, Selim Zilkha passed away, also at the age of ninety-five. He had been a sort of father figure ever since I first worked with him in 2000, and I enjoyed his company, our telephone chats about Middle Eastern politics, and his great sense of humor. I had met him with Michael in the eighties, but we grew close, I felt, after our experience with the Surf Channel. Selim, like his children, had the most generous spirit—

01.

01.
At Chris Blackwell's eighty-
fifth birthday party, June 2022

always ready to help friends and family when they needed it. He had even, as a major donor to the California Republican Party and as a host at his house in Bel Air to the Reagans, George H. W. Bush, and George W. Bush, asked the second Bush administration to hire me as an expert on Iran and on the Middle East in general, or as an ambassador, which showed a trust in me, my judgment, and my abilities that I'm not convinced I deserved.

Chapter 45

Americans in Iran

In 2019, a year after the British American Iranian environmentalist Morad Tahbaz had been jailed in Iran on charges of espionage, I met with his sister-in-law, Neda Rastegar, through my brother, who wanted to see if I could do anything to help get him freed. Neda, née Modjtabai, is the daughter of my parents' best friends from the earliest days of their marriage; their other daughter, Vida, is Morad's wife. Morad was indubitably innocent of any of the charges the judiciary pursued—he was a scientist doing his job with a love for his homeland—but got caught up as a high-profile dual (or in this case, triple) citizen in Iran's desperate ploy to gain leverage in its negotiations with the West on the nuclear issue and on the issue of the crippling sanctions that the United States had imposed (and reimposed after Trump withdrew from the JCPOA).

I talked to Majid Ravanchi, the Iranian ambassador to the U.N., who I knew as a senior member of the leadership could at least communicate with the various entities in Iran that might shed some light on whether Morad's case could be resolved quietly without the family going public, as some families of other arrested dual citizens had done in the past. I also wrote to Foreign Minister Zarif, telling him how close my family was to Modjtabai's and that in my opinion and that of pretty much anyone who knew him, it was impossible for Morad to have been engaged in espionage. Another factor in his case was that he had prostate cancer, and he required regular treatment that the prison was unlikely to give.

Ravanchi was sympathetic and agreed to see Neda and pursue Morad's case in Tehran. Zarif was also sympathetic but argued that he had little power to effect Morad's release: all he could do was ask the relevant arresting authorities—whether the IRGC intelligence division or the intelligence ministry—what the evidence was. Of course, even if he argued that the charges were flimsy or completely false, releasing any dual citizens from jail was, as the saying goes, above his pay grade. I implored Zarif and Ravanchi to at least try to lift the travel ban on Vida, who wanted to go abroad to see her children. I argued that she would always return; she was never going to abandon her husband. But it was to no avail, and the judiciary officials seemed to take a perverse pleasure in denying simple and perfectly reasonable requests by prisoners and their families, perhaps because they were resentful of their status as citizens of a Western nation and of their apparent wealth, or because they were simply cruel. I suspect it was a combination of both.

As with Jason Rezaian, there was in reality very little I could do other than champion his cause, but Ravanchi, to his credit, took Neda's calls and met with her whenever she wanted. But in the end, no dual citizen was going to be released and allowed to leave the country without Iran getting something in return; it appeared to have become state policy starting sometime after Rouhani was elected. By 2023, when dual American citizens were transferred from jail to a hotel in an agreed prisoner and asset-freeze swap, Morad Tahbaz had spent five years in jail, and Siamak Namazi, the longest serving, eight years. They, along with three other jailed Iranian Americans, left Iran for Qatar and then went on to the United States on September 18, 2023, just as Iran's president, Ebrahim Raisi, arrived in New York to attend the U.N. General Assembly.

It wasn't that the foreign ministry officials could do nothing, as was shown by Zarif's enabling Mary Rezaian's Christmas visit and personally

01.

01.
With my brother (on the right) in the courtyard of our apartment in Barons Court, London, late 1950s

intervening to allow Jason Rezaian's wife (not a dual citizen then) to leave on the private jet with him after his release. Yeganeh left quickly without a passport and was given special dispensation to arrive in the States with Jason. After a couple of months of getting nowhere with the Iranian authorities in their issuing one while she was in Washington, she called me and asked for my help. I called Khoshroo, the Iranian U.N. ambassador at the time, and said the foreign ministry had to intervene and sort out the Rezaians' issue—they had suffered enough. He promised to sort it out, and he did.

I had, like Neda and her family, thought that Sadegh Kharrazi, the one person close to both the reformists and the conservatives—even the IRGC and its intelligence division's then head, Hossein Taeb—could have done something about the prisoners, perhaps even pleaded with the supreme leader, but despite being a friend of Morad's he was unable to effect any wavering. My own situation with respect to Iran is part and parcel of this policy. As a relatively high profile Iranian American (to the Iranians) in the media, I am a good target for extracting concessions from the United States should I be foolish enough to appear in Tehran. Taeb, no longer the head of IRGC intelligence, presumably due to his having presided over the arrests of dual citizens while Israeli agents seem to have had carte blanche to come and go in Iran with ease, assassinating scientists, blowing up facilities, and stealing nuclear documents—all dutifully reported by the Western and Iranian media—and who is also close to the supreme leader's powerful son, Mojtaba, has reportedly said I'm high on his list of dual citizens he'd like to welcome to Evin.

My brother and I had lunch in 2021 with Mr. and Mrs. Modjtabai at Neda's house in Connecticut, on one of the occasions that they visited from Tehran. I hadn't seen them since I was a child. Maryam Modjtabai told a story of when we were first in London in the late 1950s. One evening my mother happened to say to her that she wasn't going to a party with my father, because she had to stay home with the kids. Mrs. Modjtabai insisted she go and said *she* would stay with us. And of course, the one time both my parents were away, I apparently fell off my tricycle and cut my head, something Maryam thought, knowing my mother, could mean the end of her advice being followed, if not the end of a friendship. As she told the story, I reached for my phone and clicked on my photo library, showing her a photo of me on my tricycle in London in the late 1950s, and she exclaimed, "That's it!"

Chapter 46

Home, Revisited

When someone boasts, or bemoans, that he or she is "married to their work," it means their work, or job, is a second home if not their primary one. While in the music business, I *was* married to my job(s)—the workplace was a home of sorts for me, especially after my separation and divorce—and my work in music and film was also the only time I ever had a "real" job. The unexpected end of that career was vivid proof that, much like the Iranian revolution had upended an expected life, one should never take anything for granted.

From my first visit back to Iran since childhood, my repeated trips—whether on assignment to interview the president, to report from inside the country, or to compile my observations and memories into books—each gave me further perspective on the country of my ancestors and allowed me greater comfort in thinking of that distant land as my home. And after decades in New York, I instinctively call the city my home, too; I miss it when I'm absent and reply "New York" when asked where I'm from—even if asked in New York, which often makes me feel like a fraud.

In truth, I've never really known what home is. I thought I was looking for one when I applied for and received my Iranian passport, and that perhaps I had found it when I first traveled there as an adult in 2004. But I know that home is more than a geographical location. My mother and father had homes—my father hating his and happy in his escape, my mother longing for hers and dying without seeing it again—but I don't. I know that for my sister England is home, and I suspect my brother simply doesn't mind not having one. But for me, if I could relish being a *minister without portfolio* throughout my career, I can also accept that home will remain an unknown concept, and that that's just the way it is, and always will be.

Tamam shod (finis)

Acknowledgments

I would like to thank Michael Zilkha for thinking my life story interesting enough to warrant a book; Nathan Rostron, my deft editor; my agent Andrew Wylie for his guidance; and my friends and family who are all named in the book, without whom it could not exist.

About the Author

Hooman Majd is an author and writer based in New York, and a contributor at NBC News. He has written for *The New Yorker, The New York Times, TIME, Newsweek, Financial Times,* and *Interview,* among others. Majd is the author of the *New York Times* bestseller *The Ayatollah Begs to Differ* (Doubleday, 2008) and *The Ayatollahs' Democracy* (Norton, 2010). His most recent book on Iran, *The Ministry of Guidance Invites You to Not Stay,* was published by Doubleday in 2013. Majd has appeared on numerous television and radio shows, including *Real Time with Bill Maher, The Daily Show with Jon Stewart, Charlie Rose, NBC News,* and many others, and on numerous NPR programs.